Scratch-Building Model Railway
TANK LOCOMOTIVES

Scratch-Building Model Railway
TANK LOCOMOTIVES

THE TILBURY 4-4-2

Simon Bolton

THE CROWOOD PRESS

First published in 2016 by
The Crowood Press Ltd
Ramsbury, Marlborough
Wiltshire SN8 2HR

www.crowood.com

© Simon Bolton 2016

All rights reserved. No part of this publication may be reproduced or transmitted in any form or by any means, electronic or mechanical, including photocopy, recording, or any information storage and retrieval system, without permission in writing from the publishers.

British Library Cataloguing-in-Publication Data
A catalogue record for this book is available from the British Library.

ISBN 978 1 78500 141 3

Dedication
To Don Wilson and Angela Leonard for their care and understanding.

Acknowledgements
My thanks to the following: Paul for his unending help and support; David Coasby for his wit and wisdom; Sam Manley and Jonathan Clay for their superb artistic contributions; the members of Shropshire & Herefordshire Area Group for their advice and biscuits; Richard Stanton and Neil Briggs for the use of their photos; Sophia Brothers from the Science & Society Picture Library; the various credited photographic companies for curating such a great resource; all of the readers and reviewers of my first book for their helpful and enthusiastic feedback. I'd also like to thank all those society members and website forum contributors for their assistance and kind comments.

All photos and drawings, unless otherwise credited, are by the author.

Disclaimer
The author and the publisher do not accept any responsibility in any manner whatsoever for any error or omission, or any loss, damage, injury, adverse outcome, or liability of any kind incurred as a result of the use of any of the information contained in this book, or reliance upon it. If in doubt about any aspect of railway modelling readers are advised to seek professional advice.

Typeset and designed by D & N Publishing, Baydon, Wiltshire

Printed and bound in Malaysia by Times Offset (M) Sdn Bhd

CONTENTS

PREFACE	6
CHAPTER ONE: **SCRATCH-BUILDING FUNDAMENTALS**	9
CHAPTER TWO: **TILBURY TANK RESEARCH**	15
CHAPTER THREE: **THE WORKPLACE**	22
CHAPTER FOUR: **DESIGNING THE CHASSIS FRAMES**	26
CHAPTER FIVE: **BUILDING THE CLASS 51 FRAMES**	33
CHAPTER SIX: **FILING AND FORMING THE FRAMES**	41
CHAPTER SEVEN: **FITTING THE LEADING AND TRAILING TRUCKS**	52
CHAPTER EIGHT: **FITTING THE MOTOR AND DRIVING WHEELS**	59
CHAPTER NINE: **THE CYLINDERS AND CONNECTING RODS**	64
CHAPTER TEN: **CLASS 51 FOOTPLATE AND CAB**	74
CHAPTER ELEVEN: **CLASS 51 BOILER AND SMOKEBOX**	83
CHAPTER TWELVE: **BUILDING UP THE CAB SIDES AND TANKS**	90
CHAPTER THIRTEEN: **TANK TOPS, BUNKER END, CAB DOORS AND BEADING**	100
CHAPTER FOURTEEN: **BUILDING THE CLASS 79 CHASSIS**	116
CHAPTER FIFTEEN: **CLASS 79 BODYWORK**	134
CHAPTER SIXTEEN: **BUNKER, TANKS AND A WRAP-OVER CAB FOR THE CLASS 79**	149
CHAPTER SEVENTEEN: **DETAILS, DETAILS**	162
CHAPTER EIGHTEEN: **PAINTING AND DECORATING**	174
POSTSCRIPT	186
FURTHER READING AND RESOURCES	188
INDEX	190

PREFACE

Mica Levi, one of the very few contemporary female film-score composers, once said:

> To me, a good way to spend your time is doing something that's exciting and challenging, something you can't get quite right.

I think that's the finest reason for scratch-building model railway locomotives and the best definition for it that you are likely to find.

Levi wrote the stunning score for the film *Under the Skin* which is a chilling tale of dastardly alien goings-on in downtown Glasgow. Her music adds a truly disturbing dimension to the film (especially for the Glaswegian men who meet Scarlett Johansson for the first and only time).

Since my previous book *Scratch-Building Model Railway Locomotives* was published I've been privileged to receive a great deal of informed and lively feedback. Besides some very pleasant compliments, a common comment was that starting off in scratch-building might be more daunting than I had hinted at. Starting anything that you are unfamiliar with is often daunting; I just didn't want to put you off.

The author at his workbench. RICHARD STANTON

I think Levi expresses the feeling beautifully of being daunted and excited by what you are attempting to do, something that you can't get quite right.

For another perspective, I recently read Mary Roach's brilliant book *Gulp: Adventures on the Alimentary Canal*, which describes the journey that food takes through the human digestive system. It's an alarmingly good read. At one point the author cheerfully tells us that the most nutritious part of any animal is the gizzard. Those gory bits and pieces are so full of vitamins that they are happily regarded as vegetables in plant-poor environments. It seems we are only stopped from regularly necking wholesome viscera because of cultural pressures. Apparently, we can become accustomed to and grow to like almost any foodstuff as long as we persevere – even liver (the curse of many a school dinner), or perhaps kiviaq (auk, left to ferment for a few months in a seal skin), which wasn't regularly served up with our mashed spuds.

'What's the point of all this?' you shriek, soldering iron quivering in your expectant paw. When do we get to touch metal?

Well, the argument I'm trying to construct here is that if you can open yourself to new experiences – new *difficult* experiences – then with a bit of work you will find that you really like them. And after a while you will become really good at them.

In the same light I would like to pay tribute to Don Wilson, to whom I have dedicated this book. When I was at secondary school, where he and his lovely wife Angela taught, I and some other waifs and strays attended a model railway club at their nearby home. Don had only recently lost his sight through diabetic complications, yet he seemed to treat this as only a minor impediment to his modelling. He nurtured the skills of each of us with humour and great patience, encouraging us to scratch-build rolling stock and buildings for his O-gauge garden line. This had a flavour of the London & North Western Railway (LNWR) in North Wales after the 1923 grouping and the locos tended towards the London, Midland & Scottish (LMS) with a LNWR pedigree. They were professionally built for him and he would eagerly feel the detail and form of each new model to test the accuracy of their construction. He could tell by memory and touch if the slightest detail was missing or misshapen.

Don died of further complications tragically early and I have never forgotten the inspirational effect that he had on me, both personally and in my modelling. He and Angela provided an environment of care and trust which allowed us to be challenged and to accept that mistakes were an important element in improvement and eventual success. Angela, incidentally, provided her own challenges for Don by having an enormous pond constructed in the centre of the garden. It was stocked with majestic koi carp, and occasionally Don himself would have to be fished out – always in good humour, as far as I was aware.

This then is my ongoing mission to inspire you, as Don did me; to hone your scratch-building skills, make mistakes, persevere and boldly go where no model locomotive modeller has gone before. The book complements and develops beyond my first book, which detailed the building in OO gauge (4mm scale) of a London & North Eastern Railway (LNER) J15 0-6-0 loco and tender. Only here you get to build a Tilbury Tank (or two).

While some of the methods are necessarily the same – there are only so many ways you can turn a big bit of metal into a collection of smaller bits joined together to form a model locomotive – I have incorporated some alternative ways of doing things along with ideas and techniques that I've come across more recently. New hand tools, further methods and some slightly more expensive machinery are described and introduced in a manner that I hope you will find entertaining, informative and inspirational enough for

Don Wilson getting to grips with his latest gift, a very welcome Christmas present from Angela. ANGELA LEONARD

Tilbury Tank No. 41961 on night duties, by Jonathan Clay, based on a photograph by E. E. Smith in the N. E. Stead collection.

you to get to the work surface and have a go at some scratch-building.

Learning never stops, you know; it is a product of our inbuilt curiosity that we strive to improve the skills that we already have. Otherwise, why would I spend so much valuable time practising the violin? We are never going to stop making things with our hands, and one reason why we are such a fantastically successful species is because we are driven to pass on skills to each other. Our hands twitch to make objects. If you doubt this, try reading *Touch: The Science of Hand, Heart and Mind* by David J. Linden, which describes why we like doing stuff with our fingers and how we have an emotional connection to the things we make.

While you digest that philosophical outburst, let us continue gently on our way to matters railway modelling.

CHAPTER ONE

SCRATCH-BUILDING FUNDAMENTALS

Scratch-building can be great fun, very satisfying – and absolutely infuriating. It calls on a variety of skills and attributes, so before we get into the creative and practical side of things, here are a few thoughts on the fundamentals of scratch-building to help you on your way.

Since I produced my last book, a very pleasant ready-to-run model of a J15 has come on to the market, which is a good thing as they are charming little locos and I'm glad to see more of them. A small part of me felt slightly miffed that, having lovingly and laboriously produced something that most other people didn't possess, suddenly there was one available to everyone. But when I look at my own model, especially since I painted it (see Chapter 18, Painting and Decorating), I'm even more pleased to have invested time and skill in making the one I have.

I must admit here that a reason I chose to build some Tilbury Tanks was because although they often appear on most wanted lists for ready-to-run locos, they're generally not so high up that they won't appear immediately this book is published.

WARTS AND ALL

Scratch-building, for me, is an exercise in continuous problem-solving, one solution informing the foundations of the next problem. The more experienced you become the less time it takes to come up with a viable solution (as opposed to a number of non-viable ones that end up in your 'useful' scrap box). As we progress through the book I will outline some of the problem-solving processes I went through in order to produce the models. You will find that with experience you can make things up as you go along. The key is not to be daunted by the possibility of making mistakes. I firmly believe that you can learn a lot through making mistakes. The next time you try something you'll probably do it better and it should take a lot less time. If you have

Preserved Class 79 Tilbury Tank **Thundersley.** DAVID COBBE

a memory like mine, try writing it all down as a book – I've found that process very helpful. Or you can plan things properly before you start, which sounds ideal in principle but just doesn't work for me.

PATIENCE

Another biological imperative: we all have a facility for patience derived, presumably, from the ability to wait patiently in a bush in anticipation of supper strolling innocently into grabbing distance. Patience is a virtue. Sometimes it walks out on us and we have to recognize that and give the soldering iron a rest before things turn nasty.

INSPIRATION AND LEARNING

I'm constantly amazed that craft knives can cut brass and nickel; after all, they are all made of metal. It comes as a bit of a revelation to understand that some materials are harder than others; that hack-saw blades can cut through copper pipes, and diamonds through glass. An understanding of the materials and processes that you are using can help things along nicely and you really only get that through experience. So, where to start?

The methods I use are ones that I have been taught and practised, read avidly about, or watched other people demonstrating, on video or in real life. I invite you to pick and choose, to practise and find preferred methods that work for you. I find that my construction skills evolve and improve continually. I can trace their beginnings back to making a model of Tracy Island for my Thunderbirds by watching Anthea Turner do it on Blue Peter. I thought: well, I can do that. And I did.

TOY PROJECTS

Have fun and enjoy the freeing effects of making toys. It's marvellous; you can try out methods you've been wary of using in case you wreck a cherished project. Simply allow your mind to take a flight of fancy that is normally more appropriate to the corridors of a science-fiction convention. I've had a go at a number of ideas and proudly produced an 0-gauge Dalek train for a local bookshop's window display (featured on my website if you're curious). It's a remarkably freeing exercise. Or have a go at something unrelated to railways. Military modelling in particular is a cornucopia of good ideas.

THE REAL THING

Well obviously you have to like the real thing and where better to go for inspiration than a preserved steam railway. I am fortunate to live near the Severn Valley Railway and any excuse finds me standing on the platform at Bewdley. There are plenty of themed galas across the network of heritage railways nowadays which means you get a chance to dress up, too, if you like that sort of thing.

You'll discover fabulous steam and diesel locos and rolling stock and get to experience (and breathe)

'1940s Weekend' at the North Norfolk Railway. 'Don't tell him, Pike.' PAUL SAYERS

that special atmosphere unique to steam railways. One autumn, in the early evening, I stood on the station overbridge at Bewdley and amidst the mist and fog a goods train clanked and squealed underneath. I'm too young to have any memories of those noises and it was quite a revelation.

Nothing quite beats the excitement of going on a drivers' course to provide unmatched memories, although all of the goings-on during a visit will help you understand how a real railway works. This then feeds back into how you run your own trains.

THAT MODELLING FEELING

Shropshire & Herefordshire Area Group are a talented bunch of finescale modellers. I've been lucky enough to become a member and seen some fantastic layouts *and* been permitted to operate them. Besides benefitting from the advice of highly experienced modellers, I've recently learned a great deal about operating model railways the way they were in reality, or thereabouts. I now (nearly) know all the signal-box bell codes from the Lancashire & Yorkshire Railway operations manual. Where else can you learn that sort of thing, other than at a model railway club?

RESEARCH

As with all projects I very much enjoy the research process. The more facts and figures you amass the more likely you are to make a good job of the finished product. It can be a good excuse for putting off making a start so make sure you get out of your armchair and start waving some tools.

PICTURES

Get lots and lots of pictures from books, magazines and the internet. That will help you choose the look of the loco. Read up on its history to find out how it changed throughout its life – like us, they certainly do.

DRAWINGS

Find or produce your own drawings to appreciate the size and shape of your project. The proportions of the component parts are particularly important in order to capture the character of each unique locomotive. There are lots of drawings available from back numbers of magazines and a fair number of books are dedicated to the subject of locomotive drawings.

The National Railway Museum (NRM) is very obliging and will provide you with a great deal of information

Operating the P4 layout 'Kerrinhead' in Gavin Clarke's spacious loft.

Research materials for the Tilbury Tank: books, photos, magazines and drawings.

by email, phone or in person at their dedicated research library and archive centre in York. Just ask them, they are there to help. There are a huge number of diagrams available with lovely General Arrangement (GA) drawings that can be supplied in paper or digital form. The digital version is fantastic as you can enlarge it at will on the computer screen, and if you are good with computers you could even print it at exactly the size you want. I use a photocopier instead.

GAs are difficult to follow: they have a huge amount of information on them, rather like an X-ray or a CAT scan of your own multi-interlocking innards – and they are equally fascinating. Versions known as 'pipe and rod' drawings can be simpler and could well have all the information you need; ask the NRM if you are not sure.

What you can easily do with either type of drawing is read off the measurements of key elements such as the length of the footplate, the outside diameter of the boiler and the size of the wheels. Knowing these fundamentals helps you to work out everything else.

I bought a huge paper copy of the GA for the Tilbury Tanks from the NRM in addition to the digital version because I like paper and I like putting stuff up on my workshop wall.

Warning: having lots of different drawings can be confusing, so do try to stick to one or you may end up taking all of the right measurements but not necessarily from the same drawing.

Some drawings can be less accurate than others and here is where photos of the original are so important. If something looks wrong on your drawing, check it against the photos. Digital photos are great for zooming in on. You can make reasonably accurate estimates of an unknown span, such as the depth of the cab window, by measuring directly from a photo if you are aware of some of the larger measurements.

Beware of creeping errors. It has been pointed out to me that you should always start from the same place, the 'datum', and measure everything, as far as you can, from there. That is sound advice. However, you don't need to worry too much about a half-millimetre here and there – life's too short. And anyway, as you creep

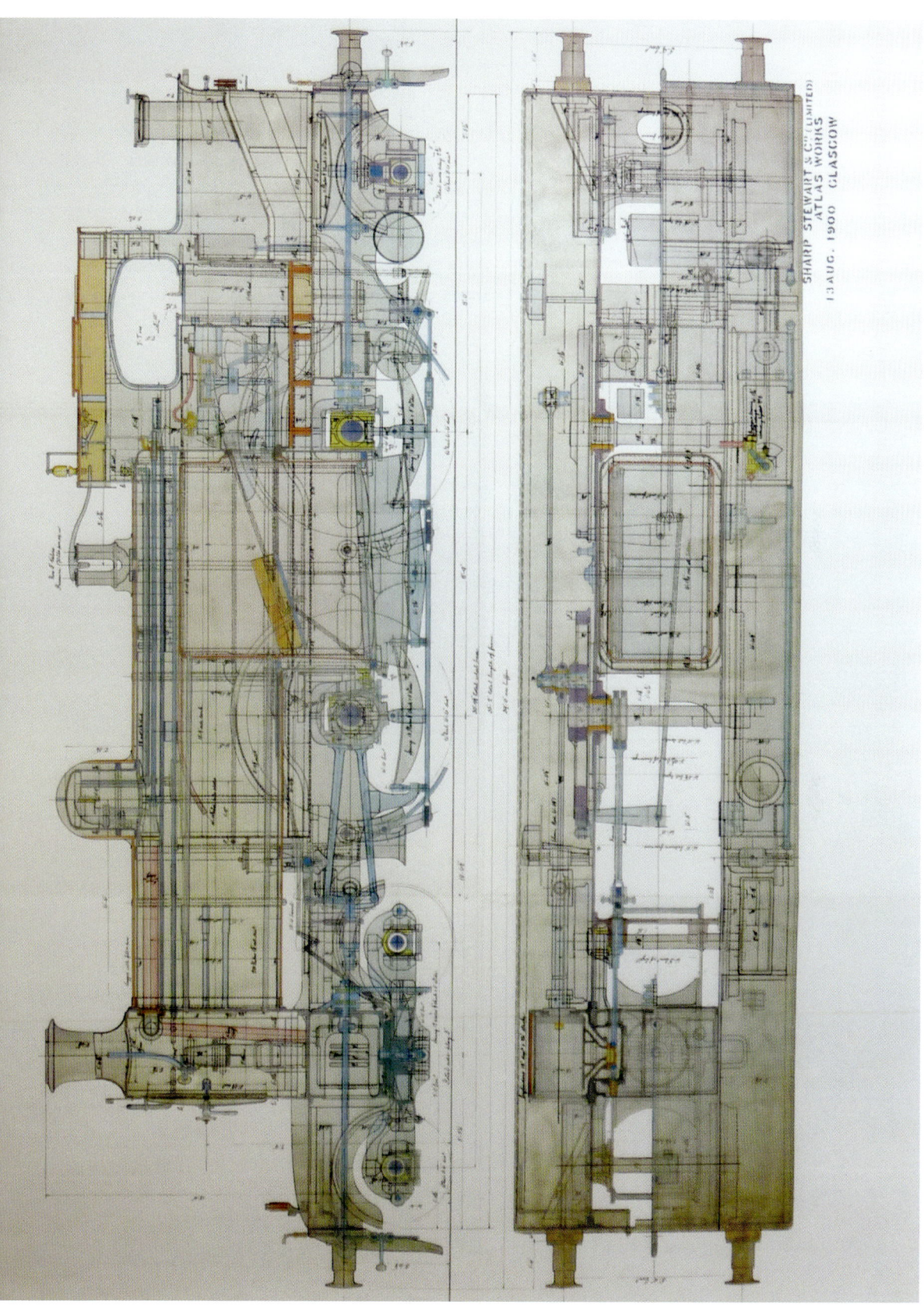

A beautiful example of a tinted GA drawing for the Class 51 Tilbury Tank. NRM/S&SPL

SCRATCH-BUILDING FUNDAMENTALS

along making further errors in your build you will have to do a bit of cunning compensation as you go.

If you would prefer to spend your modelling time modelling rather than drawing, I have included my own diagrams for the builds in this book. Exactly the same warnings apply.

KIT-BASHING

When you have mastered the skills of scratch-building, you will find kit-making comparatively easy. After all, the tricky bits in kits are simply scratch-built items pre-shaped for you; they just need to be married together in pleasing harmony.

Many kit manufacturers supply you with lots of spare bits and pieces to make the many subsequent variations that were only dreamed of by the initial locomotive designer. So what are you going to do with all of those spare parts? Why not use them to build another loco?

One final diversion before we turn our thoughts once again to Tilbury Tanks: scratch-building involves all of the skills and attributes I have mentioned and more. While there is a worry that these skills are being irrevocably lost, you only need to look at the initiatives of various preserved railways as they take on new apprentices, passing on the knowledge of steam locomotive engineering to people too young to have ever seen the real thing in revenue-earning service, to know that this is not the case. I find that very encouraging. And think about the resurgence of vinyl records. And books. The future is out there, ready to be scratch-built.

SCALE

Please note that while the scale drawings in this book are all reproduced to a scale of 4mm/ft, they may not have ended up being entirely accurate after printing. Use the scale bar on the drawings to check; each foot should come out as 4mm long, so 10 foot should be 40mm. Resize them by photocopying if necessary. In fact, it's a good idea to get into the habit of checking all your drawings wherever they come from.

A beautiful Class 1 Tilbury Tank. From the London Road Models kit, superbly built and painted by Neil Briggs. NEIL BRIGGS

CHAPTER TWO

TILBURY TANK RESEARCH

If you are being put off scratch-building because of the prospect of having to do lots of research, don't be. It can be as simple as getting hold of a single drawing or you could go and measure the real thing, if you are lucky. This is how I went about the very enjoyable task of investigating the Tilbury Tank.

MY RESEARCH PROCESS
DECIDING WHAT TO BUILD
When I was looking for an interesting locomotive to scratch-build, I ran a few searches on model railway websites under the words 'wish list' and 'wanted ready-to-run'. A number of less well-known alternatives came up including small industrial steam and diesel locomotives, medium-sized steam cranes, tramway engines and metropolitan steam locos.

After checking various possibilities, I narrowed the search down to large mainline tank locomotives and came up with the London, Tilbury & Southend Railway's Tilbury Tank. These were very attractive 4-4-2 tank locos with outside cylinders and simple motion. They were sufficiently long-lived to survive into the post-war British Railways era from the early days of the LTSR through (rather surprisingly) the Midland Railway and LMS. Suprisingly, because the line runs through stalwart Great Eastern territory. The line and the tanks have a fascinating history and a list of relevant books is included under Further Reading and Resources for those wishing to delve further.

I remember being taken by my gran from West Ham to Southend along the line to see the pier. I don't recall any steam locos but the green-liveried electric multiple units were rather atmospheric. So there's an emotional connection of sorts. And, brilliantly, I found out there was a preserved example – No. 80 *Thundersley* – currently on loan from the NRM at Bressingham Steam Museum in Norfolk. It fitted the bill exactly.

There were, as usual, a number of different classes and rebuilds and so on and I wasn't sure exactly what *Thundersley* was. I asked for advice on sourcing drawings on RMweb and was instantly provided with lots of drawings, a very reasonable offer for an excellent book and some lovely old photos of *Thundersley* in steam in the open air at Bressingham. Fantastic.

It turned out that *Thundersley* was essentially a Class 79 tank, modified under the ownership of all and sundry and then retrofitted back to its original(ish) form before being preserved.

I emailed Search Engine, the library and archive centre at the NRM in York, asking for help in identifying a GA drawing for a Class 79 loco. They swiftly got back to me with exactly what I wanted. It can take a few months for your copies to arrive but they are well worth waiting for. The Class 37 and 79 locos are essentially the same; it even says so on the drawings.

WORKING OUT HOW TO BUILD IT
Once you have decided what you want to build you then have to work out how to build it. Experience helps: the more models you have built before, the more likely you are to have a strategy. Modifying ready-to-run locomotives and building kits will give you an insight into how models are put together – where motors are fitted and so on.

A good way to continue is to see how the real thing is constructed. You won't be able to build a model that is an exact scaled-down version of the original – the physical properties of the universe just won't let you. However, you will be able to see how various constructional problems were solved by the locomotive engineers of the day.

For an understanding of how steam locomotives work, I can recommend two very good books.

16 TILBURY TANK RESEARCH

An atmospheric painting of **Thundersley** *by Jonathan Clay.* JONATHAN CLAY

R. Barnard Way's *Meet the Locomotive* is a classic, first published in 1947 and reprinted in recent years by Ian Allan. This layman's guide has a series of simple, charming line drawings and concise descriptions of how a steam locomotive works, and was written at a time when they still did. On a more ambitious scale, Drew Fermor's Haynes 'Owners' Workshop Manual' for the *GWR/BR (WR) Castle Class* is an ultra-modern working manual on how to build, run and maintain a Great Western Railway (GWR) Castle class locomotive – should you wish to. It is, quite simply, brilliant.

Luckily for me, *Thundersley* is easily accessible. If there isn't an example of the precise loco you want to build then look for something similar. There are only so many ways of building, for instance, an efficient pony truck and the engineers of the real things were not shy in using the ideas of others.

For example, GWR's chief mechanical engineer G. J. Churchward happily 'adopted' the bogie design of the French engineer Alfred de Glehn on his very successful standardized 4-6-0s – I think he asked him first. In fact he purchased a couple of locos, brought them to the Swindon works, tried them out and copied bits of them. It happens all the time. In the same vein, you could look at how kit manufacturers tackle various constructional problems.

SITE VISIT

Before you take your camera and head for a preserved railway line or appropriate museum, it's a good idea to make a list of all the things you want to take a look at, otherwise when you get home you will inevitably discover that you have missed something vital. (Mind you, even if you find a suitable photograph to resolve that particular problem, you might well be looking for an excuse for a second visit.)

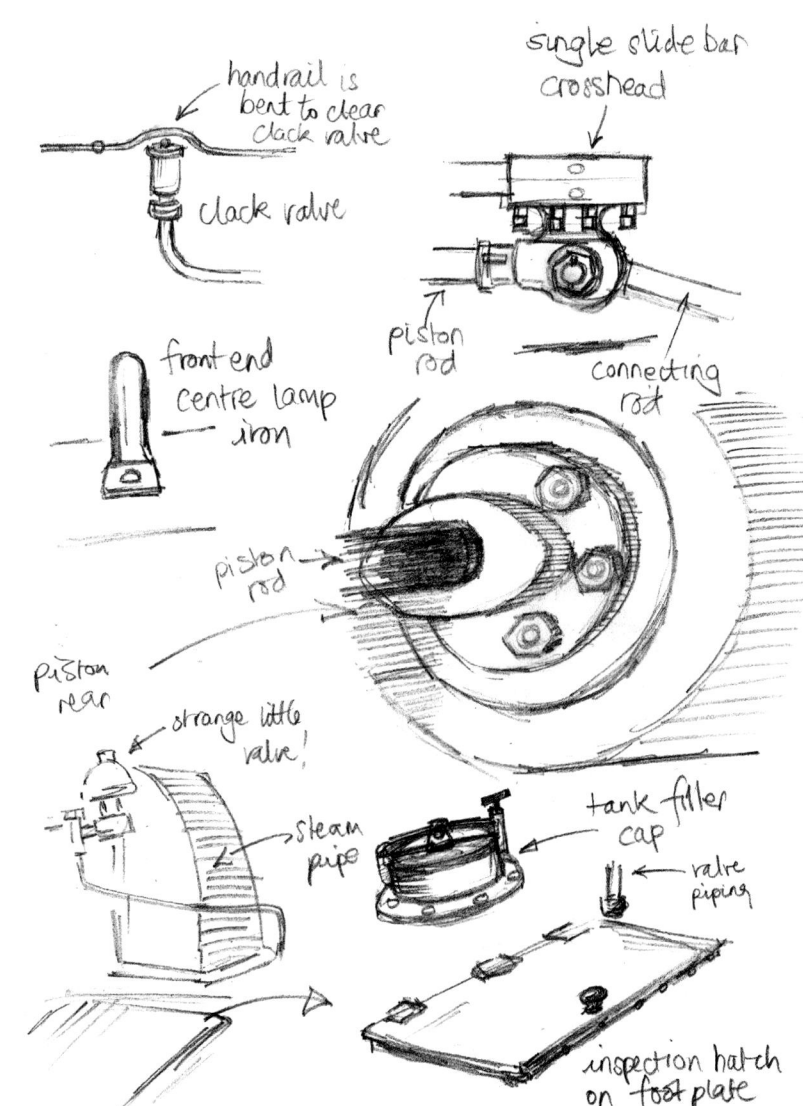

Thundersley *details sketched in situ.*

For my Tilbury build, I wanted to know how the 'wrap-around' cab was constructed. It surely couldn't have been made in one enormous piece with the tank and cab sides bent round, which is how I might have attempted it on the model. The later rebuilt locos at least must have had their roofs attached to the existing cab sides in some way. Photos showed evidence of a suspicious row of rivets and a joint line at the cab sides, so I particularly wanted to make a close inspection there. (By the way, the correct name for the cab 'sides' and so on is, I believe, 'sheets'. As a sailor used to applying that term to the sail ropes of a dinghy, I find this confusing. So 'sides' it is for me.)

Another item on my checklist for Bressingham concerned the chassis. It was difficult to determine the exact shape of the chassis frame, particularly in the area between the driving wheels and the bogie, so I wanted a good poke around under there when I got to the museum.

Which brings me to accessibility. It's great if the object of your attention has been left outside in the sunshine to allow you easy access and good light for photography but you can't guarantee that. When I visited the Bluebell line and wanted to take a look at their lovely Adams Radial tank loco I wasn't so lucky. It was tucked away in the back of a shed with rather poor lighting and not much space around it. The photos were not particularly good, though still helpful. Preserved railways do occasionally give their less commonly seen stock a bit of an airing and it's always a good idea to make contact in advance to ensure that what you want to get at is at least accessible if not running about outside.

Regardless of accessibility, it's always a good idea to take a sketch pad in addition to a camera. You don't have to be Leonardo da Vinci, just make sure you understand your own drawings and annotate them to help you remember what you have drawn.

It's also advisable to take a tape measure. Failing that, stand an acquaintance of known height up against the loco so that you can make an informed estimate of various measurements. For the smaller bits and pieces, I sometimes use my arm or fingers as a point of reference.

An amicable acquaintance stands at 5ft 8in against the side tank of **Thundersley**.

The information I gathered from my trip to Bressingham was extremely useful. It answered many questions and I'm grateful to David Atkinson for arranging an out-of-hours visit in exchange for a donation to the museum. In fact everyone I have dealt with while researching this project has been enthusiastically helpful. So no excuses, get out there and research. Unless you are going to build a Tilbury Tank, in which case it's all here. Or nearly.

Let's find out a bit more.

THE TILBURY TANK

The Tilbury Tanks are 4-4-2s. They have four little wheels at the front, four big driving wheels in the middle and a pair of small, carrying wheels at the back. This means that we can have a good look at making and setting up leading trucks (the front four wheels) and trailing trucks (the back two). Not only that, unlike the J15 tender loco, the Tilburies have outside valve gear, so we will get to construct some cylinders and the single slide-bar operating system with its collection of connecting rods.

Tank locos are by their very definition different to tender locos in that they carry all their water in tanks dotted about the loco and their coal in a bunker behind the cab. As there is no tender trailing loyally behind them, they don't have to be turned around in order to run in the opposite direction – as long as it is reasonably easy to see out of the back. If they needed to be bigger to cart larger loads of people or goods around, or travel greater distances, then further sets of wheels at the back or front were necessary to carry the extra weight of water, coal and locomotive.

The LTSR had a variety of other locos including a couple of 0-6-0 tender locos (which you could build using my previous book), some 0-6-2s and some truly magnificent Baltic tanks that were 4-6-4s and real whoppers.

In homage to *Meet the Locomotive*, I have included a drawing in the same style showing the Tilbury Tank's outside working parts.

I'll now take you on a brief journey through the different types of Tilbury Tank.

CLASS 1

These were the original and most diminutive of the 4-4-2 tanks, with narrower boilers and smaller wheels than their later cousins. They were gradually rebuilt by the Midland Railway and the LMS with (besides other bits and pieces) various different chimneys, domes, smokebox doors and extended smokeboxes. Some of them were smothered in rivets, others had theirs discreetly disguised. A few had their cab roofs changed to the wrap-around or 'hooded' model that all the final forms took. They carried a wide range of liveries and looked great in all of them. They also had a fantastic selection of names derived from places on the line, the best by far being 'Barking'.

We don't need to scratch-build a Class 1 because London Road Models do a very nice kit (see Chapter 1).

CLASS 37

Class 37 locos had larger wheels and a wider boiler; the cylinders were very slightly bigger too. They were a couple of feet longer than the Class 1 and as all of the subsequent 4-4-2 tanks were of the same length with a basically identical chassis it makes building more than one type much easier for us. The usual chimneys and so on were gradually replaced and many were extensively rebuilt with larger boilers and wrap-around cabs. You can tell a rebuilt 37 from a 79 by the ledge under the widened side tanks allowing some foot room for the cleaners.

CLASS 51

These were virtually the same as the un-rebuilt Class 37 with a slightly larger boiler, tanks and coal bunker. They are thought by some to be the best-looking of the lot.

CLASS 69

These were the exception to the 4-4-2 tanks and were used as freight locomotives. With their 0-6-2 wheel arrangement, I don't think they look anywhere near as striking as the others. There is a set of body and chassis etches available from Worsley Works Models so we don't have to worry about this one either.

CLASS 79

This is where *Thundersley* comes in. Four of these were built by the LTSR and they are virtually identical to the Class 37 rebuilds (on which they were based) with a bit of jiggery-pokery to the side tanks and bunker. They also had very slightly larger cylinders (we are talking scant inches here). The design was so successful that the Midland Railway built some more, as did the LMS. In their later lives these locos could be seen all over the country, including the Midlands and East Anglia, and some even made it up to Scotland. They just managed to sneak into the 1960s before being withdrawn.

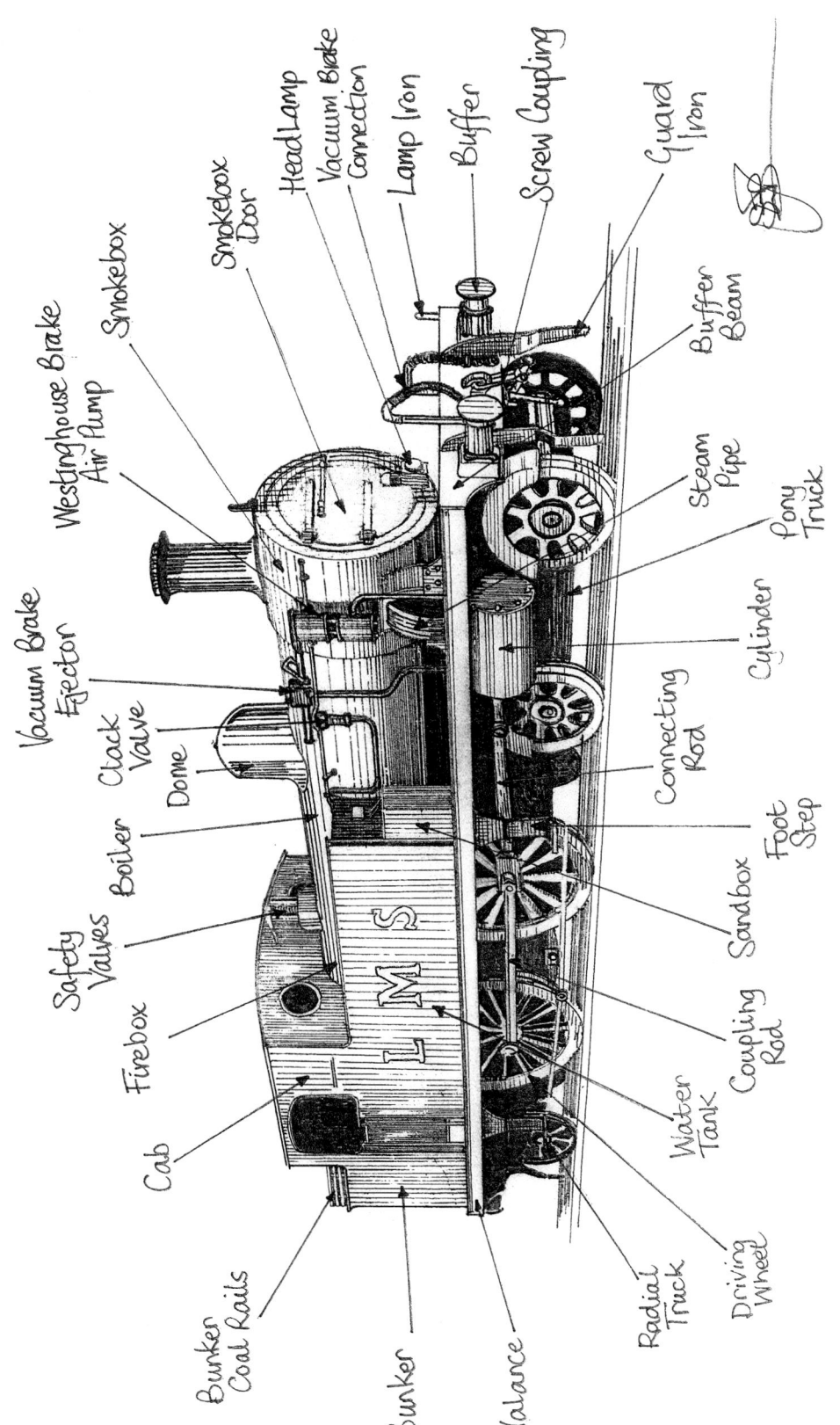

The outside working parts of a Class 1 Tilbury Tank.

DECISION TIME

I have photographs of both Class 51 and 79 hauling passenger trains on St Pancras to St Albans services, a line I have used a great deal, which endears them to me even more. As I have detail photographs of *Thundersley*, a Class 79 would be the obvious choice although I wanted a loco from the BR era (I'm not a fan of the more ornate liveries; I like simpler styles of painting). That would mean I would have to build a loco with extended smokebox and hooded cab, both of which are slightly more complex than the earlier versions.

Inspiration struck: as the Class 51 locos are almost the same, with more or less the same chassis, I could build a Class 51 with ordinary cab and smokebox and a later-type Class 79.

For a more detailed description of all these locos, I can thoroughly recommend *London, Tilbury & Southend Railway and its Locomotives* by R. J. Essery. Buy it, borrow it or order it from your local library; it's a brilliant read with lots of lovely pictures.

I will close this chapter with a mention of the Baltic Class 4-6-4 tanks of the LTSR. They are magnificently huge and I thought my drawing might whet your appetite for a further scratch-building project.

Baltic Class 4-6-4 LTSR tank.

CHAPTER THREE

THE WORKPLACE

THE SCRATCH-BUILDER'S NATURAL ENVIRONMENT

As I am presently living in a large rented house, I have graduated from the kitchen table to a spare bedroom that serves as a workroom. My current bench is a base-board, destined one day to become part of a layout but in the meantime being pressed into alternative service. As it is nearly at chest height it is also very good to stand at, which improves sight lines, is better for your back and can add numerous knee miles to your worn-out cartilages. A bar stool serves for when the cruciate ligaments need a bit of a rest. (By the way, you use lots more calories standing up than sitting down.)

There is lots of natural light in my workroom during the day and I've got various daylight bulbs and work lights for close-up viewing when things get a bit dim. My head-based magnifier is invaluable too. The window is large and supplies abundant ventilation for a variety of fumes and even allows for airbrush painting, neither of which were at all popular when I worked in the kitchen.

WORKBENCH ORGANIZATION

Try to keep the tools you use most frequently near to the work area and those you use less often further away. Those that you use very rarely can end up on the other side of the room as long as you have a good idea where they are. No doubt everything will creep forward like wolves around a campfire and your work area will shrink until it becomes the patch of floor at your feet. We can but try, though.

If it wasn't for gravity, how would we know where to find all those missing bits and pieces? Protecting the rented carpet I have a plastic/canvas car cover that makes a pinging sound as small and irreplaceable objects hit it, much aiding their recovery, though some of them still manage to ricochet into the middle distance. Without such protection, anything

An ergonomic work area.

THE WORKPLACE

The horrible reality.

white-hot escaping from the bench, after paying brief attention to the fingers, would hit the carpet or parquet flooring and leave indelible marks.

I have tried laying out my tools on paper with the outlines of each tool drawn on it, so tempting me to return them to the correct place. This is a good idea that can work for a while, though the paper does get very dirty and it is of course inflammable. A recent acquisition in the fight against disorder is a plastic cutlery tray in which to keep oft-used tools near to hand. We'll have to see how it copes with sharp edges and hot solids.

SOURCES OF DANGER

This is a good moment to advise you how dangerous scratch-building can be if you don't apply a degree of common sense.

HEAT
You do need to think about heat sources, particularly your soldering iron. Use a proper stand, keep it away from the edge of the bench and remember the iron is hundreds of degrees hot. You can be burned very badly if you touch it or any metal that has come into contact with it. Take great care.

Mechanical work, such as drilling and sawing, can also heat metal to surprisingly, and painfully, high temperatures.

CUTS
Scratch-building involves lots of sharp things. Handle craft knives and scalpels carefully in order to avoid cutting your fingers. Always put them down away from the general work area with the blade facing away from you. When you rummage through your tools you don't want to find a blade pointing towards you. The same goes for drills and the smaller broaches – they'll go deep into your fingers if you let them.

A plastered finger shows up occasionally in the photos, evidence of when I discovered how sharp a piercing saw blade can be – there's a clue in the name. Keep your fingers out of the way, particularly as you reach the end of a cut. Gardening gloves can offer a certain amount of protection for your precious digits.

EYES
Always wear eye protection when you are using slitting discs in the mini-drill: they can disintegrate at high speed. You are also advised to use goggles while drilling and wire-brushing.

FUMES AND GASES

Keep the window open, or at least make sure you have adequate through ventilation. Almost everything in scratch-building seems to produce some sort of noxious vapour – and that includes permanent marker pens. Watch out for fizzing flux, glue fumes (especially from superglue) and paint spray. Cellulose paint fumes are particularly poisonous; wear a mask and spray outside.

Never smoke or light a candle (why would you?) when you are working.

POISONOUS MATERIALS

Lots of the materials used in scratch-building – including lead, flux, solvents and solder – are poisonous or caustic and can give you chemical burns or even kill you. Don't drink or eat them. That might sound obvious, but take care that you don't accidentally expose yourself to them. So be careful what you dip in your tea, always wash your hands carefully afterwards and don't eat while you are working – quite apart from the safety aspects, you'll get crumbs everywhere.

I hoover up any dust that I make from filing materials such as resin or plastic. It keeps your workspace clean, too. Just watch out for small tools and components that can shoot straight up the nozzle.

TOOLS AND MATERIALS

I will describe the materials and the tools used to shape them as we come across them in the building process. For those of you who like to be pre-prepared, here are a couple of lists of the things you could be getting hold of.

The lists could be endless: you will pick up new tools as you go along and discover new ways of doing things, discarding previously adored tools. More esoteric tools and materials are mentioned throughout the book and there is an extensive list of suppliers at the back.

My recent tool acquisitions include:

- Garryflex abrasive block
- Jewellers' clamp or hand vice
- Large triangular file
- Fibreglass burnishing pencil

BASIC TOOLKIT

Measuring
- Steel rule
- Dividers
- Digital calipers
- Set-square

Gripping
- Bending bars (mini folders) – or large-jawed bench vice
- Pliers – long, round and square-nosed
- Tweezers

Cutting
- Craft knife – Stanley type, scalpel and 'scrawker' (a hooked craft blade) plus cutting mat
- Piercing saw – with a selection of fine to coarse blades
- Pin-chuck hand drill – and/or electric mini-drill
- Hand reamers and broaches

Fixing
- Soldering iron – powerful, high wattage, ideally temperature controlled with a digital read-out

Filing, finishing and cleaning
- Files – small flat, triangular and square; medium and large flat
- Sharpening stones and oilstones
- Wet and dry paper, assorted grades
- Brass brushes
- Scrapers
- Fibreglass burnisher

- Round, triangular and rectangular fine-grade sharpening stones
- Tiny needle files
- Half-round brass wire
- Tapered broaches
- GW Models 4mm finescale wheel press and quartering jig
- Screw thread taps and dies
- 10BA nut spinner

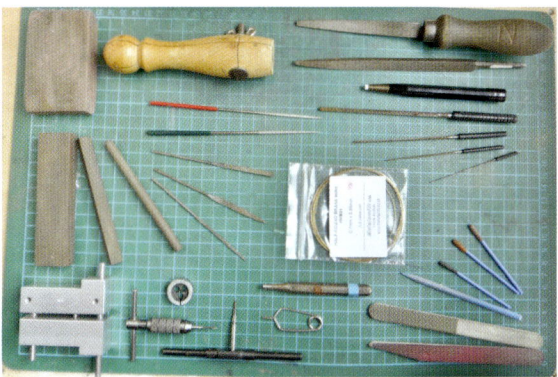

Some tools that are new to me.

> **BASIC MATERIALS**
>
> **Brass and/or nickel-silver sheet**
> - 12 x 6in sheet is a good size – it is cheaper to post and easier to use
> - 0.015in and 0.020in thickness are all you will need
> - 0.010in brass can be useful
> - Brass is easier to bend, nickel is springier and easier to solder
>
> **Other shapes**
> - 2 x 2mm L-section brass is good for valances
> - A variety of sizes of telescopic brass tubing – anything from 1mm diameter upwards
> - Straight brass wire, mainly 0.5mm and 0.7mm diameter
> - A variety of small U and square-section rods and tubes are handy
>
> **Solders and flux**
> - 180°C solder for main construction
> - 145°C solder for detailing
> - Flux – I use water-based safety flux
>
> **Nuts, bolts and washers**
> These are very helpful for holding things together and great for detailing work
> - 10BA, 12BA and 14BA
> - 16BA are really tiny, nice for details although fragile and very fiddly
>
> **Miscellaneous**
> - Various wooden blocks
> - Cocktail sticks
> - Clamps such as clothes pegs
> - Blu-tack
> - Masking tape
> - Permanent marker pens

- Angler's fly-tying clamp
- Variety of shaped abrasive sticks

TAPS AND DIES

A quick word about taps and dies before we move on. If you are not keen on soldering nuts into confined places, which happens in this book more often than you might think, taps and dies provide a possible alternative. These are magical little tools that cause a screw thread to appear, either within a hole – by tapping it – or on the outside of a rod, using a die. A certain thickness of metal is required for a reasonably secure screw thread so extra material may need to be soldered to the area to be tapped.

Once a hole is drilled you can cut a screw thread; specific hole sizes are needed for each tap (they are generally stated on the tap). If you haven't got a dinky little tap holder like mine you can use your pin vice – not a powered drill! Things need to be taken very slowly or you'll strip the thread or, worse, break the tip of the tap off inside the hole. (You don't want to do that too often as they are quite expensive.)

Enter the tap into the hole, keeping it as perpendicular as possible and very carefully, with a little pressure, rotate it until you can feel it 'bite'. Continue to turn it gently as it cuts the thread and screws its way through, like the mole that used to be delivered from the underbelly of Thunderbird 2 whenever there was a bit of subterranean jeopardy. That was always getting stuck too. You might want to practise on a disused mine working or spare piece of thickish brass. If only those Tracy boys had thought of that first.

The dies work in a similar way, travelling around the outside of a tube, and can make any number of useful bits and pieces, which we may come to later.

Ready? Tilbury Ho!

CHAPTER FOUR

DESIGNING THE CHASSIS FRAMES

One of the many great things about scratch-building is that you can decide exactly what you want to build and how you are going to do it. Whatever works for you is best and you can research and refine your methods, tools and skills as you progress. How I decided on the design of the frames of the Tilbury Tank is a good example.

It is usually maintained that 'the frames maketh the loco', which is why everyone gets so excited when those of a new-build locomotive are completed. While there is still the not inconsiderable problem of having to create all the rest of the bits, it's a great starting point for celebration.

As we've discovered, the family of 4-4-2 Tilbury Tanks – classes 37, 51 and 79 (rejoicing generally in the rather apt nickname of 'Universal Machines') – have essentially the same chassis design with some minor differences in such things as cylinder size. This is handy if you want to build examples of each. What isn't handy is that you can't see the shape of the frames very well: hardly at all on any photos or drawings, tricky to follow on the GA and almost impossible even on the real thing.

Steam locomotives sometimes have cut-outs at the front end, shaped to accommodate the wheels that guide the loco as it passes through curves in the track. See how the front ends are shaped on this

ABOVE LEFT: *A fine example of new-build loco frames in the raw on the Severn Valley Railway at Bridgnorth. These are of the Riddles BR 3MT 2-6-2 tank loco, No. 82045. There is a fascinating website showing the progress of the build at www.82045.org.uk.*

Wonderful front ends.

DESIGNING THE CHASSIS FRAMES

How to accommodate overtight curves.

majestic line-up of Great Western locomotives at Didcot.

Curves on real railways are, in most cases, very much less sharp than those on model layouts, which can be excitingly acute in order to negotiate such obstacles as furniture. Many model locos therefore require larger cut-outs in the frames than those on the real thing and may also be fitted with smaller-than-scale wheels to allow running on non-prototypical curves. There's nothing wrong with this kind of compromise if it meets your requirements.

Here on the lovely Tri-ang *Lord of the Isles* even the valance is given a cut-out to clear the tiny bogie wheels allowing the loco to rocket around scale equivalents of a 90-degree bend.

THUNDERSLEY'S FRAMES

Peering closely at *Thundersley*, what with all the wheels, pistons, rods and dinky little mudguards, there is scarcely a whiff of the frame. I tried to get a look from the inside but you can barely see a thing.

The GA drawing isn't that much help either as so many lines converge at the front end of the frames that it's hard to work out what's going on. Following a particular line with a highlighter on a photocopy of the GA makes things a little clearer, and if you've got the GA in digital form you can blow it up to individual pixel size on the computer screen, but the actual make-up of the frames remains a bit of a mystery.

> **MODEL REQUIREMENTS AFFECTING THE FRAME SHAPE**
>
> - What is the minimum radius of curves you want the loco to run through?
> - How complicated or simple in shape do you want the frames to be?
> - Do you want to include provision for springing or compensation systems?
> - What sort of pickups do you want to use?
> - What amount of detail do you want to include?
> - Are you prepared to compromise on wheel size or other diversions from the real thing?

That's not a problem as far as we are concerned. If you can barely see the frames on the real thing – and therefore on the model – then a few sensible adjustments can be made to allow for small-scale running. In fact, if you can't see it you can make it all up. Excellent. The most important considerations are, therefore, your requirements for the model.

DESIGNING THE FRAMES

A good start is to get a close look at some solutions devised for the real thing. For example, here is some modern steam traction on the Severn Valley with the

28 DESIGNING THE CHASSIS FRAMES

The LMS Ivatt Class 4 No. 43106 delights in the nickname 'The Flying Pig'.

LMS Ivatt Class 4 No. 43106 showing off her frames in a rather un-Victorian manner.

Everything is very clear as these locos were built for ease of maintenance; no hiding things under the railway equivalent of skirts for designers in an age of austerity. There isn't really a valance, in fact hardly a footplate at all, just a shelf high up on the boiler, presumably to allow for a bit of cleaning and upkeep without the use of a ladder. The boiler seems to sit directly on the frames and all of the 'motion' (the moving parts that transfer the movement of the piston to the wheels) is hung off the sides, so it is not too difficult to get at with a spanner.

In particular, you can see that the frame is 'humped' up over the wheel axles to provide extra metal for added strength in those areas that would otherwise be weaker. In a model it is simpler just to have a nice straight top edge to the frames. The disadvantage of this is that you can end up with potential weak points above the axle – not too much of a problem if you are careful.

In fact, in the olden days of the mid-twentieth century you might have found a pair of model loco frames that are simply two brass strips with holes in.

With Computer Aided Drawing (CAD) programmes and modern metal-etching techniques, things have become a tad more sophisticated and the results can now faithfully mirror the real thing.

Looking at the Adams Radial frames opposite demonstrates another little trick for scratch-building as employed on the real thing, that of standardization of components. Using the same design over and over again saves time and allows you to become very familiar with the construction methods of various bits and pieces. The Great Western Railway in particular really loved standardization. William Adams (1823–1904) was the locomotive superintendent of the North London Railway from 1858 to 1873, the Great Eastern Railway (GER) for a few years until 1878 and finally the London & South Western Railway until his retirement in 1895. During his tenure with the GER, Adams seems to have had quite a strong influence on Thomas Whitelegg, who worked there at around the same time. While Whitelegg is the credited designer of the Tilbury Tanks, his association with Adams can be seen particularly in the shape of the frames and associated bits and pieces. Parts of the Adams Radial and the Tilbury locos are almost identical. It's nice to imagine the pair of engineers sketching loco designs on the back of a fag packet over a pint in a Stratford pub.

Some more clues here for our scratch-built design.

DESIGNING THE CHASSIS FRAMES

The simple frames of a much-loved first kit.

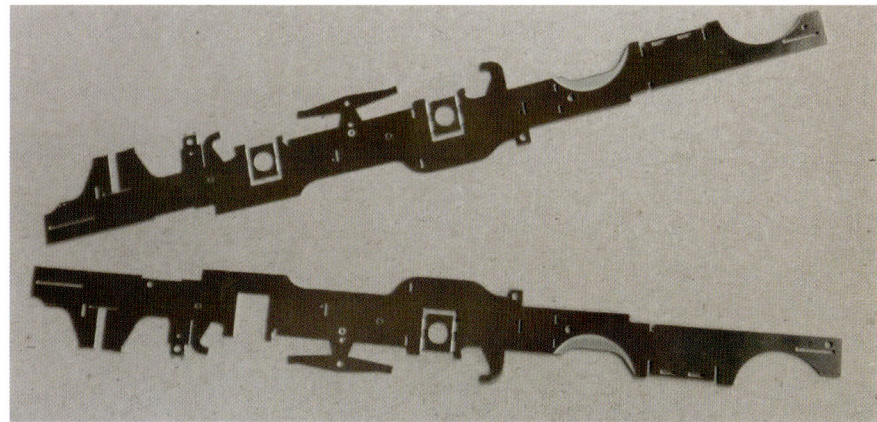

Martin Finney's fine Adams Radial frames from his superb O-gauge kit.

DRAWING THE FRAMES

Although I have provided the drawing that I used (*see* Chapter 5 describing the frame build for the Class 51) – which you can photocopy or trace – I thoroughly recommend that you produce your own. Drawing can be very rewarding in its own right and you get to learn a great deal about how the subject is put together as you study its shape.

I use a small portable drawing board for sketches and have an architects' drawing board for larger-scale drawings. It's fantastic as you can draw parts to, say, four times the size you need in order to include more detail, then reduce them on the photocopier to the size you want. Always check that the copying process hasn't distorted anything and beware of your paper stretching. I always include a ruled scale on the drawing, which makes checking easier.

You can pick up good drawing boards very cheaply at the moment as plan drawing has become largely superseded by CAD programmes. For old-fashioned types like me, the sharpened pencil will do nicely.

If you are concerned that you haven't had the advantage of technical drawing classes (which were

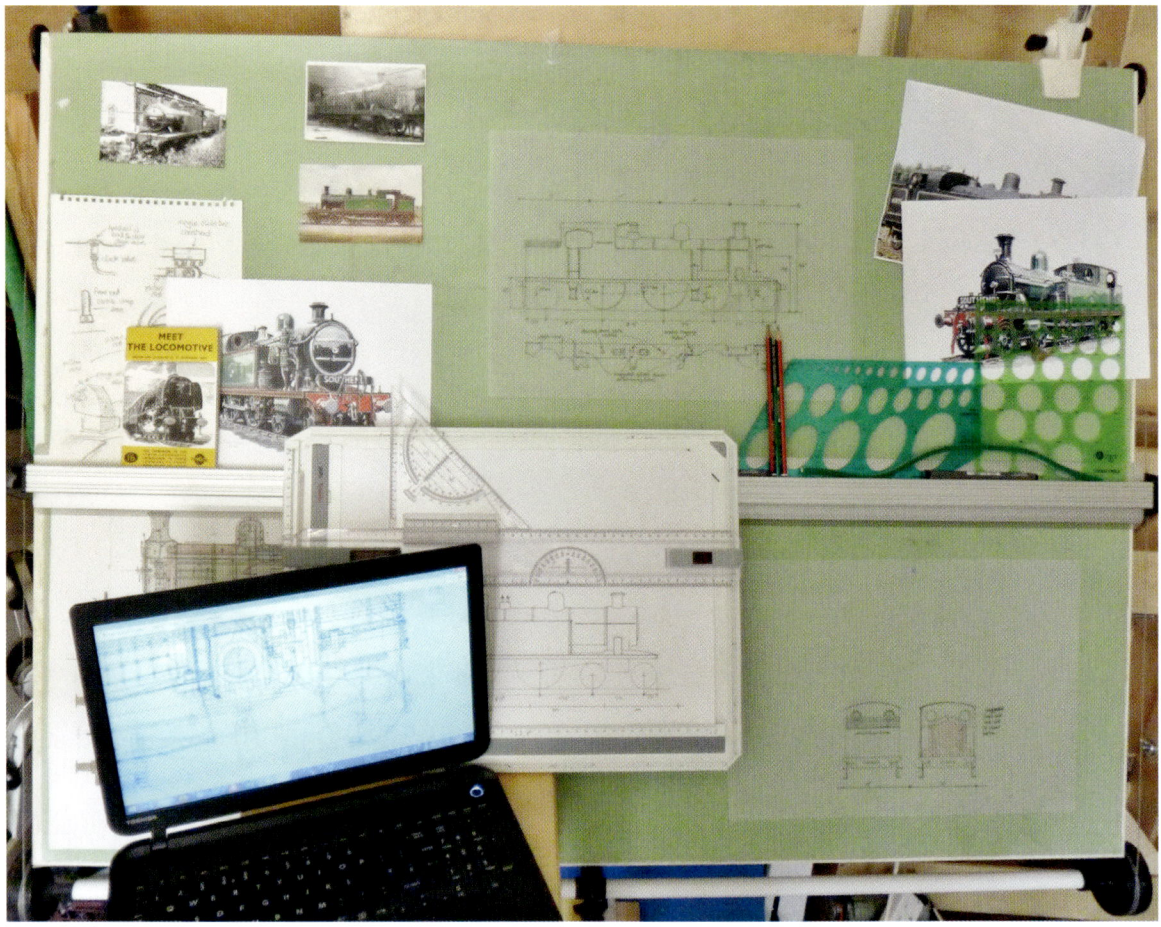

Various aids to drawing and design.

definitely long gone by the time I got to secondary school), there are some excellent videos on YouTube – how ironic. All you really need is a large plastic set-square with at least one edge ruled in millimetres; some good-quality pencils and fine fibre-tip pens; a reasonably steady hand; a rubber; and quite a lot of patience.

Very basically, you draw horizontal lines with the guide on the drawing board and then add the verticals with the set-square resting on the horizontal guide. Wiggly bits can be plotted using French curves, which are still widely available. I usually estimate curves by eye from photos and drawings.

Once you are happy with the work in pencil, go over it in fibre-tip and you are ready for the photo-copier. Tracing paper is thoroughly recommended as you can scrape off mistakes with a curved scalpel blade. Tippex always shows.

SHAPING THE CHASSIS FRAMES

Before I cut any metal I made some preliminary sketches, keeping in mind my requirements for the model. They show the progression of my ideas for the final drawing of the frames.

Once the sketches were made and I had decided on what I wanted, I produced my finished drawing (see Chapter 5). I say 'finished', but as I built the first chassis I went back to the drawing quite a few times to make modifications.

DESIGNING THE CHASSIS FRAMES

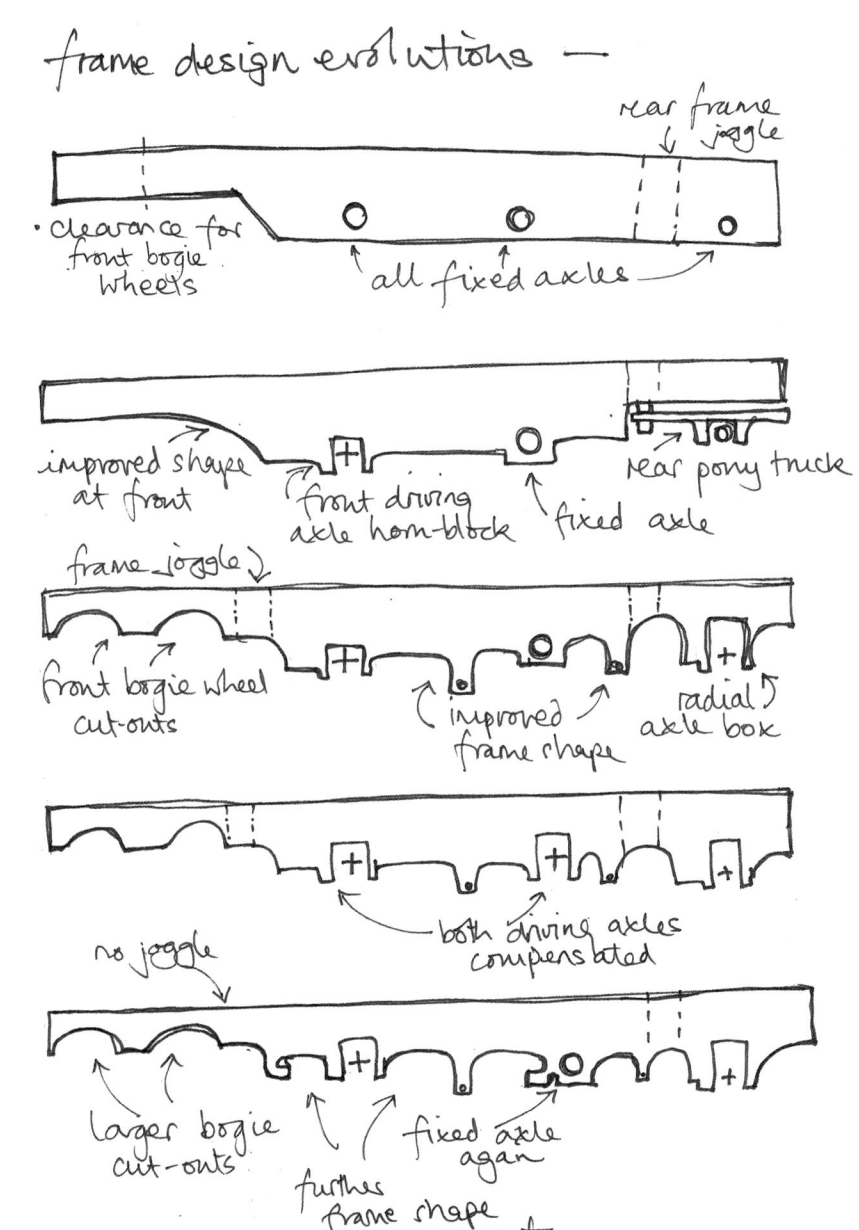

Preliminary design sketches.

'No battle plan survives contact with the enemy' is one of my favourite scratch-building quotes. Helmuth von Moltke the Elder might have had things military on his mind when he observed this but it applies perfectly to scratch-building, which involves a constant series of feedback loops as you respond to various problems and produce new solutions. That's why it can take so long. Planning can help to cut down the actual building time; it doesn't always. However, when you want to build the same thing a second or third time over, keeping notes of improvements can help considerably. So I've done it for you with the drawing. There's no reason why you shouldn't modify and improve on it yourself, but here are my reasons for why I produced the frames in the way that I did:

- I wanted to have the prototype joggle that accommodates the movement of the wheels in the radial truck and bogie.
- The front cut-outs are just big enough to clear the bogie wheels. You could make them larger to completely clear the wheels but be careful that you don't end up with a nickel-silver doily. If your layout curves are particularly tight then the dodge of fitting smaller wheels might be a more appropriate solution.
- The various little downward projections are for hanging equalizing beams and brake gear that appear on the real thing. They could be omitted if you don't want to go into so much detail but they don't take much extra time or effort to cut.
- I've tried hard to put the holes for the spacers in places where they can't easily be seen or where they will allow you to use plunger pickups.
- The various other holes are for the brake gear and anything that needs to be drilled while the frames are soldered together.
- The axle holes have dotted cut-outs showing where you can saw to make provision for the radial truck and compensation beam or sprung horn blocks. The rear driving axle is 'fixed' as the motor is going to be attached to that one. See Chapter 14 for a description of compensation beams and horn blocks. Horn blocks, incidentally are the brackets fitted to the loco frames to act as guides for the axle boxes, allowing them to move slightly up and down as the loco passes over less than perfectly laid track.

If you want to make any modifications to suit your own requirements, it is best to do so at this point as it is a lot easier to change a drawing than to modify metal after it's been cut.

CUTTING AND STICKING

Having produced your drawing you might want to have a little think about what you are going to do with it.

Many modellers simply cut out the drawing and stick it to a handy piece of metal. The main advantage of this 'sticky-paper' method is that you don't have to draw everything out all over again. If you don't like drawing, that's a particular plus point. The disadvantages, which can be overcome with care, are:

- If you haven't checked properly, your drawing – and therefore the pieces you cut out – may be inaccurate
- The paper might stretch and distort as you stick it onto the metal
- The lines on the drawing may be rather thick and they can become ragged as you saw against them, making it difficult to finish off accurately
- It can be difficult to cleanly remove the paper and glue residue afterwards
- The glue can jam the saw blade (or is that just me?)

I find that glue sticks (such as Pritt Stick) work best for this method as the glue isn't liquid so the paper doesn't distort and it's easy to remove. Just smear a thin layer onto the metal and position the paper carefully without sliding it about too much. You don't need to cut the complex shape out in paper first, which is quite tricky. Simply make sure the top edge is straight and true and cut the rest out as a reasonably accurate rectangle.

When I started scratch-building I always used the sticky-paper method. However, as I became more confident in my draughtsmanship I began to transfer the drawings directly to the metal. It is quite simple to coat the metal surface with a thick black permanent marker. Taking the measurements directly from the drawing with a pair of dividers is easier than measuring with a ruler and you can scribe directly onto the surface.

What I like with this method is that you get very fine lines that show up brightly against the background and are very good to file to and to finish off. Of course you can still make mistakes, so check.

All this can be seen in detail in the chapter that follows.

CHAPTER FIVE

BUILDING THE CLASS 51 FRAMES

In order to include a variety of modelling techniques, I'll describe the build of a Class 51 loco first and then that of a Class 79, giving you a choice of two Tilburies.

While the main construction techniques are the same, the Class 51 is arguably simpler to build than the Class 79, the construction of which illustrates some of the more complex options. Perhaps you'd like to pick and choose? As with many tank locos they both consist of an agreeably simple selection of rectangular boxes and cylinders complemented by

Class 51 tank in near mint condition.
SAM MANLEY

THE DIFFERENT BUILDS

The following construction elements are covered:

Class 51
Rigid chassis
Etched leading truck
Simple sprung trailing truck
Folded-up cylinders
Etched coupling rods
Scratch-built connecting rods
Romford wheels
Ready-made gearbox/motor
Wheel wiper pickups
Tube boiler
Folded-up smokebox/saddle
Simple cab roof construction

Class 79
Beam-compensated chassis
Scratch-built leading truck
Etched radial trailing truck
Solid cylinder construction
Etched fluted coupling rods
Scratch-built connecting rods
Alan Gibson wheels
Fold-up High Level gearbox
Plunger pickups
Boiler rolled from sheet
Extended smokebox/saddle
Wrap-over cab roof
Embossed rivet detail

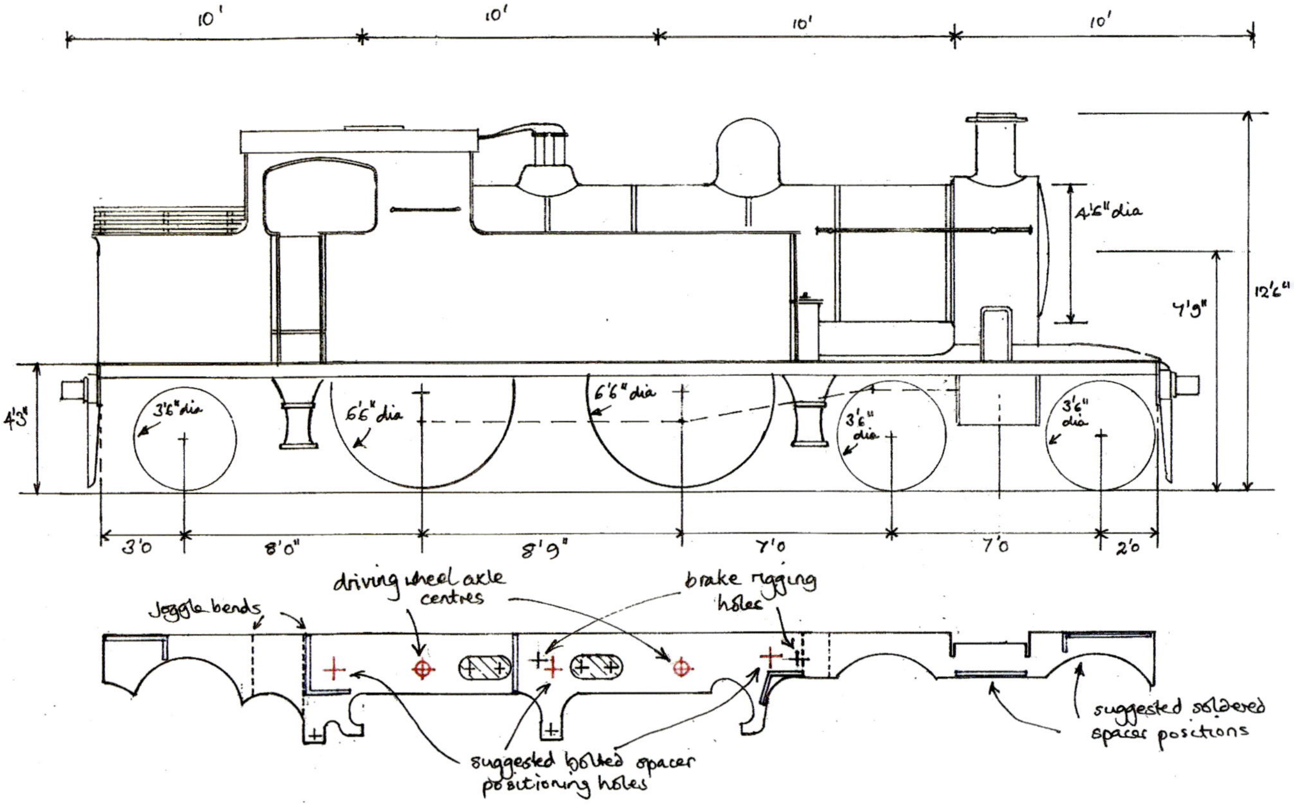

34 BUILDING THE CLASS 51 FRAMES

Class 51 drawings.

MOTIVE POWER: CHOOSING THE GEARBOX/MOTOR

I like to build the loco frames first as any clearances necessary for the motor, wheels and motion can be incorporated into the body design. There is a wide range of motors and gearboxes available, which can be somewhat confusing, so it helps to consider what you want to do with your loco and how you are going to achieve it when choosing your set-up.

Generally it's good to have the largest motor you can fit into the confines of the frames and loco body without being able to see alien tech anachronistic to a steam locomotive. I like my locos to be capable of smooth slow running and tend to choose high gear

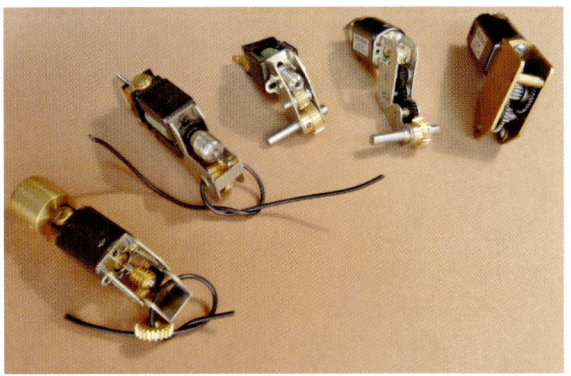

A selection of motors and gearboxes.

ratios on my gearboxes, which helps to achieve this. The higher the ratio the slower the running; the compromise is that you lose a bit of power. A great big brass flywheel is always good for smooth progress too.

BUILDING THE CLASS 51 FRAMES

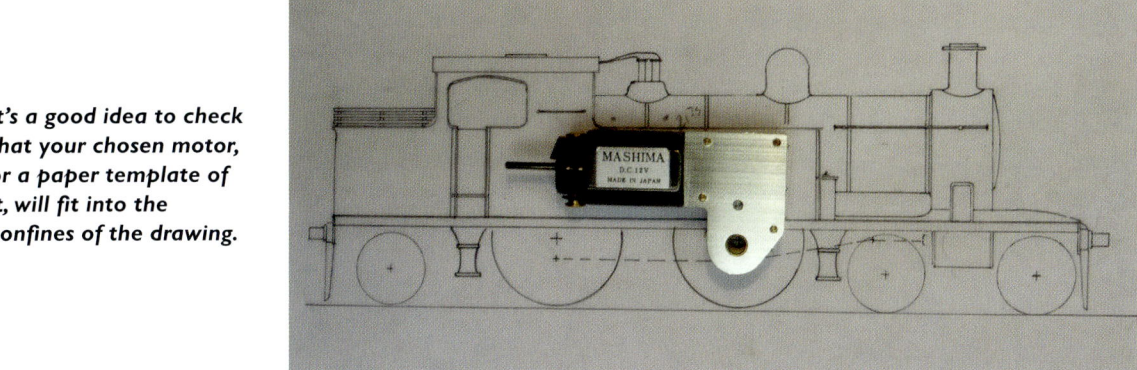

It's a good idea to check that your chosen motor, or a paper template of it, will fit into the confines of the drawing.

Class 51 tanks were designed for suburban passenger traffic and needed to haul heavy loads with a reasonable amount of acceleration. The combination of motor and gearbox I chose for this build – a DJH GB2 gearbox and M1124D Mashima motor with 50:1 ratio gears – gives me what I want. It takes up a lot of space in the cab so there's not going to be much left for added detail. In OO gauge the wheels take up a lot of the interior space anyway and if you fit some doors and a crew you can barely see inside.

My choice for the Class 51 build is ready-made and quite pricy; you could go for a simple soldered-up gearbox, which can be cheaper. The Class 79 build illustrates the build-it-yourself gearbox, with the added extra that it will give you more space inside the cab for detailing if you are so inclined.

Now these choices have been made, we can make a start on the frames.

MAKING THE FRAMES

The frames of a locomotive are the big metal sides underneath that hold the wheels in place and support the locomotive body. They are hefty pieces of metal, usually around 1in (25mm) thick in real life (each railway company had their preferred thickness). They are a good place to start a locomotive; you can't really have a chassis without them and they are reasonably simple to make.

PREPARING THE METAL

First you'll need some pieces of metal; it's a lot quicker to make both frames simultaneously and of course they'll be identical if you cut them as a pair. And that's important. I use 0.020in nickel silver as I find it stiffer and easier to solder than brass. It also looks pretty.

Make at least one strip the length and widest breadth of the frames. Two strips are unnecessary, unless you've already got some. Just line up the straight edge of one strip with the straight edge of a wider piece of metal and cut two frames out from that. In fact you could just solder together two roughly sized rectangles along one straight edge. It depends on how much metal you are prepared to waste.

Please watch your extremities when using knife blades and metal rulers; it's very easy to slice your fingertips. It never fails to make me feel faint and plays havoc with my violin practice.

It's a good idea to have another check that your drawing is correctly scaled. As we're working in OO gauge, at a scale of 4mm to 1ft, a good rule of thumb is to multiply the real (imperial) measurement by four to see if everything is OK – so 10ft on the drawing should be 40mm on the model. Or check against a given scale rule.

Ready? Here goes, breaking the metal to size:

- Find a good straight edge and 90-degree corner on a piece of 0.020in nickel silver, using a set-square.
- Mark off the length of the frames against the drawing with a scalpel blade.

36 BUILDING THE CLASS 51 FRAMES

- Use a set-square to keep your marked line perpendicular across the metal surface.
- Use a scrawker (or hefty craft knife) to deepen the cut. I find that if you can see the line faintly on the other side of the metal you are likely to get a good break.
- Clamp the metal in the bending bars with the scrap piece poking out of the business end of the bars. This should stop you from distorting the piece you want for the frames.
- Use a solid file to support the piece as you bend it up and down until it breaks along the line.
- Smooth the broken edges by rubbing gently on a piece of wet and dry paper supported on a flat surface; this will remove any burrs.

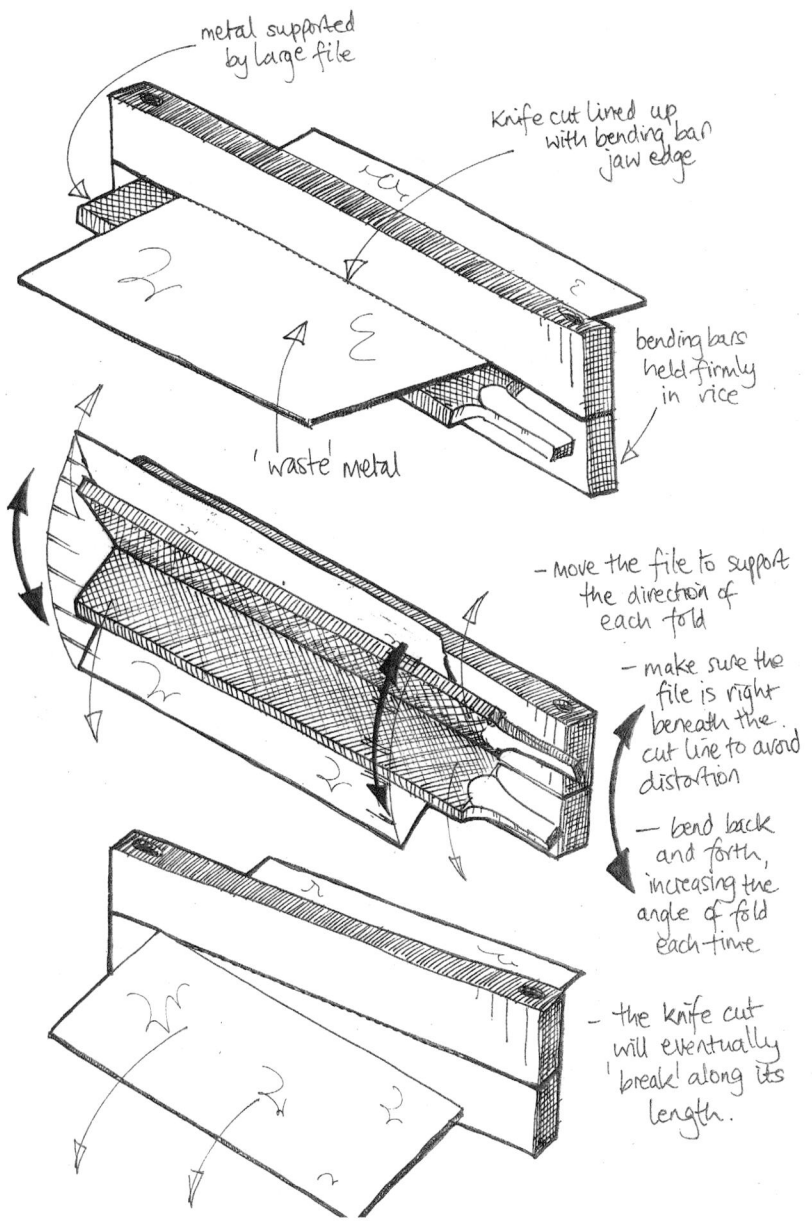

How to break the metal by bending.

BUILDING THE CLASS 51 FRAMES

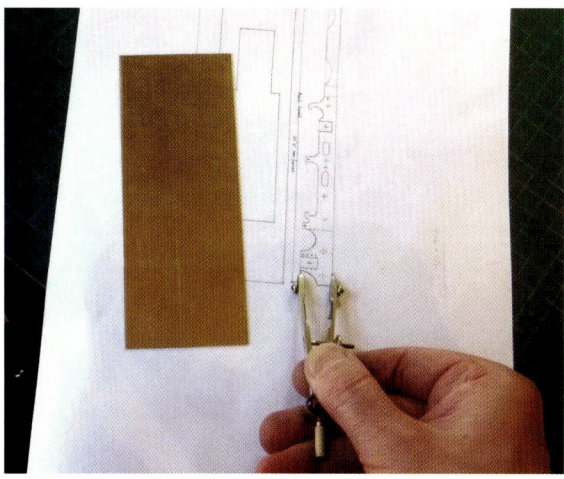

Use the dividers to take the frame width from the drawing.

Clamping the frame strip using clothes pegs.

Transfer the measurement, carefully running the dividers along the edge of the metal.

- Repeat the marking, bending and breaking process to produce a strip to the correct length and width of the finished frames.
- Clean all metal surfaces with a gentle rub of wet and dry paper.
- Clamp the strip to the remaining original piece. Using a flat surface, line up the sides and bottom carefully. Clothes pegs make handy clamps. It's important that you have the top edges of your frames straight and true as it helps keep

> ### SOLDERING TIPS
>
> - Keep everything clean and brighten the metal surfaces that are going to be joined with some fine wet and dry paper. Solder doesn't take to dirt or grease.
> - Use a powerful soldering iron that is good and hot. Small irons lose heat to the metal very quickly; high-wattage ones can really pump it out.
> - It's handy if you have a digital temperature read-out on your iron. I usually keep mine at 395°C – you'll soon find a temperature that suits you.
> - Use a suitable flux. My preferred one is Water Based Safety Flux from Building O Gauge Online. It doesn't seem to produce noxious fumes or too much tarnish if you don't wash it off. It does tend to spray itself about the place and cause rusting on treasured tools. And boy does it sting when you get it in a cut.
> - Use 180°C solder for the main construction.
> - Use 145°C for secondary construction and detailing.
> - Always give everything a good wash after each soldering session.
> - Soldering is swift, efficient and satisfying but requires great care if you want to avoid nasty burns.
> - Ask a demonstrator at a show to let you have a go (or you could watch my demonstration on YouTube via www.artfulengineering.co.uk).

everything square when you build up your chassis.
- Tack solder the two pieces together in three or four places where the lumps of solder won't get in the way later.

Tack soldering temporarily holds the pieces of metal together and consists of swiftly applied blobs of solder – it doesn't have to be pretty. It is very good for initially soldering a joint, holding things together while you check everything is in the right place. See box on the previous page for some basic tips.

PREPARING THE FRAMES

Here you can choose to either draw the frame shape directly onto the metal or cut out a copy of the drawing and stick it on as a cutting template. A complex shape like these frames can be time-consuming to redraw so I've gone for the stick-and-saw solution.

It isn't necessary to cut the complex shapes out from the paper as you'll do that bit with the saw. A careful rectangle is fine. Try hard not to distort the paper as you stick it on and don't rely on any of the drill holes to be in the right place; they will be measured accurately after cutting and removing the paper.

A glue stick is a good adhesive if used sparingly. Or try double-sided tape, which though fiddly to get right doesn't wet the paper and avoids stretching. It also seems to saw easily, forming small balls of fluff. A real plus is that provided you haven't wrinkled the template it is stuck universally firmly and you can file right up to those thin lines without the paper fraying and blurring. In fact I like using double-sided tape so much I've rather stopped drawing onto the metal. The main problem with the tape is that you only have one go to get the template down in place correctly, otherwise it's rip and strip and start again. Another problem is getting the stuff off when all is fine and filed. We'll come to that.

Anyway, carefully tape the template nice and square and level at one end and judiciously place it so that the straight edge matches that of the metal strips. We are now ready to saw the frames.

SAWING THE FRAMES

As with other techniques, people develop their own favourite ways of sawing. Some like to saw against the jaws of a vice for straight lines, others like to saw up and down or side to side. It's up to you. As you get better you can saw closer and closer to the lines to reduce the amount of final shaping and gradually you will break fewer and fewer blades.

This is how I set up for sawing the frames.

Thin metal can be supported even more by placing a piece of card underneath and cutting through that simultaneously.

Saw the frames roughly to shape. Take it gently around tight corners. Always saw in the waste side of the line – things can be tidied up later.

Glue stick or tape – your choice.

Piercing saw, blades and sawing table.

BUILDING THE CLASS 51 FRAMES

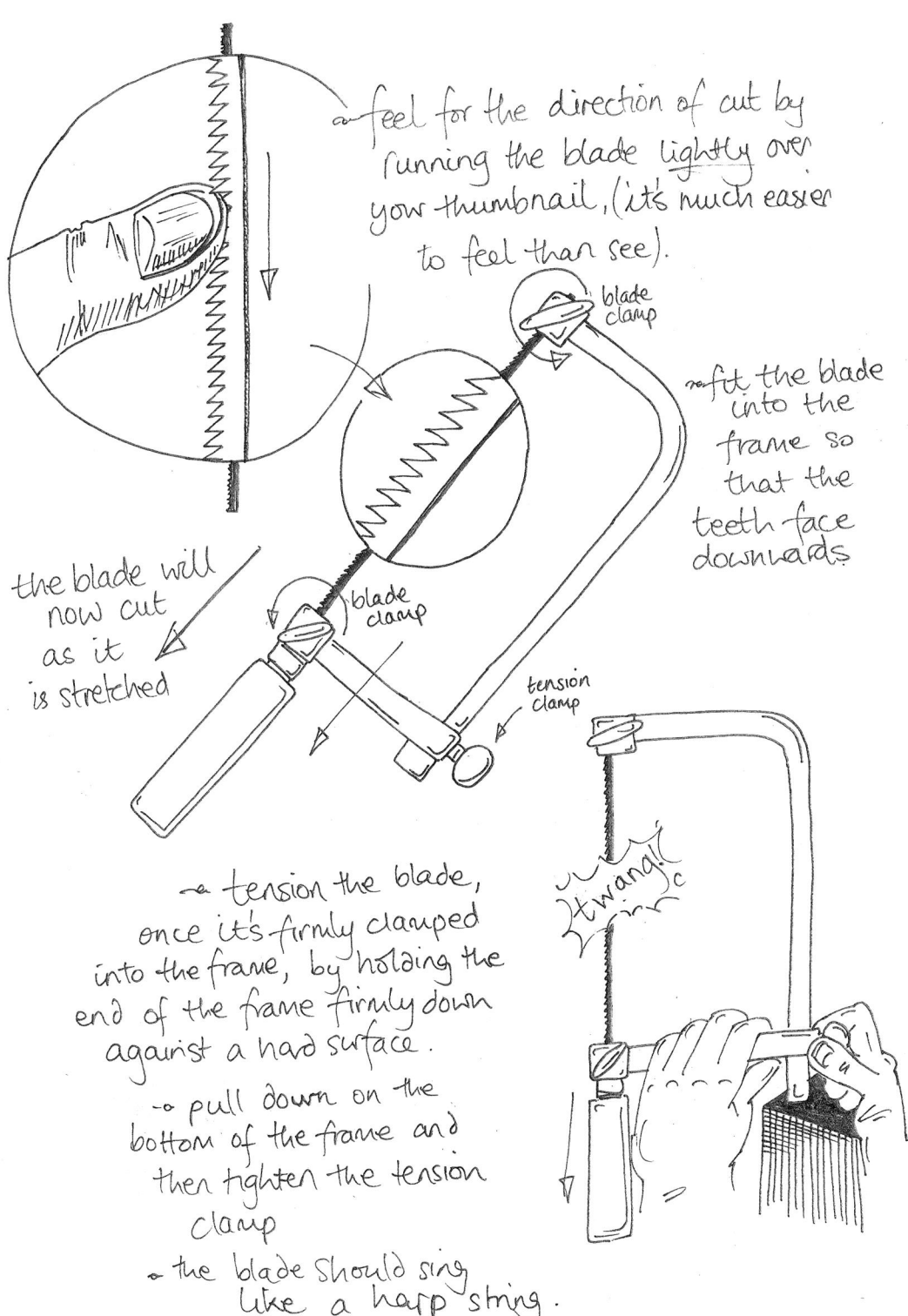

Setting up for sawing.

PIERCING SAW TIPS

- Use fine blades, say 6/0 (the larger the number the more teeth per given saw blade; you need about two teeth to be in contact with the metal edge).
- The metal you are sawing needs to be supported to prevent vibrations that will break the blade. Use a little sawing table and hold the work down firmly *and* gently.
- The blades will break anyway – take it gently, like tickling for trout.
- Drill a starter hole somewhere in the waste area of the metal if you are cutting a shape out of the middle.
- You can saw around tight corners if you saw up and down in the same place and *gently* twist the saw frame round as you go.
- Cutting corners is a bit like steering an oil tanker: the blade doesn't twist as quickly or as far as the frame does. Try letting go of the work piece, it will probably swing around to where the blade would like to be.
- Plan the directions in which you are going to cut if the piece of metal is large and the frame of the saw won't fit. You may have to start again from another place.
- The blade will always snap just before you finish. Take deep breaths and change the blade.
- The blade can be lubricated by rubbing on a candle.
- The blades are astonishingly sharp. Watch your fingers.
- Sawing can be satisfying.

If at any time it looks as though the two pieces are going to come adrift, just add another soldered tack joint or two where you have worked already.

So now we have a roughly shaped pair of Tilbury Tank frames, ready to be beautifully shaped and drilled for the axles, brake hangers, spacers and so on. Don't separate them yet.

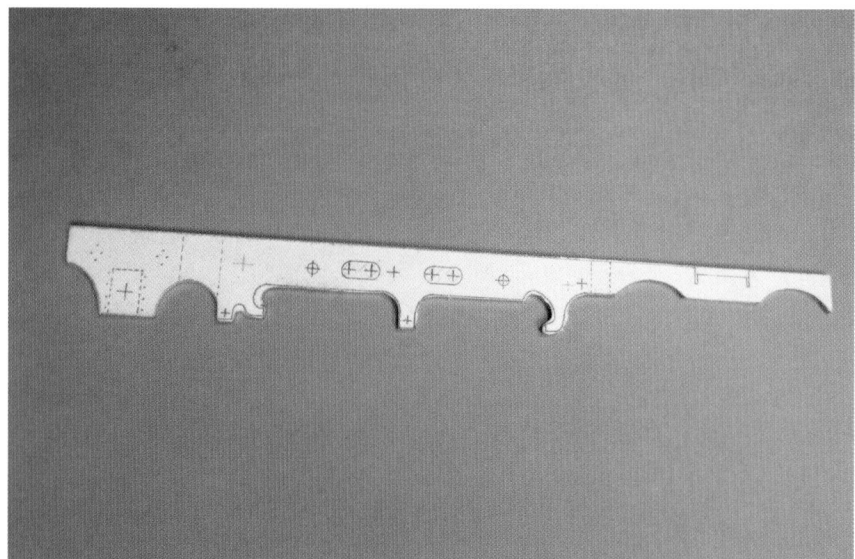

A lovely pair of roughly cut frames, ready for shaping and drilling – note that the frames are yet to be separated.

CHAPTER SIX

FILING AND FORMING THE FRAMES

Before the frames are separated they can be filed to a crisp, finished shape and then drilled, using the coupling rods as templates for the axle holes.

FILING THE FRAMES

There's not too much to say about filing – after all, most of us have some experience of it, if only in the pursuance of good pedicure or when grating cheese. Files smooth and shape surfaces by removing small pieces of material, a little at a time, from whatever you are filing. If it is cheese, you would choose a coarse cut for cheddar and those smaller holes for parmesan. Filing is just about as simple as that.

Finishing off the frames is a good place to practise your filing skills. As long as you leave the flat top surface alone you can't really go wrong. Aim for an accurate and artistically pleasing look. A good tip is to keep turning the work over. The side without the template gives a clearer view of the real shape. Make small adjustments without being led astray by the printed line.

DRAW FILING AND FURTHER TIPS

To finish everything off neatly and get rid of file and saw marks on the edges, use draw filing. This has nothing to with tidy documentation; it consists of simply moving the file lightly across the edge of the metal at 90 degrees. It gives you that baby's bottom smoothness. I use it all the time.

Take care if using round and half-round files. They can be useful to get into curved spaces but try not to dig too deep as you can get unwanted notches. A triangular file worked around the curve at about 45 degrees can do the job just as well. Try to get straight lines straight, curves curved and good square right angles.

FILING TIPS

- Use the coarser files to do the main shaping; the bigger the better. You can see how coarse they are, they look rough. They are called 'bastard' files.
- Double-cut files have two rows of teeth, like a shark. Like a shark, they can take out large lumps more roughly – take care.
- Single-cut files are smoother and gentler for finishing off.
- Good files for fine model work are generally No. 2 and No. 4 files – the larger the number, the more teeth per inch.
- Straight, flat 'hand' files are the most useful to have, followed by triangular and half-round needle files.
- Flat files aren't always flat on both sides; look closely at them, edge on; there may be a taper.
- Flat files can have a 'blind' side with no teeth, which is great for filing up against a surface without removing it.
- Files can become clogged very quickly with solder and white metal; keep your old ones for that sort of work. They can be unclogged with a brisk wire-brushing or poked with a piece of sharp-ended brass strip.
- Experience, as with everything, will tell you what files are good for you

For an excellent article on file facts see www.2mm.org.uk/mag2000/files.htm.

42 FILING AND FORMING THE FRAMES

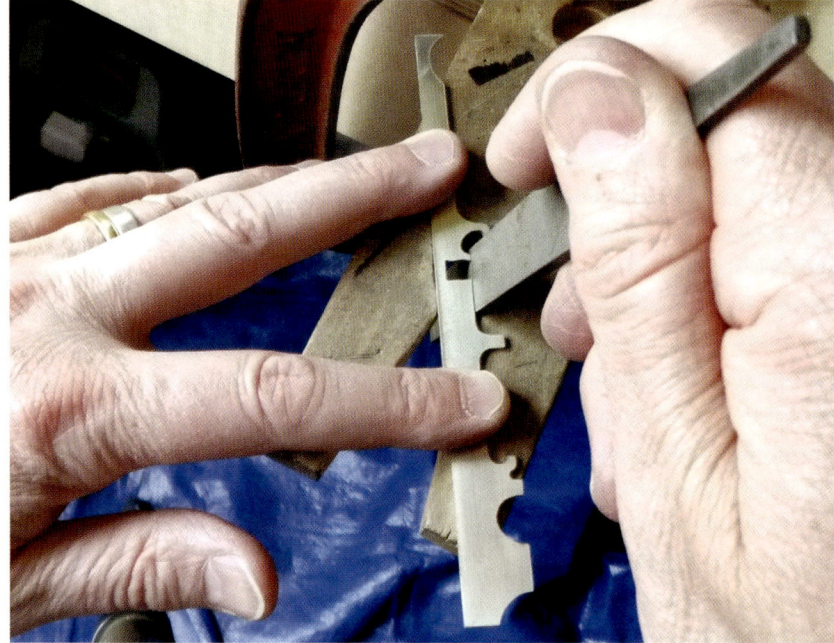

Use the largest file you can manage to begin with.

Finish off with diamond or needle files. A few decisive strokes can make quite a difference.

Finally, for all sorts of metal-working tips, have a look online at car restoration videos. I learned a brilliant way to file curves from one: don't follow the curve with the file – instead, move the file in the opposite curve to that of the metal, a bit like the action of a rocking horse. It's counter-intuitive, hard to do at first, but very satisfying once you have learned it. Here is a sketch showing how to do it.

Draw filing.

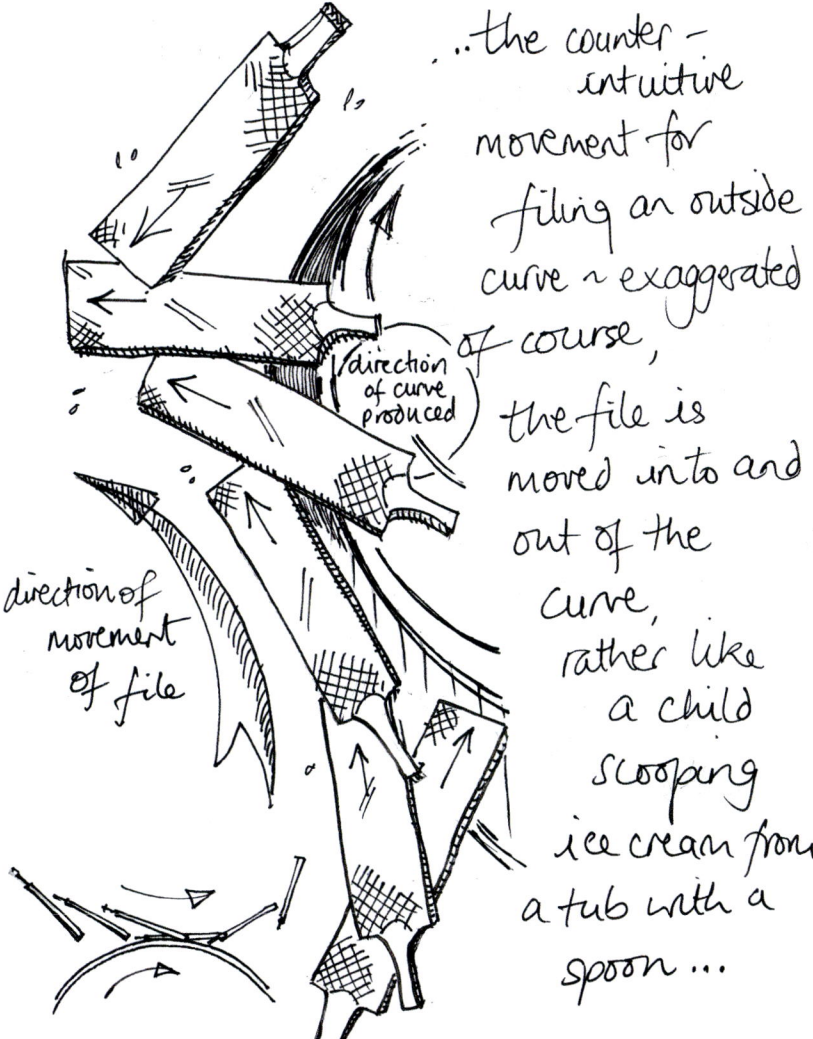

Filing curves the car restoration way.

...the counter-intuitive movement for filing an outside curve ~ exaggerated of course, the file is moved into and out of the curve, rather like a child scooping ice cream from a tub with a spoon...

direction of curve produced

direction of movement of file

After you have completed the filing, clean everything up with wet and dry and there you are. Beautiful. This set took just a few hours including the trip to the stationery shop for the photocopies.

REMOVING THE PAPER TEMPLATE

Glue or tape can be very stubborn and you will need to remove all trace of it and the template from your frames. The tape can be particularly obstinate. I start by scraping off any remnants with a wooden spatula so as not to mark the metal surface. If all else fails, use a scrap piece of metal of the same type so that it won't scratch. Then wipe the metal with a solvent like meths or cellulose thinners.

DRILLING THE FRAMES

COUPLING RODS

The coupling rods are used to decide the final position of the holes for the axles. This virtually ensures free running which, happily, is comparatively easy with a 4-4-2 tank as there are only two driving wheels on each side. The rest of the wheelbase is set by the position of the bogie wheels at the front, which are nicely independent of the drivers, and the rear carrying wheels at the back. Quite a bit of balancing and weighting is necessary to get everything running sweetly – that's something to look forward to later.

You can make your own rods quite easily if you wish. However, I wanted to demonstrate soldering a pair of Alan Gibson's offerings (other makes of coupling rods are available). These are fluted on one side; if you want them plain, just turn them over. They take some pleasant effort in making so you can assuage your guilt for not concocting a pair of your own.

- Use the piercing saw gently to remove the pieces from a delicate etch like this. Once the pieces are free don't bother to clean off any tags as it's much easier to do this when everything has been soldered.
- Make yourself a soldering jig from a wood block and a couple of small drills to fit the etched crankpin holes. (A jig, by the way, is any contraption that makes life easier – usually by holding things still and making repetitive work simpler.)
- Tack solder the fluted front to the plain back on each pair using a tacked joint.
- Once tacked in the centre, remove the rod from the jig and, holding carefully in a pair of pliers or

Detaching delicate etched parts with a saw.

FILING AND FORMING THE FRAMES 45

Tack solder the fluted front to the plain back on each pair using a tacked joint.

jewellers' clamp, finish and fill the joint by flooding with plenty of 145°C solder. Avoid getting solder in the fluting, otherwise you'll have to spend some extra time cleaning it out with a scraper.
- Draw file the edges, holding everything steady in a vice. If you have added enough solder you will get a solid-looking pair of coupling rods.

- Clear any solder from the holes with a small drill. Clean up with a wire brush and wet and dry.

DRIVING WHEEL AXLE HOLES

Now we are going to use the coupling rods as a jig to drill the axle holes.

The completed rods surrounded by all the things I used to clean them.

46 FILING AND FORMING THE FRAMES

- Take the horizontal depth of the driving wheel axle holes from the drawing, using the dividers to transfer the measurement from the top surface of the frames.
- Clamp the coupling rod blanks in place to establish where your axle holes are going to be.
- Drill one 0.7mm hole through the coupling rod hole and bolt the rod to the frames using that hole. The other hole can then be drilled very accurately.
- Carefully drill through the holes with a 0.7mm drill – keep the drill horizontal and at 90 degrees to the work. I find it perfectly acceptable to drill these holes by hand, keeping the drill horizontal by eye. If you own a drill press for your mini-drill all the better, although I do like to have the feel of the drill in my hand while I'm working.
- Remove the coupling rods and put them somewhere safe.

Carefully drill through the holes with a 0.7mm drill – keep the drill horizontal and at 90 degrees to the work.

OPENING THE HOLES OUT – TIPS

- Support the work on a wood block as tiny drills break rather easily, especially when breaking through the back of the metal.
- Always clamp the work down or hold it in a jewellers' or hand clamp. If a drill 'snatches' the piece of work it will whizz round and take your fingers off.
- Start with a pin-chuck and use a mini-drill to finish, if you wish, to speed things up a bit.
- Use a succession of very slightly larger drills to about 2.5mm. Anything much larger on thin metal will tear and snatch the metal.
- Open the holes out to the correct measurement using broaches – a large tapered broach to start with and a much finer parallel broach to finish. When you are nearly done, slowly and carefully twiddling the broach in your fingers will give you a fine fit.
- Measure the appropriate diameter on the broach with electric calipers and mark with a permanent marker.
- Check frequently that the hole is a tight fit for the bearings so as not to over-enlarge it.
- 'Break' the edge of the holes to help the bearings sit properly and remove burrs by twiddling a large-diameter drill around the edge by hand.

FILING AND FORMING THE FRAMES

- Open the axle holes out carefully to fit the outside width of the bearings.

SCRIBING HOLE POSITIONS

Now that the axle holes are done, the next stage is to mark out the position of the holes for the frame spacers, the weight-relieving holes and those for the brake hangers.

- Take the measurements from the drawing with the dividers and scribe them directly onto the metal. You will end up with a series of crossing lines. Run a scriber or centre punch gently along each line until you reach a cross and that's where your hole needs to go.
- A gentle tap with a small hammer will give you a little lead-in dimple for the drill. Drill them all out starting with a 0.5mm drill and then open them out with the appropriate sized drill as specified on the drawing. Be careful not to mix up the holes and drill them to the wrong size.
- The lozenge-shaped relieving holes need to be sawn and filed to shape; good practice for your filing and sawing.

For further reading on metal marking I can thoroughly recommend the Workshop Practice section on www.clag.org.uk, the website of the Central London Area Group of the Scalefour Society. There is a lot of other fascinating stuff on their site.

SEPARATING THE FRAMES

The two frame pieces can now be parted by resting one edge on a wood block and gently sliding a craft knife blade between them. Slide it lightly down with a gentle rocking motion. If the solder is reluctant to relinquish its grip, very cautiously heat the joint with the soldering iron, holding the iron just in front of the knife blade.

Now you have got the frames apart, remove any solder, clean them up and label them left and right with a marker.

JOGGLING THE FRAMES

As the Tilbury Tank has a long wheelbase (the distance between the centre of the front and rear wheels) it's going to have difficulties going round curves. We can add an extra trick here to help it navigate them successfully. By 'joggling' (a pleasing term to describe the process of putting a kink or notch into something) the frames at the front and rear, extra clearance can be provided before the leading and trailing wheels make contact with them.

You can sometimes see evidence of this on the real thing. Have a look at the frame of a similar locomotive

Separating the frames.

(if you can): there may be circular marks where rubbing has occurred without apparent disaster. On the model this can cause derailments, short circuits or extra friction, none of which are particularly desirable.

- Use a copy of the drawing to mark the position of the bend. Those that bend inwards should be marked on the inner sides and the bends that come back out are marked on the outers.
- Score the lines deeply with a knife running against a square (the bends need to be at a true 90 degrees), or use a skrawker to make the cut even deeper.
- Deepen the cut with the edge of a triangular file to make the fold more accurate. Use carefully

Filing the fold line.

Folding the metal.

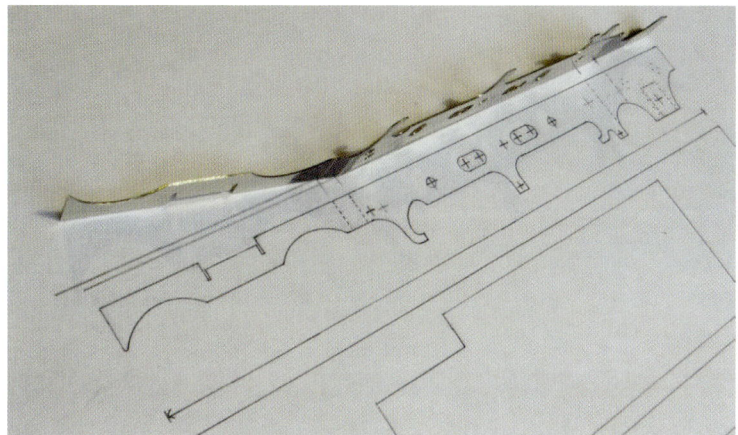

Comparing the fold to the drawing.

controlled strokes. When you can see evidence of the line on the back of the metal, things should be about ready. Or look carefully on the edge and you should be able to see a nice triangular cut that you can imagine folding up crisply.
- Use bending bars or straight-edged pliers lined up along the fold and with gentle, firm finger pressure form the bend. It won't take much.
- Check against the drawing that you've got the right angle of bend and then repeat to bend back the other way. It can be pretty easy and requires only minor tweaking to get it just right.
- The frames should lie level on a flat surface after bending – more minor tweaking may be necessary.
- Repeat for the other frame, checking against the first one to form a mirror image. They don't have to be precise as the driving wheels won't be affected. It looks nice if they are though.

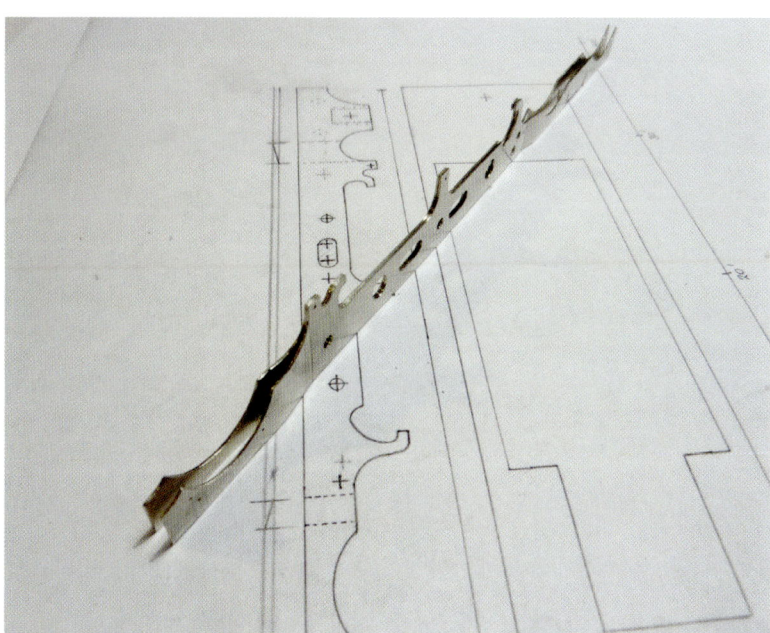

The completed joggles.

FRAME SPACERS

The frames are held a fixed width apart by spacers. There are lots of different ways of achieving this. You can simply screw them together with turned frame spacers and leave it like that. Or some etched spacers can be soldered in for further security and strength.

Comet Models do a very nice jig, consisting of two turned cylindrical spacers and a couple of threaded rods, some nuts and a really useful instruction sheet. The cylinders locate over axle bearings that are pushed, not soldered, into the axle holes, the rods are slipped in and the nuts tightened. This holds the chassis frames rigidly in alignment while you get on with the job of soldering the spacers. (If you like scratch-building your own tools then this is an opportunity for you to make your own jig.)

Test the chassis on a flat surface, mirror, glass or ceramic cooker hob to see if the whole thing is flat

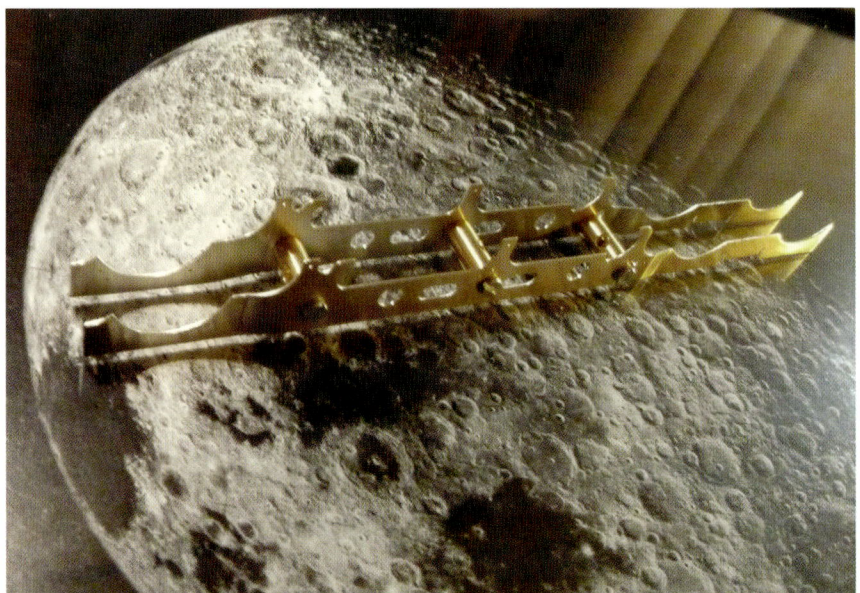

Turned frame spacers bolted in place and the chassis checked against a flat glass surface.

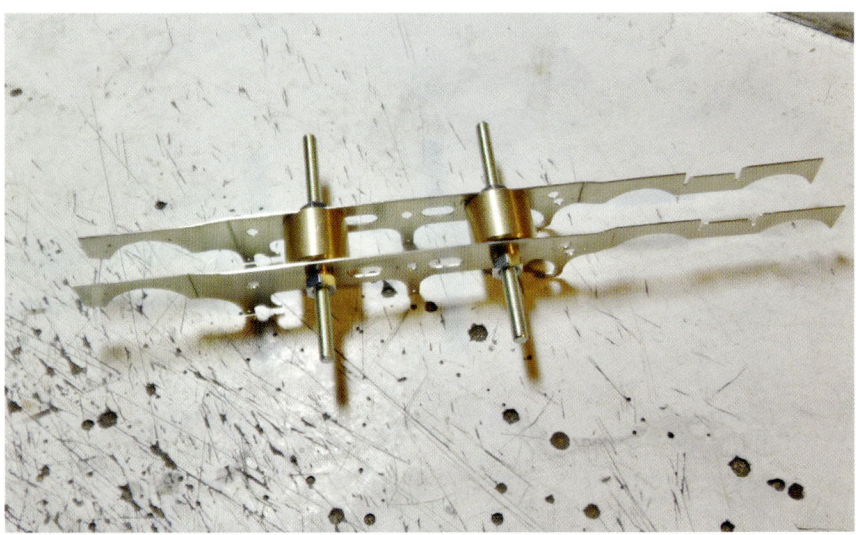

Use the temporary Comet jig spacers to bolt the frames together.

FILING AND FORMING THE FRAMES

Solder etched spacers in position on one side. These are from an Alan Gibson fret.

Solder the spacers into the other side. Remove the jig and check for squareness.

and without a twist. It shouldn't be twisted as the holes are in exactly the same places, but if it is a bit of manipulation should be enough to fix it.

Beware of using too much heat when soldering as you may get unequal expansion of the frames giving you a banana-shaped chassis. Just make quick dabs with the iron, soldering first one side then the other. If all else fails, remove the solder, clean up and start again.

I find this method of chassis frame construction to be very effective as you drill the frame spacer holes at the same time as the axle holes. When bolted together, the axle holes will remain in alignment. With the flat spacers soldered in, the frames will be exact and the loco should run properly. It's a good foundation for the rest of the model.

CHAPTER SEVEN

FITTING THE LEADING AND TRAILING TRUCKS

You may be raring to fit the driving wheels and motor at this stage. A word of warning though. If you put the driving wheels on now, you will almost certainly have to take them off again as there's work to be done on the chassis to fit the leading and trailing trucks. The fewer times you have to dismantle everything the better for the wheels and your patience; so let's have a look at the little ones first.

The Tilbury Tanks actually had devices called radial trucks supporting the rear trailing wheels. The rear carrying wheels are held in a curved rectangular box-like structure that includes the axle bearings. The box slides sideways in a set of curved guides allowing the wheels to follow the curvature of the track. In the photo above you can see the rectangular end of the curved guide and the truck itself within (the attractively painted wheel hides almost everything unless you look really closely).

Radial trucks present a nice little scratch-building challenge. If you would like a bit of a rest from hewing your own, there are some excellent etches available – I describe how to use the London Road Models offering when building the Class 79 tank (see Chapter 14). If you want something simpler, with the possible added bonus of allowing for sharper curves in your trackwork, you can build a lovely little basic pony truck to act as your trailing truck.

PONY TRUCK

TUBE AND STRIP CONSTRUCTION

This is simple and satisfying but you can't get away with sloppy soldering – things need to be accurate.

All you need is a piece of brass tube with an inside diameter of 2mm to act as an axle bearing and a 0.020in

MAIN COMPONENTS

- One pair 3ft 6in (14mm) Gibson or 14mm Romford bogie wheels
- 2mm inside diameter brass tube
- 0.020in brass/nickel-silver strip
- 8BA nut and bolt
- 0.5mm phosphor-bronze or brass wire

Close-up view of Thundersley's radial truck.

Simple components for a pony truck.

FITTING THE LEADING AND TRAILING TRUCKS

strip of brass or nickel silver as the pivot. There are a few other bits and pieces – the trimmings you might say – and you'll have a lovely little truck for nought.

- Cut the axle-bearing rod a millimetre shorter than the back-to-back setting of the wheels to allow for a tiny bit of side play. You could have more by making the tube a little shorter but you don't want to let things get out of control.
- If you want really tight corners on your layout file the wheel arches of the frame a little bigger to let the wheels pass beneath them.
- To cut the tube you can just roll it beneath a sharp knife blade to cut it to length. Or use the piercing saw.

- Smooth the ends with a file.
- Check that the tube fits snugly between the wheels and marvel at your engineering prowess.

The next bit requires a bit more thinking:

- Take a strip of 0.020in brass or nickel (I used a piece of etched kit fret) about 5mm wide and 25mm long. A little over length is fine as you can always trim it back; too short and you'll have to make another one.
- Solder the strip at 90 degrees to the tube, otherwise you'll get things running diagonally. I used graph paper to position everything. A good tack of solder holds everything in place to allow some checking and then give it a good seaming too. If you value your fingertips, hold the components down with a piece of wood.
- Clean up with a brisk wash and wire brush.
- Gently twist one wheel from the axle, thread the axle through the tube and just as gently pop the wheel back on. A back-to-back gauge or electronic calipers will help you reset the wheel distance.
- To work out the correct place to attach the pony truck to the rear frame stretcher hold one of the wheels against the slot of the stretcher

ABOVE LEFT: **Soldering the pony truck.**

Marking the pony truck pivot point.

54 FITTING THE LEADING AND TRAILING TRUCKS

and mark the centre of the hole onto the pony truck pivot.
- Drill a 0.5mm hole and enlarge it to take an 8BA bolt.

FITTING THE PONY TRUCK
- Solder an 8BA nut over the hole in the rear stretcher. This is most easily done by screwing the nut onto a cocktail stick or wooden skewer. The nut can then be held centrally over the hole and a good splash off flux and a dollop of 180°C solder will hold it there without getting solder into the screw thread.
- If the nut is slightly off-centre, or you do get some solder in there, gently widen the hole by twiddling a larger drill around the edge. Clear the solder by twiddling a bolt or 8BA tap very slightly in and out of the nut.

MAKING A SHOULDERED BOLT
It's good to have a bit of controlled up-and-down flexibility in the pony truck, for better traction. A shouldered bolt is a handy device for this.

- Cut a 1.5mm piece of the tube that you used for the axle. This will fit nicely onto the bolt to form the shoulder.
- Screw the shouldered bolt to the nut fixed to the stretcher leaving a smooth tube for the pony truck to slide up and down on and pivot around.

ABOVE LEFT: *The finished item.*

Soldering a nut over the spacer hole.

FITTING THE LEADING AND TRAILING TRUCKS

- The hole in the pony truck pivot may need to be widened slightly to accommodate the shoulder tube.
- Check that all is nice and flexible and reasonably wiggly.

Now we need to add a bit of springing. The pony truck has to stay on the track without propping the rear drivers up so that they lose traction. The real things guide the loco through curves when running backwards and support the weight of the loco above. You want the wheels to bear down on the track a little to stop them flapping about. A simple piece of springing will do the job nicely.

- Solder a length of phosphor-bronze wire (brass will do) to the rear stretcher.
- Bend it at about 90 degrees and again to pass it through a small hole drilled in the pivot just in front of the axle tube. It doesn't need to be soldered here, a loose fit is good.
- The springing can be adjusted when the driving wheels and front bogie are fitted. It's all about tweaking.

FRONT BOGIE

The two pairs of wheels on the front bogie are the first to encounter curves and other track irregularities. Their job, besides carrying some of the weight of the loco, is to guide it through these irregularities. There is some springing and so on visible and this can be added cosmetically after building the main structure of the unit.

After the excitement of building your own pony truck, I thought we could have a look at an etching as a useful aid to scratch-building. If you are fired up with the excitement of making your own, *see* Chapter 14 for how it's done in the description of the Class 79 build. However, I'm perfectly content to indulge a spot of cheating now and then and Comet Models (besides others) do a nifty little etched bogie at just the right 7ft wheelbase. You don't need all the bits and pieces supplied in the etch – it's got armour-plated sides for Great Western locos. We just want the delicate bits.

Follow the instructions and, using your best soldering and bending skills, fold up the main etch and you'll end up with a fine base for the Tilbury bogie. A few tweaks and modifications will make it just right.

The beauty of this little etch is its simplicity. The wheel sets are merely fitted into the

Thundersley's *front bogie.*

56 FITTING THE LEADING AND TRAILING TRUCKS

Comet 7ft bogie etch.

FITTING THE LEADING AND TRAILING TRUCKS

A little judicious filing of the inside bearing faces will ensure smooth running.

For extra side play use the piercing saw to enlarge the central pivot slot. Also remove any unwanted brake rodding and so on.

slots in the bearings, and lengths of 0.5mm brass wire are threaded through the obligingly placed holes in the bogie baseplate to hold the wheels in place and add a nice bit of sprung compensation.

The bogie can be easily fitted to the front spacer on the frames in the same way as the pony truck using an 8BA nut soldered to the front spacer and a bolt passed through the bogie slot. You can add a bit of extra springing if you wish: a coil spring on a collared bolt and some more brass wire to control the sideways movement.

In the next chapter we have more excitement with wheels – it's time to fit the drivers.

58 FITTING THE LEADING AND TRAILING TRUCKS

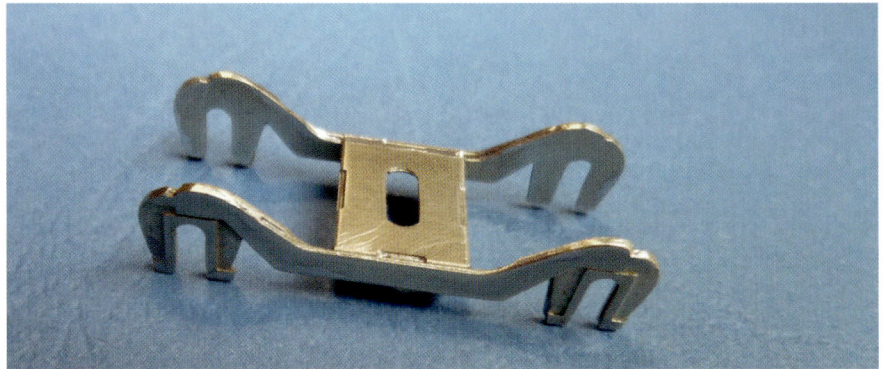

Solder on the cosmetic sides, lining them up carefully, and clean up.

The sprung bogie ready to fit to the frames.

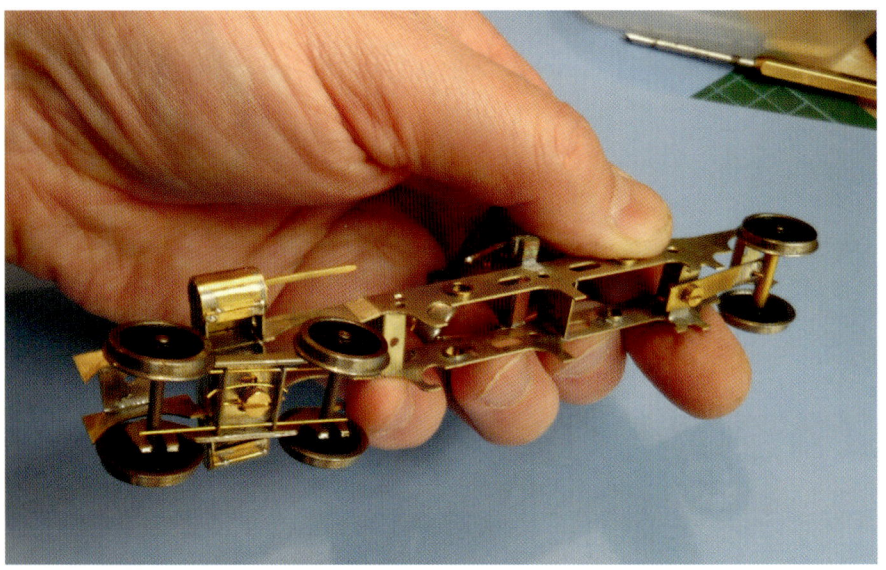

The front bogie and rear pony truck in position.

CHAPTER EIGHT

FITTING THE MOTOR AND DRIVING WHEELS

MAIN COMPONENTS

- Two pairs of 26mm insulated Romford driving wheels
- Two OO-gauge Romford axles
- Pack of slotted crankpins and Romford axle-nut screwdriver
- Pack of axle bearings
- The coupling rods that you made earlier
- Comet axle bearing jig
- GB2 gearbox and Mashima motor, ready assembled (DJH model loco ref. AM10)
- 1mm phosphor-bronze strip or 0.5mm brass or nickel-silver wire
- Gold wire (optional)
- PCB (printed circuit board) strip

Important note: check for free running after each stage of chassis construction; if it is affected, you'll know exactly what caused it and be able to remedy it.

DRIVING WHEELS

Romford driving wheels are the easiest to use and the favourite of many. They locate squarely onto the ends of the axle and are simple to 'quarter' so that the coupling rods are positioned properly in relation to each other. The wheels are held onto the axles by little slotted collars that are screwed on easily with a slotted screwdriver, also supplied by Romford. The screwdriver is also used to attach the crankpins for the coupling rods. This is a great system to use and a good base from which to move on to more finescale wheels such as those from Alan Gibson.

SOLDERING THE BEARINGS

To begin with, unscrew the bogie and pony trucks and put all the bits somewhere safe. I have a labelled box for each loco build and put all the loose bits in there before I lose them.

When soldering in the bearings, remember that the shoulder is on the outside face of the frames. Everything should be nice and square: you can check by either using an axle/coupling rod jig with the coupling rods or just threading two 2mm tubes through the bearings and laying the chassis down on some graph paper. The tubes should be exactly parallel to each other and to the surface of the paper.

FITTING THE DRIVING WHEELS

You might want to do everything over a plastic tray to stop things rolling away into oblivion.

- Thread the axles through the bearings, fit the wheels on to the axles, thread the slotted collars onto the axle ends and tighten them up with the screwdriver. The last bit is a little fiddly: I lay the collar over the axle end before tightening it up.
- The wheels need to be a quarter turn further round on the right-hand side on each pair – which is why it's called quartering. The laws of physics don't cope very well with anything much different.
- Fit the crankpins and finally the coupling rods and crankpin nuts, which slip inside the holes in the rods. If you've quartered correctly, when the rods are at the bottom of their travel on the left-hand side (as you look towards the front of the loco) they should be as far forward as they can go on the right-hand side.

The loco should run along under light finger pressure or on a gentle slope. If it's sticking you may have the holes in the coupling rods a wee bit tight. When you undo everything – which you will in a minute – very, very slightly open them out with a broach. They shouldn't be really tight and they shouldn't be at all sloppy. There are more running tips at the end of this chapter.

MOTORIZATION

Once everything is working smoothly, it's time to attach the motor. There are myriad motor choices but I've included the DJH combination because almost everything is done for you and it's quite a compact little combo. Make sure you read the instructions about oiling it and so on.

- Take the driving wheels off again. You'll become adept at doing this.
- Check that the gearbox slips in easily between the bearings of the front axle. You may need to file them slightly to get a nice snug fit. If you do this precisely you won't need to use washers to stop the gearbox moving from side to side, which will really cut down on the fiddle factor.
- Clean everything up (you don't want metal dust in your gearbox) and then, holding the box inside the frames at the front wheel position, slide the axle in so that it traps the final gearwheel. The little grub screw should be loose enough to allow the axle through; not too loose, otherwise you'll lose it. (It's always good to have a packet of spares as they are murder to find once they drop out of the gear.)
- Reattach the wheels and coupling rods (quartered properly). Tighten the grub screw.
- Prop up the chassis on some wood blocks and attach a couple of wires from a suitable controller to the motor terminals. Bingo – locomotion. Let it spin for a while to run it in. Keep a watch out for the crankpins coming undone or any other such misdemeanour. Try it on slow and fast speeds and backwards and forwards.

Now we need to arrange for a more elegant way to get the power to the motor.

CURRENT PICKUP

There are many different pickup systems. Some – such as the split-axle pickup – are more complex than others; some you can build yourself and some you can buy. It's really up to you to find something that suits you and is appropriate to the job. Experiment; have fun – more pickups are described in Chapter 14.

Filing the inside of the wheel bearings to a snug fit for the gearbox.

FITTING THE MOTOR AND DRIVING WHEELS 61

The gearbox in place between the frames.

Test running the chassis.

With the Tilbury Tank's large driving wheels disappearing into the bottom of the side tanks, a fitting method of power pickup here seemed to be to have wire wipers bearing on the tops of the wheel treads. They are cheap, easy to instal, easy to adjust and hidden away from accidental damage and prying eyes.

Wire wipers, besides being ubiquitous, are very simple. They are made of wire and are lightly sprung. They also double up as wheel cleaners. You may, if you wish, use some precious metal (gold) – I'll explain later.

The top-wiper method was championed by Allan Sibley, one of my modelling heroes. In fact they are sometimes named for him as 'Siblups' – there's immortality for you. I believe Mr Sibley is now a big fan of split-chassis current collection.

Back to the basics.

TOP-ACTING WIPERS

These are formed from short lengths of either 0.5mm brass (or nickel-silver) wire, or, in this case, phosphor-bronze strip. I like phosphor-bronze strip: it is strong and springy and easy to use and it conducts electricity well. Its only downside is that it may react badly to steel wheel tyres in the presence of electricity. This means that we can use some gold as a preventative measure. The cavernous side tanks provide lots of space for the assembly to rest on the top of the wheel treads.

- Check the photographs to help here.
- Saw a 20 × 3.0mm strip of double-sided printed circuit board (PCB). Don't make it too long, to avoid the ends being hit by the revolving coupling rods.
- Saw a gap across the centre of the copper surface on both sides to prevent electrical short circuits.
- Solder two small pads of PCB strip (approx. 6.0 × 3.0mm) across the ends of the longer strip.
- Solder a 28mm length of phosphor bronze strip centrally to each pad.
- Now for the gold wire (a snip at £5 for a short length from the local jewellers). Turn the wiper assembly upside down and holding a length of wire across the end of phosphor strip splosh on some flux and a quick dab with the iron and 145°C solder should hold everything nicely in place. Then trim the wire to length with a pair of cutters; it is surprisingly hard.
- It is much easier to do it this way than to fiddle about with tiny little pieces of gold, which you will inevitably lose. In fact it's a good idea to keep the wire in a bag or container, proudly labelled 'gold', and it should last a lifetime.

- Solder two short lengths of electrical wire to the pads. I like to solder copper spiral clips to the ends of the electrical wiring, which make good temporary connectors to the motor. They can be soldered securely in place when everything is set up properly.
- Solder the whole wiper assembly across the frames centrally between the driving wheels.
- Reattach the wheels and motor. Now tweak the phosphor-bronze strip so that the gold-laden ends bear lightly on the wheel treads.
- Clip or solder the wires to the motor terminals and test by propping up the chassis and touching the wheel treads with your controller wires. Amidst sparks and excitement it should run just as well as it did before. If not, check everything again – constant checking and fettling is, I'm afraid, all part of the process. You may find that the motor tends to lift itself as the chassis runs. It can be restrained with a loop of insulated wire or insulating tape gently wrapped around it and the wiper assembly crosspiece.
- Reattach the leading and trailing trucks and off you go: a running chassis. More infernal fiddling with the springing of the trucks will probably be necessary here. Do remember, though, that the weight of the body – once constructed – will certainly help things along.

For now just glory in your engineering skills and have a break from all that hard work.

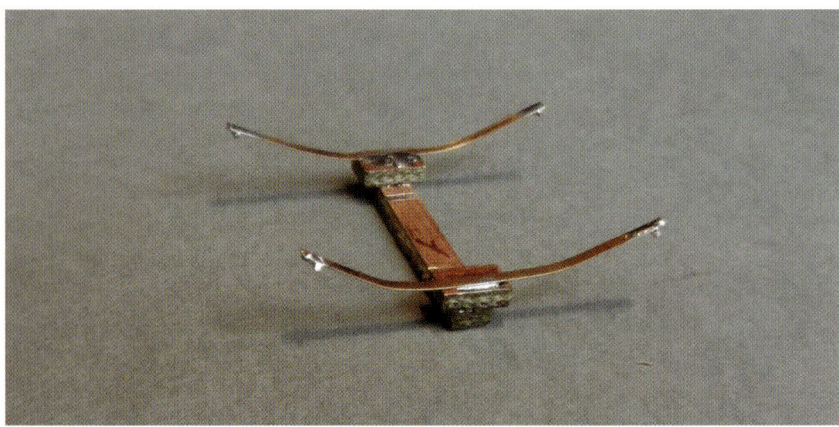

The wiper assembly

FITTING THE MOTOR AND DRIVING WHEELS

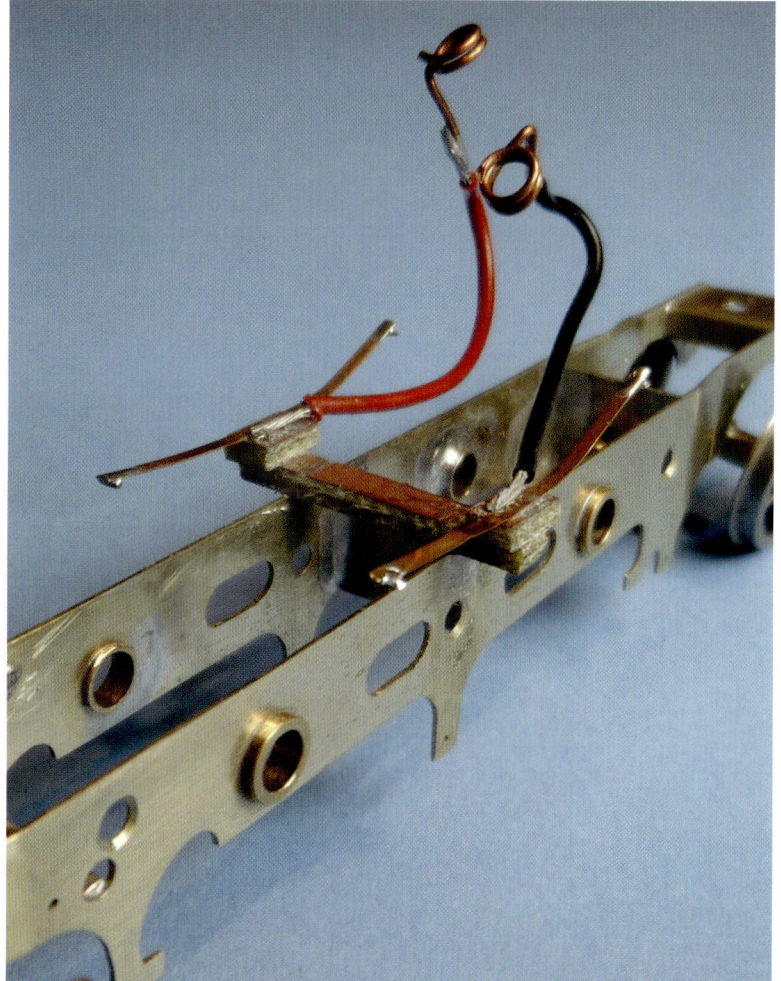

The wiper assembly soldered to the frames.

Up and running.

CHAPTER NINE

THE CYLINDERS AND CONNECTING RODS

MAIN COMPONENTS

- 0.020in nickel-silver sheet
- 1mm square brass rod
- 1.1mm inside diameter brass tube
- 8BA, 12BA and 16BA nuts and bolts
- 0.010in brass sheet
- Pair of London Road Models single slide bar crossheads
- Steel or brass dressmaker's pins
- Alan Gibson shoulderless handrail knobs
- 0.5mm brass wire

BUILDING THE CYLINDERS

The cylinders – or, to be more precise, the cylinder casings – on Tilbury Tanks are obligingly tubular, lending themselves to being made either from nested telescopic tubing or from thin sheet brass wrapped around formers. Both have pros and cons. The Class 79 build describes how to construct solid cylinders; for the Class 51 I chose to form them from sheet. Take your pick, or try both. The slightly smaller cylinders (18 x 26in) on Class 51 locos were one of the few things that distinguished them from their very slightly larger cousins, the Class 79s.

First you need to form the formers. You can cheat the shape of the whole unit into a lozenge that will give the impression of two cylindrical blocks. It is a lot easier to make than you might think.

FORMING THE FORMERS

- Tack solder two 0.020mm pieces of nickel silver together and using the drawing as a guide either scribe the cylinder formers and spacer and piston tube hole positions, or paste a template onto the

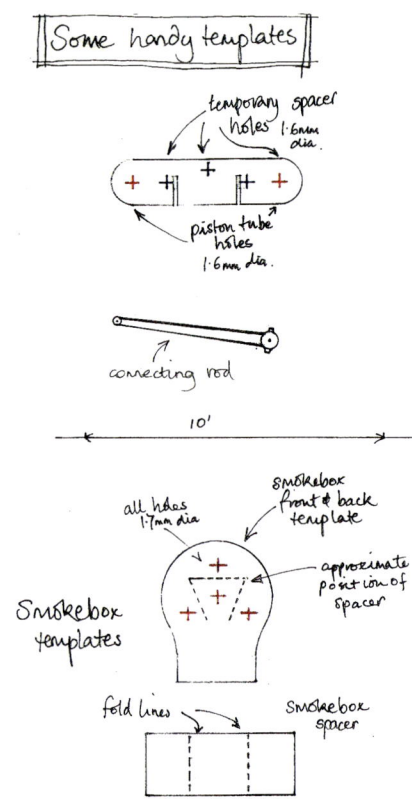

The cylinder formers, connecting rod and smokebox templates.

metal. Centre-pop the holes and progressively drill all of them to 1.6mm diameter as specified on the drawing. File the slide bar notches as shown on the photo opposite.
- Carefully grind out the slots that locate the block into the frames with a cutting disc in the mini-drill. Don't forget to protect your eyes. Try and be as exact as you can, then file to shape.
- Separate the two pieces and cut a spacer 8.5mm × 12mm to hold them apart. Fold the spacer down the middle to about 90° so that it clears all the holes and notches.'

THE CYLINDERS AND CONNECTING RODS

- Tack solder the stretcher in at one side to keep everything in place. If you want to remove it later you may need to give it a bit of a push with the soldering iron; if it's not interfering with anything, leave it in place. Then bolt the two formers together.
- To prevent the piston rods flapping around, cut two 12mm lengths of 1.1mm inside diameter brass tube to act as guides. If you have the correct diameter tubing, skip the next step.
- If you have some tubing that is not quite the right diameter and want to drill it out a bit then a good ruse is to solder a length of tube to a chunk of scrap brass. This acts as an excellent base to hold things still. Do take care not to break drills or broaches. Take things slowly, use copious amounts of spit and withdraw the drill every now and then to clear the swarf. When you have finished opening out the tube diameter, unsolder the tube from the scrap base, cut the tube to length and clean up.
- Fix the tubes into the cylinder block with 180°C solder. Leave a bit projecting at the rear end; this helps to stop the piston rod falling out of the tube at the furthest reach of their travel. (The projections are known as piston glands and have something to do with oiling on the real thing.)

Opening out the inside diameter of a tube – hold it still by soldering to some scrap brass.

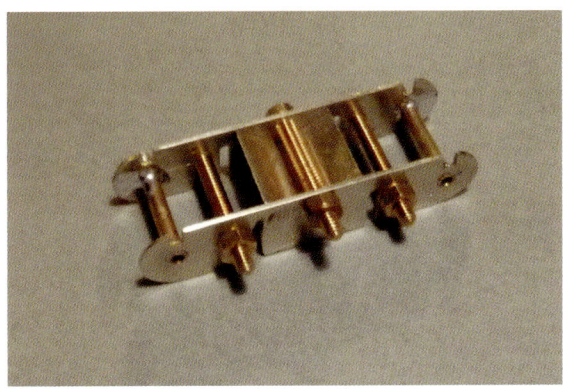

The piston rod guides soldered in place.

The two cylinder formers bolted together with a spacer between to keep them parallel. Note slide bar notches have been filed.

SLIDE BARS

On the real thing, these hefty chunks of metal guide the crosshead and piston rod along its all-powerful journey as it converts the steam pressure in the pistons into rotational energy in the wheels.

- The notches at the top of the cylinders will be in line and parallel with the cylinder rod guide tubes. Solder straight lengths (approximately 30mm or longer) of 1mm square brass rod into the notches, parallel with the guide tubes, flush with the front face of the cylinders and

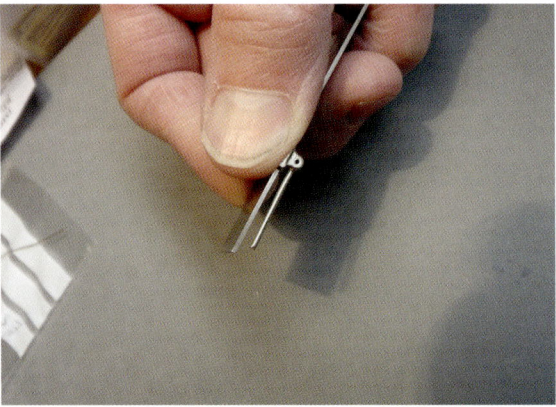

The slide bar should be slightly longer than the piston rod, plus the length of the cylinders.

- Use a piece of thin card as a template to work out the size of the two pieces of 0.010mm brass you will need to form the wrapper. Thin brass bends more easily than nickel silver so it is better to use brass for this purpose.
- Wrap the card around the cylinder block; it should be long enough to bend around the outside curve of the block and continue about 5mm past the centre line on both the top and bottom. It should be about 53mm × 24mm.
- Use the template to cut out the brass pieces. They should be slightly wider than the block to make soldering easier – they can be trimmed later. It is *much* easier to fit and then file rather than trying to line up and solder a perfectly fitting piece.
- Repeat for both sides.
- To gild the lily, solder a circular riveted cover onto the front end of each cylinder. This helps to create the illusion of a cylindrical piston. I found an etch from London Road Models had exactly what I wanted, without having to cut my own pesky circles. You can do the same at the rear-facing ends: just drill a hole to accommodate the glands and file a notch to fit around the slide bars.
- For an extra decorative touch you can make up the little cylinder draincock piping arrangements shown in the top drawing in the 'Tubes and Pipes'

The slide bars soldered securely in place. Note also the piston rod guides projecting from one side of the block.

projecting out at the back, to form your single slide bars. The photo shows how things should look.
- At the front, file the rod ends flush with the surface. Try not to bend them otherwise you will have to keep bending them back into shape.

WRAPPERS

Now it's time for the wrapping. It isn't that difficult and the results can be very satisfying.

One wrapper side – it's easier to do it in two parts rather than all in one go.

Thinly tin the inner edges of the wrappers with 180°C solder and form the curve with a suitable drill or rod.

Line up one edge of the wrapper with the rear end of the cylinder block and tack in place – mind your fingers.

sketch in Chapter 17. Use shoulderless handrail knobs and 0.5mm wire soldered into holes drilled on the underside of the cylinders.

- To check the fit, gently push the cylinders into the notches in the frames. Some sort of fettling may be necessary. You want them to sit parallel to the frame with the cylinder glands aligned with the centre of the wheel axles. See the photos on p.72. Once you have a reasonable fit, don't solder anything down yet as there are other fiddly bits to do.

Take a moment to admire this fabulous little object you've just fabricated.

68 THE CYLINDERS AND CONNECTING RODS

Continue all the way round the edge.

Seam when satisfied; the projecting edge of the wrapper can then be filed smooth, after removing the temporary nuts and bolts.

THE CYLINDERS AND CONNECTING RODS

Soldering the etches to the cylinders; tin on the back first to make life easier.

CONNECTING RODS

Thundersley's connecting rods have a subtle taper to them. Look closely at the photo of her below and those elsewhere: the rods have pleasantly round ends with an oil box at the top and a nut at the bottom. They are reasonably easy to reproduce and satisfying when they turn out well. If you make a mess of them, particularly if it's your first time, chuck them in the seconds bin – they may be useful one day.

- Tack solder a pair of roughly shaped 0.020in nickel strips together.
- Draw or stick the shape of the connecting rods onto one of the surfaces, marking the centre line and the correct positions for the holes for the 'big end' (one of the more usefully descriptive terms in railway locomotive nomenclature) and the smaller end.
- Drill a 1.3mm hole to take 12BA bolts for the big end and a 0.8mm hole to take 16BA bolts for the smaller end.

Thundersley's chunky connecting rod and big end.

A pair of rough-hewn connecting rods ready for the file.

PUTTING EVERYTHING TOGETHER

THE LOCO IN MOTION

With the connecting rods manufactured it's time to set up the motion, which is called that for a good reason.

- Solder each crosshead to the little end of the connecting rod with the help of that ever-useful cigarette paper, which stops the solder from flowing into the joint.

The use of blocking agents such as paper is a useful dodge. When building up steam locomotive motion, in particular, you need to make sure that solder doesn't stray into areas you don't want it. Other blockers include metal-blackening fluid, permanent marker ink, pencil, oil and even Tippex. I don't like using oil as I find it gets everywhere and not just where I want it. As always be wary of stray chemical fumes.

- Insert the bolts, including washers of an appropriate size on both sides.
- Now for the filing. The bolted washers act as a good guide for filing the rounded shapes. Don't forget to leave protrusions for the oil boxes and bosses at the big end. If you file carefully along the length of the rods the washers stop you at a prototypical place and you end up with a nicely shaped piece of metalwork. Keep them back to back. Keep your file strokes parallel to the rod surface. Finish off by carefully draw filing with smaller and smaller files and then polishing with abrasive sticks.
- Once you've finished shaping, remove the bolts and washers, split the rods apart and clean up.

FITTING THE CROSSHEADS AND CONNECTING RODS

- Check the slide bars are parallel to the travel of the crosshead rod by temporarily inserting a length of tubing and tweaking the bar if necessary.

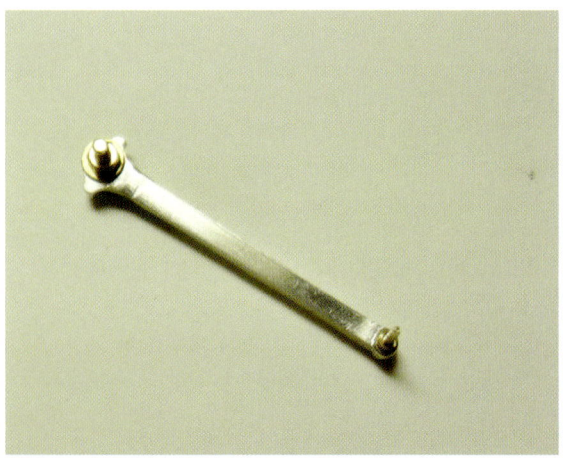

Bolted washers act as guides for final shaping.

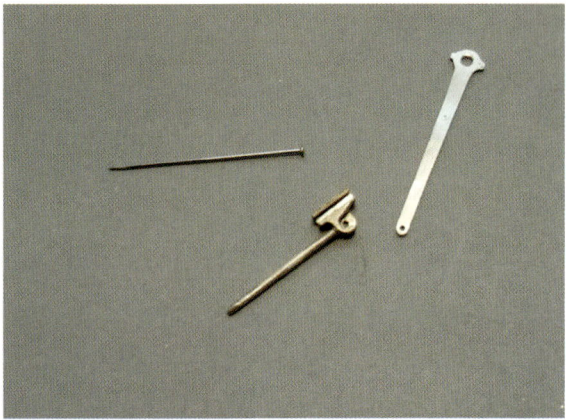

Connecting rod, London Road Models single slide bar crosshead and a pin.

THE CYLINDERS AND CONNECTING RODS

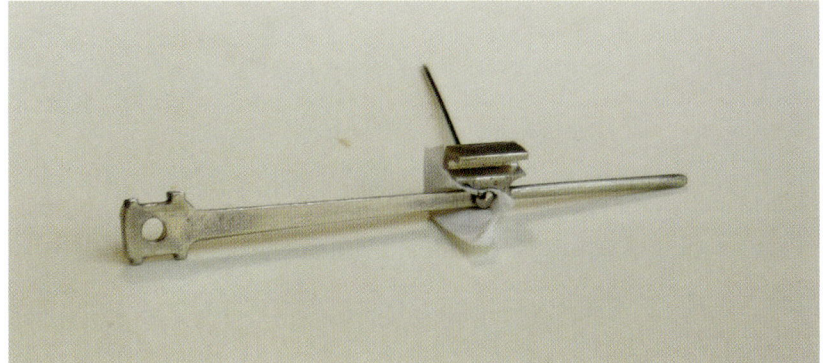

Solder with the pin head to the back of the crosshead.

- The crosshead should be a nice, not sloppy, sliding fit onto the slide bar. If it's a tad reluctant to slide it might need a very careful spot of filing to open out the slot. Do it very gently and polish off with a piece of folded wet and dry until everything glides smoothly.
- For smooth running, check the following:
  - The connecting rod shouldn't hit the slide bar
  - The crosshead shouldn't fall off the slide bar
  - The piston rod shouldn't be hitting the inside front of the piston block
  - The connecting rod should swing back and forth properly
  - The piston rods shouldn't fall out of the rear of the piston block

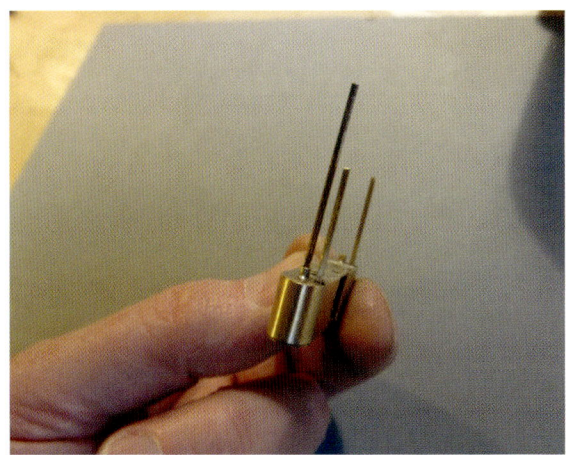

Checking for a parallel slide bar.

Some judicious filing should sort any of these problems out.

An interesting and often overlooked fact about Tilbury Tanks is that the connecting rod is positioned nearest to the wheel on the crankpin, before and under the coupling rods. You can see this on the photo of *Thundersley*'s rods earlier in the chapter. Not a lot of people know this but, if they do, they'll tell you. Various other locos sport this arrangement and you can have fun spotting it.

The only problem for modellers in OO gauge is that the wheels are closer together than on the real thing, so you can end up with a bit of a knock-kneed appearance on the model with the connecting rods at an awkward angle. You can cheat a bit by moving the pistons slightly inboard, or just accept the angle; or you could just put the coupling rods on first and then the connecting rods, as on almost every other make of loco.

I went for a little bit of moving the pistons and accepting the angle and was happy with it. Try things out for yourself. It's one of many compromises that have to be made when translating a real-life object into a jewelled fantasy.

Anyway, back to the model. It's time to fit everything together.

Romford crankpins are helpfully long enough to accommodate both rods. You can use an extra crankpin collar or cut a small piece of tubing to do the same job. It's cheaper and more in tune with the ethos of scratch-building.

72 THE CYLINDERS AND CONNECTING RODS

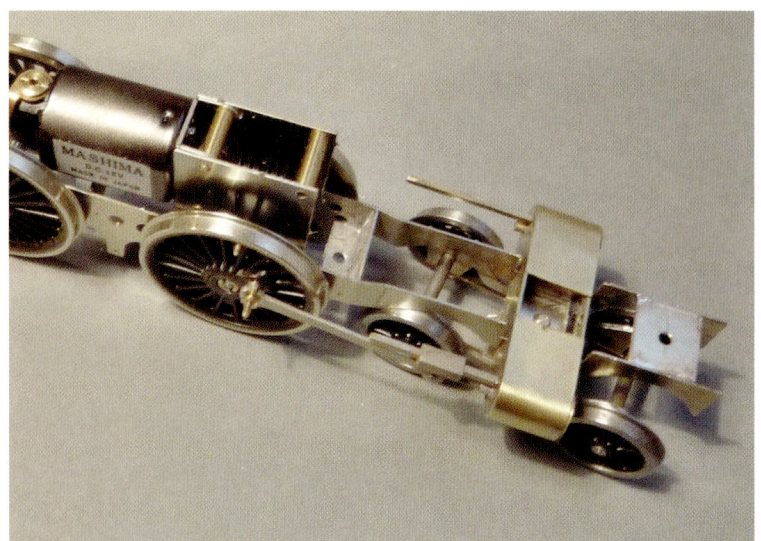

Slide bar and crosshead moving in perfect harmony.

This can all be a wee bit fiddly as you have to manoeuvre the crosshead onto the slide bar at the same time as sliding the piston rod in place into the piston and fitting the rod onto the crankpin. Things will fit eventually. You have to do this twice, once either side for each piston.

The model should now move beautifully. Run it along under finger pressure first with a loose grub screw on the drive gear. When you are satisfied all is well, tighten the grub screw and apply some power. Poetry in motion should unfold before your eyes.

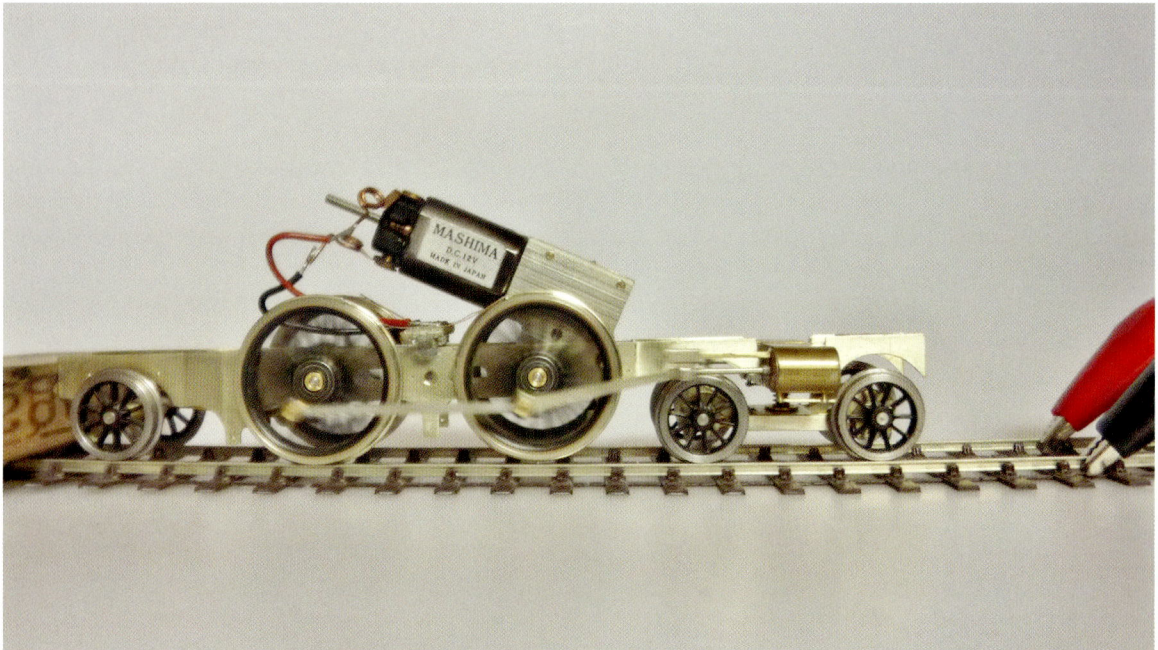

Poetry in motion.

THE CYLINDERS AND CONNECTING RODS

FAULT-FINDING

There's no escaping the fact that if you don't get the coupling rod holes and those of the axles exactly corresponding you'll never get your loco running sweetly. A sort of knock-kneed clonking will tell you if things aren't right. And things will stick. If you are in that situation, this might be a good time to step away from the workbench . . . then come back and try working through the checklist of faults I had to rectify before getting my own loco to run sweetly.

Be patient, check thoroughly, observe forensically and re-fettle. The devil is in the detail.

FAULTS CHECKLIST

- Check the wheels are quartered properly – the right-hand side a quarter ahead of the left. I had put mine back at half and half and that's not going to work.
- Check you haven't got one wheel different to the other three.
- Are all the wheels tight to their axles and running true?
- Is anything projecting from the frames and catching the back of the wheels or the connecting rods?
- Is a connecting rod bent? One of mine had bent because of whatever stresses were imposed on it from whatever the original problem was. Un-bend it.
- Are the axle and rod holes loose enough (but not too loose) to let everything revolve properly?
- Have you got a crankpin pinching a coupling rod? Loosen it and make sure it's properly placed before you re-tighten it.
- Is the front of the piston rod hitting the inside of the cylinder front? It may need shortening by a very small amount so as not to have it dropping out of the piston at the other end of its travel.

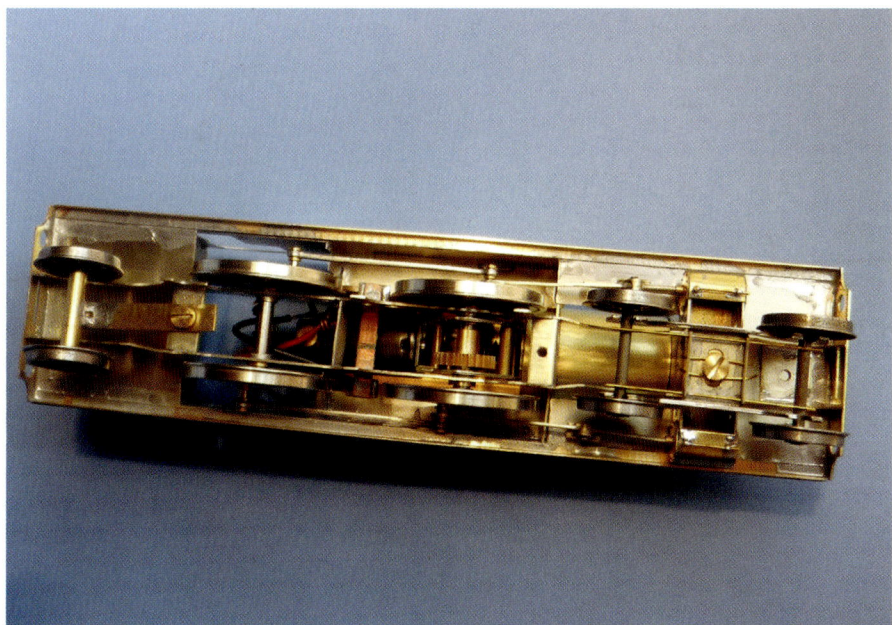

Another work of art.

CHAPTER TEN

CLASS 51 FOOTPLATE AND CAB

Now we have a fully functional chassis, it's time to move on to some delicately formed bodywork. I always enjoy this part of loco building, with its mixture of challenge and achievement, particularly in capturing the character of your chosen prototype.

Having made a chassis that will fit either a Class 51 or a Class 79, we are now going to focus on building the body of a Class 51 – so if you want a Class 79, you will need to go to Chapters 14 to 16. While I'm using some photos of *Thundersley* to illustrate various parts of the build, it's important to bear in mind that things can vary between locos of the same class. Use lots of photos in your search for authenticity; here's a good one of a Class 51.

THE FOOTPLATE

The footplate (sometimes known as the running plate) is where you stand when moving around the locomotive – usually to clean it.

FOOTPLATE SHAPE

The smokebox saddle rests on the front of the footplate with a space behind where the inside motion is accessible for maintenance. (The inside motion is the

A magnificent Class 51. WWW.RAILPHOTOPRINTS.CO.UK

CLASS 51 FOOTPLATE AND CAB

Close-up view of Thundersley's footplate.

internal version of the outside motion on locomotives, hence the name. Not all locomotives have outside motion.) The cut-out edges are just wide enough to rest on the frames and are narrower than they would be on the real thing as OO-gauge locomotives have a narrower gauge than they really ought to. Ample space is provided for the driving wheels and motion, so there is very little of the cab floor remaining – which is fine as this cab will be filled with motors and flywheels. The footplate is attached to the frames with a 'tongue' at the front and a bolt at the rear.

I discovered all this the hard way when I found that my original drawing failed to produce the footplate that I wanted to fit to the frames I had already built. This continuous feedback between what you have already made and what you are about to make is important and, for me, an integral part of scratch-building. My ability and willingness to plan in advance is not sufficient to make the building process perfect – and anyway, I enjoy the way in which the build evolves. The downside of this is that you can get a sort of creeping error where little inaccuracies can accumulate until you find that things aren't fitting or have grown exponentially to enormous size. Keep measuring.

The drawing I give here is the revised edition.

FOOTPLATE CONSTRUCTION

- Mark up a rectangle of 0.020in nickel silver and shape the cut-out with the piercing saw, using a suitably fine blade such as a No. 6. Only one relieving hole is necessary to start the saw cut, which is continued gently around the whole of the interior shape.
- Use large then smaller files to file back to the line and finally a triangular file to cut into the corners.
- Smooth the inside and outside edges by draw filing and rubbing on a sheet of fine wet and dry paper. Take care not to catch the ends while smoothing or you might bend the footplate (which I did) – in which case straighten it carefully.

It's good scratch-building practice to keep reminding yourself of the real thing by periodically looking at

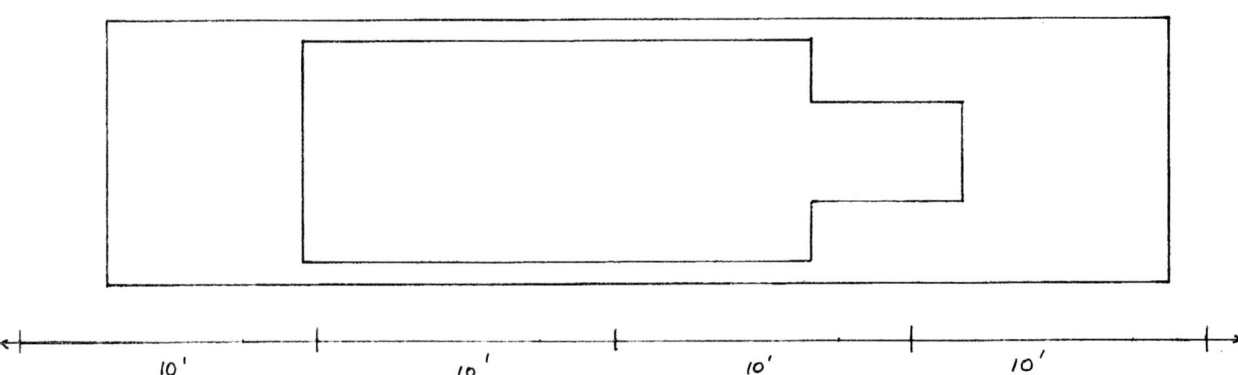

Dimensioned drawing for the footplate.

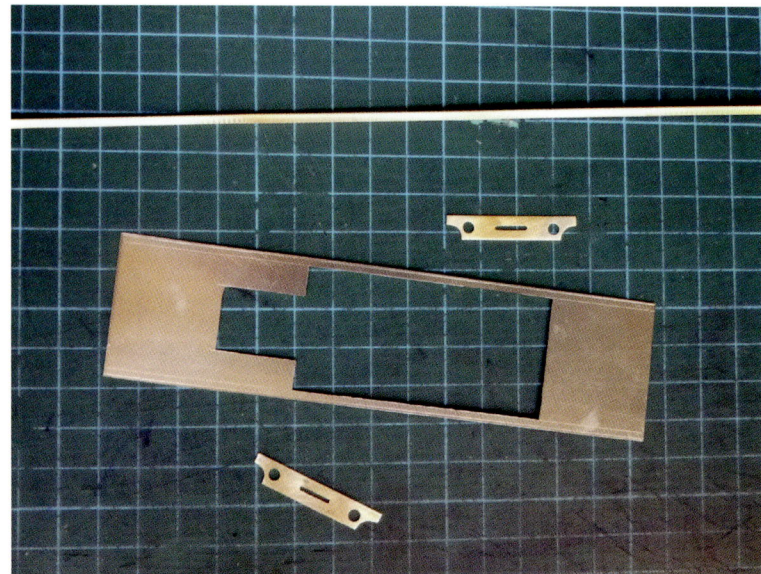

The finished footplate, buffer beams and valances. Also, see drawing on p.80.

your photographs. While looking at mine to check on the size and position of the valances, I noticed the lines of rivets on the top surface of the footplate along the side of the cab and the front that don't appear in any of the drawings.

The rivets, if you want them, need to be punched before you solder on the valances, unless you use something like Archer transfers. I like rivets; I think they add character, so any chance for riveting is good for me. For a change, though, I decided to use transfers on this build. They are easy to use and made of resin to give an excellent 3D effect. You put them on just before painting. If you are raring to emboss your rivets have a look at the Class 79 build and emboss with abandon.

VALANCES (OR HANGING BARS)

The footplate needs to be stiffened otherwise that's all it would be, a plate. In the real thing, the rest of the loco is unceremoniously plonked on top of it along with a good few gallons of water, so it needs to be strong. In the model, adding items such as the boiler and cab will help to stiffen the footplate although it's much better to have a firm foundation, so on go the valances anyway; they look good and are nice and simple on the Tilbury. No curves or anything, just straight from one end to the other, butting up against the buffer beams.

I use 2mm brass L-angle: it's strong and stays straight as you solder.

BUFFER BEAMS

First, though, the buffer beams. These add a lot to the character of the loco, having gracefully curved ends and an excitingly unusual horizontal slot in the centre for the coupling hook to pivot in.

Look carefully at the photo you decide to follow. Some buffer beams have lots of rivets, others don't – *Thundersley*'s don't. There are various mysterious holes and bits and pieces and they all have those enormous hornlike guard irons, looking as though they are ready to shove obstacles the size of a small hippopotamus out of the path of the loco.

The beams are slightly more slender at the front than the back, although this is hardly noticeable so if you want to form them at the same time, no one is going to pull you up on that one; especially not me.

BUFFER BEAM CONSTRUCTION

- Prepare a couple of pieces of 0.020in nickel silver and tack solder together.
- Draw or stick on your beam shapes.

CLASS 51 FOOTPLATE AND CAB   77

Thundersley's buffer beam with its artfully curved edges, added guard irons and central coupling slot.

BOTTOM LEFT: *Tack solder the rear beam in place.*

- Don't forget to drill the buffer shank holes to about 1mm; you can open them out once you have separated the pair.
- Cut the slot by joining two holes with the piercing saw and then smooth the slot as much as possible with a tiny file.

ATTACHING THE BUFFER BEAMS AND VALANCES

- Mark a guideline for the rear beam with dividers at the rear of the footplate – remember it goes underneath.

Check the beam is at 90 degrees to the footplate.

- Tack solder the rear beam in place.
- Check the beam is at 90 degrees to the footplate, correctly central and in line.
- Seam the joint when you are satisfied that everything is aligned correctly.
- Measure up your 2mm brass L-angle against the position for the front beam – measure between the rear and front beams rather than to the end of the footplate.
- Cut the L-angle to length, using the piercing saw to form the valance.

Seam the joint when you are satisfied that everything is aligned correctly.

Measure up your 2mm brass L-angle against the position for the front beam.

- Clamp the L-angle flush with the underside of the footplate and tack solder before seaming up.
- Add the other valance angle after carefully measuring against the first.
- Finally, solder the front beam up against the valances, flush with the end of the footplate.

The footplate should be nice and flat and tidy. You can give it a bit of a tweak and twist if it's a little bit off. Use your flat surface to check.

And there you have your footplate, buffer beams and valances, all ready to support the build of the loco body. Give it a good clean-up first.

CLASS 51 FOOTPLATE AND CAB

Clamp the L-angle flush with the underside of the footplate and tack solder before seaming up.

BELOW RIGHT: *The view from one of* **Thundersley's** *front windows. Windows in railway vehicles have any number of alternative names, from lookouts to clerestories, but we'll stick to windows.*

CAB FRONT AND REAR

Once I've got the footplate finished I like to turn to the cab. It's usually a neat box structure that seems to have evolved as a rather grudgingly provided shelter for the crew. In the early years of locomotive design the driver and fireman were remarkably windswept and exposed. They were lucky if they had a primitive windscreen to shelter them from the effects of the forward motion of the loco, let alone the prevailing weather conditions.

The Tilbury Tanks' cabs were originally enclosed and apparently quite cosy, the roof being a separate wooden construction. When rebuilt, or in later locos, the cab became a curved structure continuing the sides round and up and over. Being wholly metal, the inside became a swamp of condensation and chilly air – so much for progress. The cabs of Class 51 locomotives were never 'improved' and are easier to make.

To give us a solid foundation for the sides and the roof we'll cut ourselves the relatively simple cab front and back first. They have nice curved tops to help us fit the roof and dinky little round windows for the crew to peer through. Both sets have rather fetching

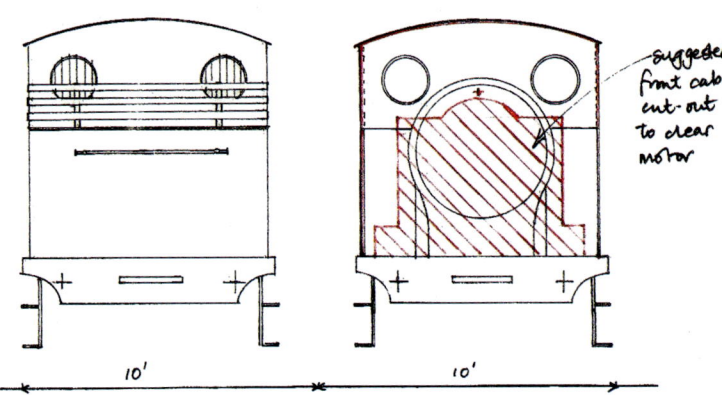

Cab front and back dimensions.

brass frames and the rear pair were later fitted with bars to prevent wayward lumps of coal from breaking the glass and making things draughtier inside the cab than they already were.

As the front and back lie within the sides of our model they need to be thinner by the width of the sides and slightly lower by the 0.25mm thickness of the roof (as provided for in the drawings).

- Draw directly onto your metal, or photocopy the diagram and stick your cab templates to two handy rectangles of 0.020in nickel silver, tack soldered together.
- Carefully saw them out – but don't saw out the front cab cut-out until after the pieces have been separated.
- Pop-mark the window centres and drill to 0.5mm, then up to 2mm. Finally, open out with a reamer to about 4.5mm. Remember not to use a big drill on thin metal – only tears can result.
- Separate the two pieces and clean them up.

Don't they look pretty? And we can make them even prettier. Time for some frames. You can either make them yourself or buy them in.

HOMEMADE WINDOW FRAMES

These brass window frames are easy to make, and pretty too:

- Open out the cab window holes to create a tight fit for some 6.0mm outside diameter thin-walled brass tube.
- Cut off four thin brass tube collars approximately 1mm long by rocking gently with a sharp knife blade.
- Use 180°C solder to fix the collars into the holes from the inside face of the cab.
- Make sure the collars project slightly from the outside surface by resting the cab on a piece of card.
- Finish off by carefully filing smooth to project slightly.

If you are really keen you can add rear window bars from fuse wire soldered into tiny holes.

ETCHED WINDOW FRAMES

If you are going for this option (and that's probably very sensible of you), you can buy a beautiful fret of etched window frames from Mainly Trains.

- Strengthen these delicate etches by giving them a fine coat of solder on the back before you cut them from the etch. Cut carefully with a sharp blade on a hard surface and remove any tags with a very fine file.
- Make sure the holes are a good fit for the inside diameter of the frames so that you have something

Homemade window frames.

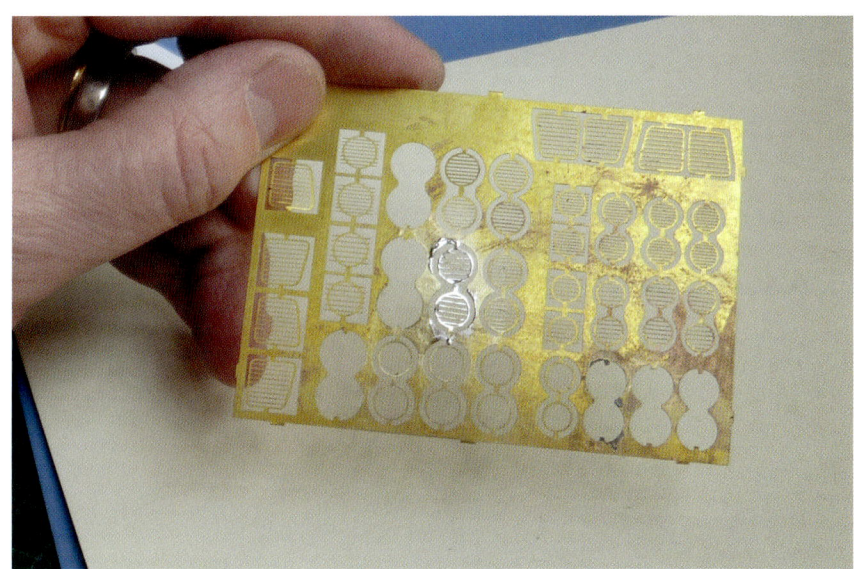

Window frame etch with solder strengthening.

to solder them on to. I tin the area with a smear of 180°C solder and 'sweat' the frames on.
- Hold them correctly in place with a cocktail stick, making sure the bars are parallel with the cab sides. Slosh on some flux and hold the iron near the etch. You'll see the solder liquefy and creep into the joint.
- Check that you are satisfied with the position of the etch and carry on until it's nice and secure. You can poke it from the back to see if it's properly attached. As you finish soldering draw any surplus

solder down and away from the grilles where you'll be able to clean it off, if you're fanatical like me. (A good dodge is to drag excess solder off the work onto a scrap of brass to get rid of it.)

FRONT CAB CUT-OUT

I had intended to fret this out before adding the front spectacle plates and only did it afterwards because I forgot. Fortunately, it made no difference.

I gave it round corners because I think it looks neater even though you won't be able to see it. Also,

Holding the etch in place while sweating the solder.

> **DEFINITION**
> **CORNER – SWEATING**
>
> When soldering, sweating means that you apply the iron near to the work, not actually on it. The heat travels to the tinned solder, which melts and does the job. Don't forget you need flux too.

do file everything smooth as you don't want ragged metal edges, especially near the expensive and delicate innards of your motor. And that's what the cut-out is for, to clear the motor.

On the real thing, the rear of the firebox protrudes into the cab, forming the back-head, where the majority of the loco's controls are situated. The rear driving wheels are in there too, taking up quite a lot of space. They are covered by rectangular splashers so they don't contribute an extra health hazard to the already dangerous cab interior.

In OO gauge, the wheels are rather close together and with the cab interior being already full of the rear end of the motor we can be thankful for the comparatively small windows. I made the cut-out nice and big in case I decided later on to have a change of motor or gearbox.

Do take care that you don't bend the narrow legs left on the sides while you are working on them.

The Tilbury cab seems remarkably free of any other details. Before moving on, give everything a careful clean and a brisk wire-brush. Put the two pieces away somewhere safe; you'll be needing them a bit later.

CHAPTER ELEVEN

CLASS 51 BOILER AND SMOKEBOX

After completing the footplate and the cab front and back you have a choice: either to continue with the cab ends and sides or to form the boiler and smokebox. As dimensions of both are to some extent determined by those of the other, it doesn't really matter in which order you choose to build them. However, as we worked on flat metal forms in the previous chapter, I thought we could turn to some more curvy bits and pieces here before attending to the body sides and cab (see Chapter 12).

The original Class 51 boiler is a nice simple affair: basically a tube with a smokebox shaped like a keyhole holding up the front end. The firebox is the same shape as the boiler, which is handy.

If you'd like to keep it simple then a piece of brass tubing is all you need: a cylinder with an outside

A beautiful watercolour of a Class 1 Tilbury Tank – smaller but very similar to the original Class 51.
JONATHAN CLAY

diameter of 18mm scales up nicely to the 5ft 6in of the real thing. If you want to roll your own then have a look at the Class 79 build and you'll find all you need.

THE BOILER

- Check whether or not the end of your chosen tubing is properly perpendicular and level so that it sits upright at right angles. Check carefully with a square all the way round. If it's good, you're lucky. If it's not, a bit of remedial filing might just do the trick.
- Assuming that the tube is not perpendicular, wrap a strip of decorator's masking tape – making sure not to stretch or twist it – around the tube just short of the end. The edges of the tape must meet all the way round to ensure the cut is straight. (Thin card can also be used.)
- Gently rest the saw blade against the edge of the tape and make a light cut all the way round. Keep going until you cut all the way through.

Checking for a perpendicular end.

- Check for perpendicularity, fine-tuning with a file until you have a good square end.
- Repeat the procedure, this time positioning the tape at the correct length of the boiler.
- Check again for perpendicularity and you have your boiler.

MAIN COMPONENTS

- 18mm outside diameter brass tube
- 0.020in nickel-silver sheet
- 0.5in length 10BA bolts and nuts
- 0.010in brass sheet

THE SMOKEBOX

The smokebox (where the smoke comes out, along with a great deal of exhaust steam) is a fine Victorian artefact possessed of subtle curves. All you need for this is a back and a front to hold the shape and then a smoothly wrapped wrapper. If you have already made your cylinders, you will have had practice doing this.

See the handy smokebox template diagram opposite.

- Draw or stick a template onto a pair of 0.020in nickel-silver pieces tacked together and saw them to shape.

Masking tape in place and ready to cut.

CLASS 51 BOILER AND SMOKEBOX

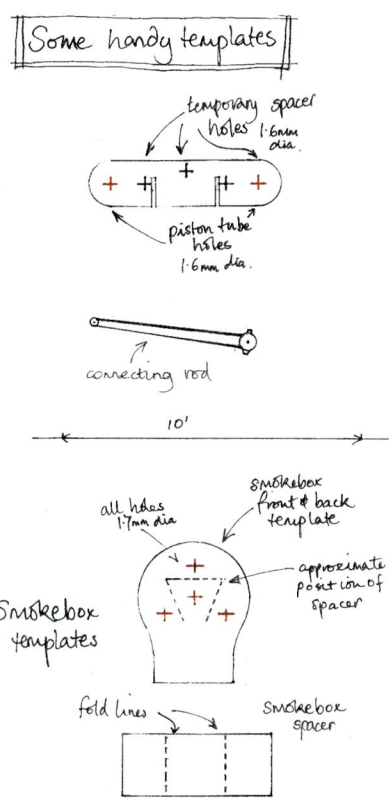

The cylinder formers, connecting rod and smokebox templates.

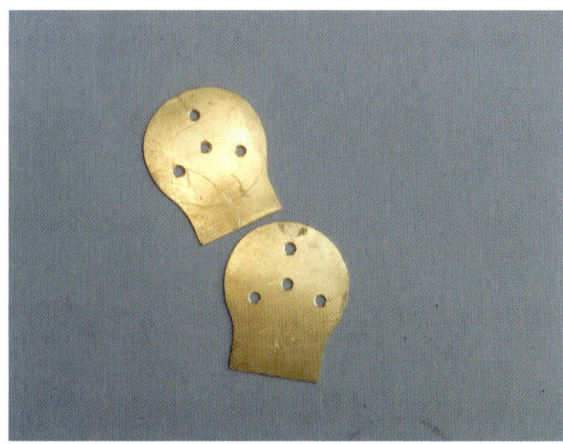

The finished pieces.

Solder a 10BA nut securely over the middle hole of the inside face of the back piece.

- Drill all the holes to 1.7mm to accommodate 10BA bolts.
- File and shape the sides and then separate. Label front and back.
- Solder a 10BA nut securely over the middle hole of the inside face of the back piece. You might wonder about the need for this nut. I assure you it is very useful for attaching the smokebox to the boiler, so don't forget it. It should end up inside the rear of the smokebox. Check that it is secure and in place by threading a 10BA bolt through from the front. Then remove the bolt.
- Cut and fold a spacer to size ensuring that the edges are parallel.
- Use three long 10BA bolts to hold everything in place. Solder the spacer in place around the centre hole. Don't get solder on the bolts, they need to come off. The spacer and bolts keep the front and back faces parallel and in exact alignment to each other. Check with a square if you wish; you can usually tell by eye if all is OK. Don't overtighten the bolts.

THE WRAPPER

The wrapper is made from thin brass which is easier to curve than nickel silver. Try not to dent it. The strip is deliberately wider than the finished article at about

CLASS 51 BOILER AND SMOKEBOX

Use three long 10BA bolts to hold everything in place. Solder the spacer in place around the centre hole. Don't get solder on the bolts, they need to come off.

Clamp the wrapper tightly around the large outside curve; any old clamps will do. Tack solder around the inside edge both back and front.

Prepare a wrapper of 0.010in brass and roll it into a curve on your thigh.

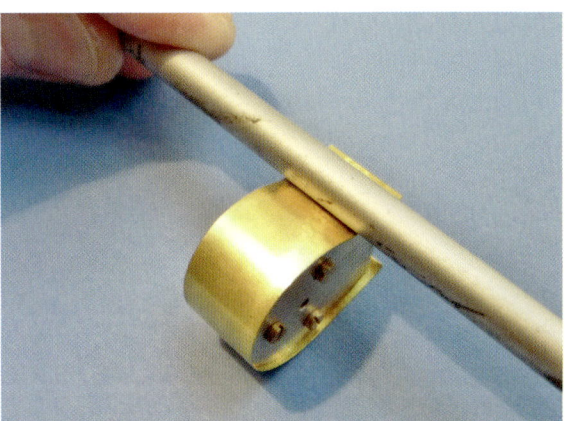

Curve the bottom edges around a suitable rod.

60mm × 12mm, making it easier to solder. The excess is filed off afterwards.

- Prepare a wrapper of 0.010in brass and roll it into a curve on your thigh.
- Clamp the wrapper tightly around the large outside curve; any old clamps will do. Tack solder around the inside edge both back and front.
- Curve the bottom edges around a suitable rod.
- Press the wrapper to shape around the lower edges using wood blocks or pegs and tack solder.
- Seam solder when completely satisfied with the fit. Remove the bolts and file the edges smooth.
- Trim and file the bottom edges smooth.

You should now have a delightful little smokebox all ready to fit to the boiler. I find that screwing these components together before finally fixing them in place makes the ongoing build more flexible. The boiler can be bolted to the rear face of the smokebox using the captive nut that is already in place.

CLASS 51 BOILER AND SMOKEBOX

Press the wrapper to shape around the lower edges using wood blocks or pegs and tack solder.

Seam solder when completely satisfied with the fit. Remove the bolts and file the edges smooth.

FIXING THE BOILER TO THE SMOKEBOX

- Saw and shape a circle of 0.020in nickel silver that will fit snuggly inside the boiler. If your tube walls are 0.5mm thick then the circle should be 17mm in diameter. A good way to start circles off is to drill a 0.5mm hole in the metal to take the point of the dividers as you draw the circle.
- Open the circle centre hole to 1.7mm and solder in a 10BA bolt from the back. Stop any solder clogging the thread by colouring it in with a marker.
- Hold the bolt (with pliers or a clothes peg) while you solder the circle just inside the boiler

Soldering the connecting bolt into the boiler front.

The boiler and smokebox introduced to each other.

tube. Keep everything parallel so that the bolt sticks out along the axis of the centre of the boiler.
- Clean it all up and then screw the boiler onto the smokebox. Again, not too tightly.
- Use the same technique to fit a rectangular base to the smokebox. This time, though, solder a 10BA nut in place over a hole in the centre of the rectangle. Screw onto a skewer and use that as a handle to solder in the baseplate, just as you did for the boiler.

The whole lot can then be secured to the bodywork, which we will build in the next chapter.

CLASS 51 BOILER AND SMOKEBOX

The baseplate situated inside the smokebox.

CHAPTER TWELVE

BUILDING UP THE CAB SIDES AND TANKS

Now we have a boiler, smokebox, footplate and cab front and back; our scratch-built kit of parts is almost complete. To pull everything together into a congruent whole (one piece) we need to make some cab and tank sides. These come in one piece on the Class 51. The bunker back can be added later and the cab roof is a separate component that clips onto the finished cab. The main challenge in this chapter is to saw and finish the sides.

Using the main drawing for the Class 51 in Chapter 5 as your point of reference, draw directly onto the metal, or stick on some photocopies if you would rather get the saw out sooner. Do just check though that the copy you are using is dimensionally consistent with the real thing – as shown by the dimensions on the GA (if you have one) – and with the bits you have already made. I made sure that the already completed cab back and front and the footplate matched the copy of the drawing I used to make the sides. At least then everything should fit together, even if they are all a bit off (as they will all be a bit off by the same amount).

MARKING OUT THE CAB/TANK SIDES

- Take the dimension for the highest point of the cab/tank sides, and transfer to the metal.
- Score the line deeply and break the metal (as previously described in Chapter 5) to produce a rectangle of the right height.
- Tack solder the rectangle to the piece you have just broken it from (if you can) as it will be of the same length and thickness. Ensure the bottom edges are exactly matched by standing them on a level surface before you clamp and solder them.
- Coat with black marker.
- Scribe with a craft blade to mark in the measurements for the sides. Check by lining up the metal accurately on the drawing.
- Use the straight bottom edge as the bottom edge of the sides; you'll have the challenge then of cutting and filing the tank tops straight and parallel.
- Mark out the shape using set-squares, steel rules and the craft knife for clean, accurate, perpendicular lines. Hatch in the waste areas so you know what bits you don't want.

I decided to make the tank fronts as part of the sides, to be folded in later at 90 degrees. You may notice from later photos that I got the measurement for the tank front folds wrong. I should stress that the published diagram is the revised version. Don't forget the small cut-out at the rear of the bunker.

I seem to have made quite a few mistakes when marking out. Luckily I noticed most of them before I started cutting.

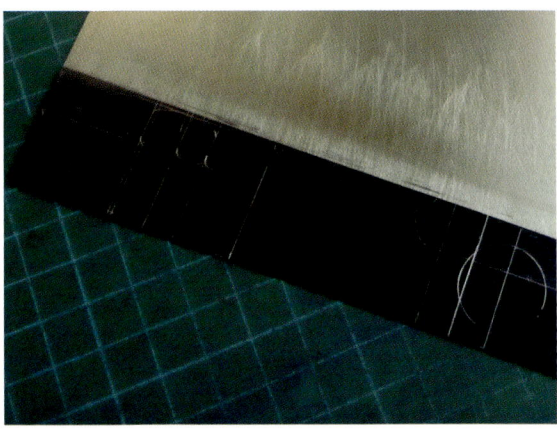

A scriber and circle templates were used to draw in the curves for the window cut-outs and tank fronts.

CUTTING THE SIDES

Don't separate the two pieces until shaping is finished. Make a few new tacks if things start to fall apart.

- Start by sawing the basic shape. Keep to the waste areas and don't try to cut the small curves accurately – they can be tidied up with files afterwards.
- Once the basic shape is cut out, compare it against the drawing before finishing.
- Leave the cab door and window cut-out until last as the thin strip at the top is rather flimsy and easily bent. Take care. A good technique here is to leave a strip about 2mm wide at the bottom of the door that can be removed later. Drill a hole in the waste area of the cab to thread the saw blade through and cut everything out smoothly.

Sawing the cab window and door aperture; the piece of card provides extra support for the blade when cutting tricky shapes in thin metal.

Clamp the sides firmly and file the curved cut-outs at the front of the tanks to shape.

- I use a large half-round file and finish with a cylindrical oilstone. The oilstones have no teeth and don't cause any drag so they are great for delicate finishing. They do make a bit of a mess and, boy, can they scratch metal surfaces. Take care.
- Once you are pleased with your delicate final shaping, turn the thing over and take a look at the back. Without the distraction of paper or marker-ink you'll get a much clearer view of the outline.
- If you haven't done so already, drill out the handrail holes to 0.5mm. If you are using a paper template it is much more accurate to mark out the holes on the back with a pen and dividers.

Check the tank front curve for fit against a piece of boiler tubing.

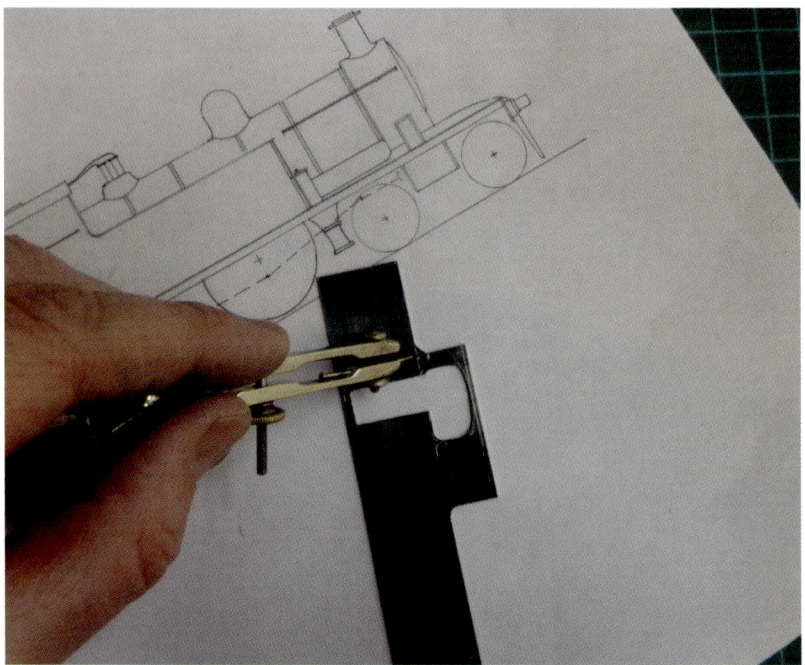

To shape the rounded corners accurately, mark off their limits with the dividers before you file them with a half-round needle file.

BUILDING UP THE CAB SIDES AND TANKS | 93

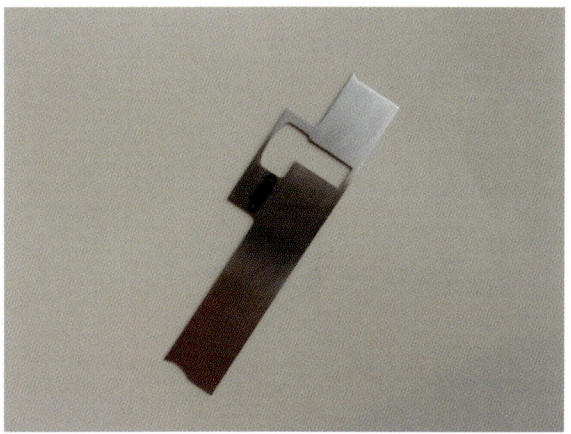

Clean up and admire – but not before drilling the handrail holes.

- Finally, oh so carefully, split the two pieces apart with the subtle introduction of a craft blade. It's always best to start at the weakest point, which in this case is the strip above the cab cut-out. Then work gently to ease everything in two, without bending the strip at the bottom.

FOLDING THE TANK FRONTS
FILING A GROOVE
A clean fold is required for the tank fronts. If it's wonky it will look bad and probably won't fit the boiler properly. It also has to be at right angles to allow the sides to sit properly on the footplate.

The corners on the real thing are quite sharp. To get a crisp fold, we need to file a triangular groove just where the metal bends – which is essentially what etched kit manufacturers do although their grooves tend to be rectangular, and etched. It takes practice to get it right, so I suggest you try it out first on some scrap.

- Mark the position of the fold line and scribe it onto the side with a sharp knife and set-square. You can use a skrawker to open the groove out a little more or carry on with the knife.
- When you've got a good groove, file it to a triangular shape with a triangular needle file.

Thundersley's *tank fronts have very tight corners.*

Rest the file against the square to help keep it in line if you wish, or file freehand. Keep going gently until you can see the line of the fold faintly appearing on the other side of the metal. If you squint at the edge you should be able to see a nice V-shaped groove, all ready to fold up neatly.

The aim of all this is to remove a triangular wedge of metal that would get in the way of a crisp fold.

MAKING A FOLD
Use your bending bars, a pair of pliers, vice or – even better – a relatively new piece of kit called a 'hold and

fold' tool, a more delicate version of the bending bars, as shown in the sequence below:

- Clamp the side into a bending device with the filed groove lined up exactly with the edge of the jaws. The square ensures the fold will be at 90 degrees.
- The bend is made by supporting the metal with a Stanley knife blade. Push it right under the groove, then bear gently upwards until you are at 90 degrees. Take great care.
- Remove and check with the square.
- And there you are. Magnificent.

Clamp the side into a bending device with the filed groove lined up exactly with the edge of the jaws. The square ensures the fold will be at 90 degrees.

The bend is made by supporting the metal with a Stanley knife blade. Push it right under the groove, then bear gently upwards until you are at 90 degrees. Take great care.

BUILDING UP THE CAB SIDES AND TANKS

Remove and check with the square.

BELOW LEFT: And there you are. Magnificent.

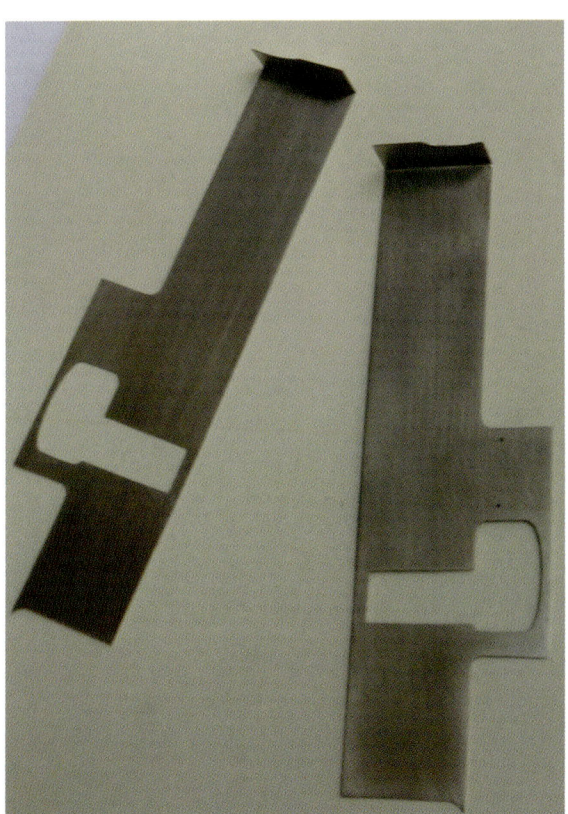

After all that hard work you might want a bit of a breather. Then back to the fray.

BODY-BUILDING

The sequence in which you fix the body to the footplate is very much up to you. I wanted to keep things as square and secure as possible and decided to solder the cab rear to one side first. The narrow strips at the bottom of the cab doors, left in for strengthening purposes, can be cut out now as it's difficult if the footplate is already soldered on and in the way.

- Place the side on a flat surface.
- Line up the cab rear almost flush in its position along the rear of the cab side; move it into the cab a fraction of a millimetre as this will make adding the beading easier.
- Make sure the cab window grilles are on the outside.
- Ensure the side and end are at right angles to each other, using a square.

BUILDING UP THE CAB SIDES AND TANKS

Soldering the cab rear to the side.

Adding the cab step strengthening piece.

- Make sure the bottom edges are exactly in line by pushing something flat up against them.
- You can just about get away with holding things with your finger, or use Blu-tack.
- Solder a tack in the middle of the joint, inside the cab.
- Check everything is in line and at 90 degrees and make another tack at the top and bottom of the joint. Check again.
- Once you are happy with that, carefully saw away the waste piece at the bottom of the cab door and solder in a strengthening step from 3mm-wide brass strip.

BUILDING UP THE CAB SIDES AND TANKS 97

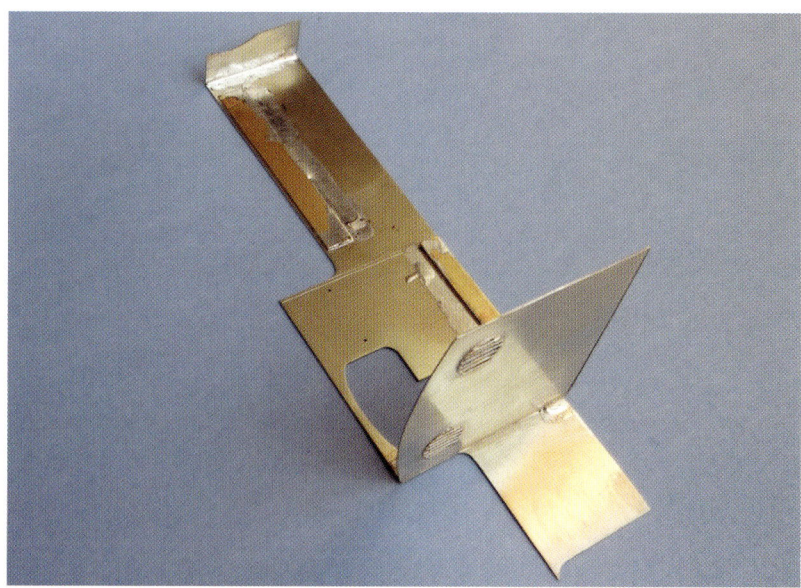

Add another strengthening piece along the inside top edge of the tank about 0.5mm down. Eventually it will support the tank top strips.

You could leave the reinforcing web at the bottom of the cab door if you are happy with the look of it. I cut it out and replaced it with a similar piece – soldered behind the door opening – to more accurately represent the cab step. There is very little visual difference; it's just one of my things. It requires you to support the side very carefully when sawing. (Remember to do this on both sides of the cab.)

SOLDERING THE SIDES TO THE FOOTPLATE

When aligning the cab and sides, it helps enormously to scribe parallel lines on the footplate with the

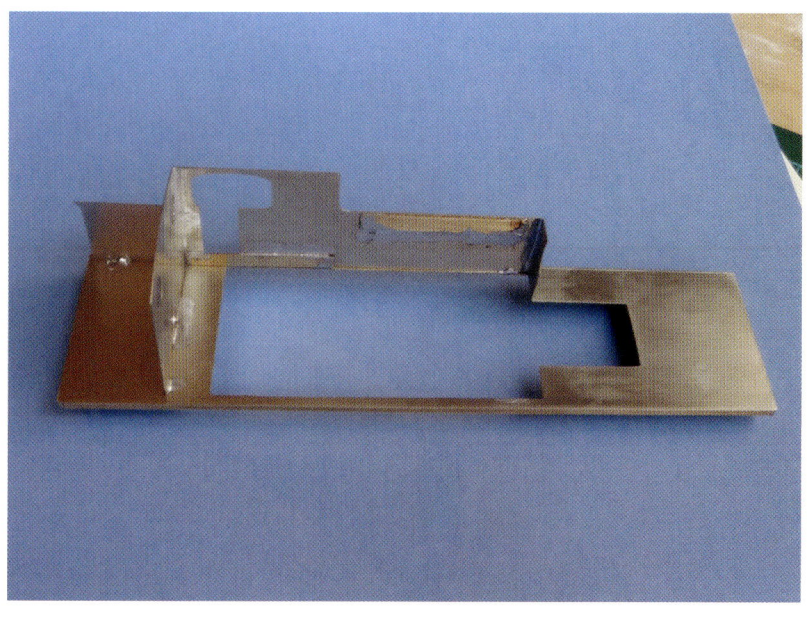

Tack solder the combined cab back and side in place, with the cab central to the footplate and the side lined up along the footplate edge.

dividers. Centre lines scribed on the cab rear and the footplate allow accurate positioning too.

- Tack solder the combined cab back and side in place, with the cab central to the footplate and the side lined up along the footplate edge.
- Check that the cab front cut-out allows sufficient clearance for the motor by temporarily placing the body assembly on the chassis.

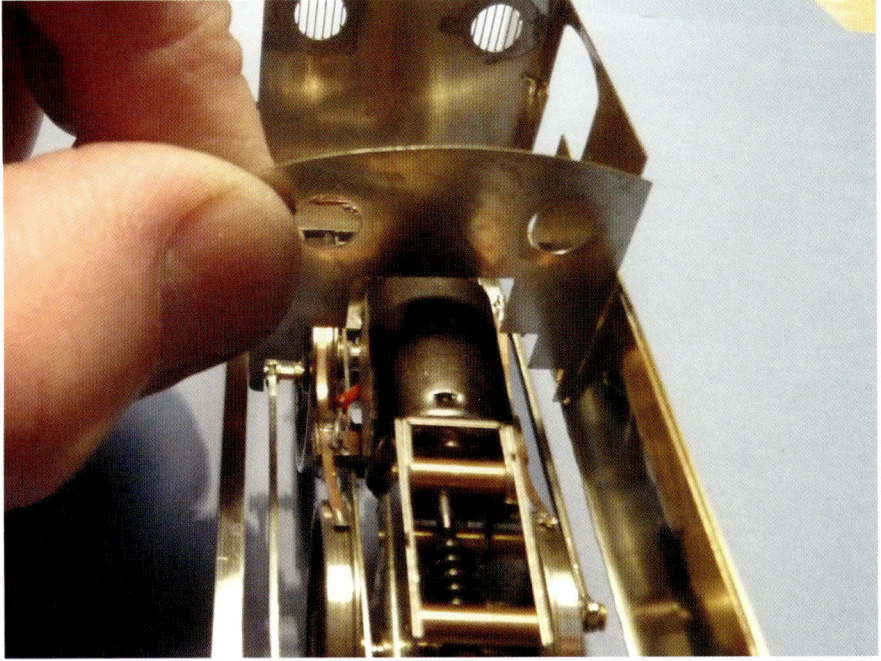

Check that the cab front cut-out allows sufficient clearance for the motor by temporarily placing the body assembly on the chassis.

Line up the other side piece and tack it to the cab rear – leave it unsecured at the front.

BUILDING UP THE CAB SIDES AND TANKS 99

- Line up the other side piece and tack it to the cab rear – leave it unsecured at the front.
- Position the cab front, align the side piece, secure everything in place with masking tape, then tack solder all joints.

It is really beginning to look like a locomotive now. Put off seaming any of the joints until the boiler assembly has been tested for a good fit. It does make things easier to dismantle if there's a problem. Well done. Give everything a good scrub.

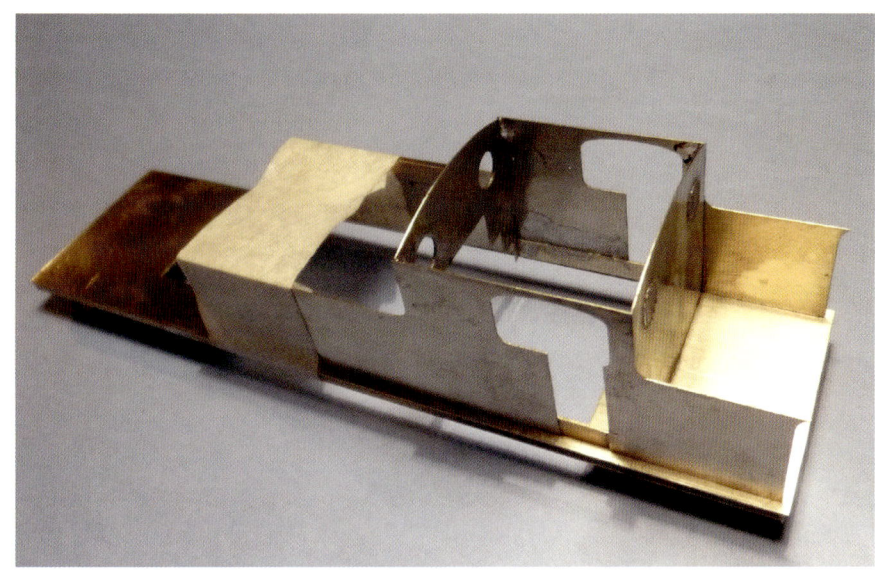

Position the cab front, align the side piece, secure everything in place with masking tape, then tack solder all joints.

CHAPTER THIRTEEN

TANK TOPS, BUNKER END, CAB DOORS AND BEADING

If you want to know exactly how the real side tanks are made, here's an educational image from the Severn Valley Railway.

You'll note that the pieces are helpfully labelled (it also says 'Made In England' on the side). To learn more take a look at www.4150.org.uk, or visit them at Bewdley.

Back to those tanks: although they are from a different type of loco, the design is much the same. Some parts of the tank have to accommodate the driving wheels while most of the rest is what it says on the tin: a tank – for water. We don't have to build all of the fascinating internal structure, just the tops, sides and fronts. We've already done the sides and front ends. So, tops it is.

TANK TOPS

CUTTING THE TANK TOPS
The tops of the tanks are two rectangular pieces of metal that fit between the boiler and the tank sides. The boiler/smokebox assembly can be used to establish the exact fit of the tank tops.

- Measure the height from the base of the smokebox to the bottom of the boiler with the handy little widget on the end of the Vernier calipers.
- Cut two temporary spacer strips to the height you have measured and tack solder them across the front and backs of the tanks. (A wooden block, as shown in the photograph, is a sound base to keep everything square and free from accidental damage as more and more pieces are added to your masterpiece. One can be whittled from balsa in a quiet moment.)
- Prop the boiler on the temporary rests and measure the distance from the top of the inside of the tank sides horizontally across to where it meets the side of the boiler with the calipers. Ensure everything is parallel and central. If it is, the strips that you cut for the tank tops should

The side tanks of GWR 2-6-2 tank No. 4150 being rebuilt by the sturdy folk of The 4150 Fund at the Severn Valley Railway.

TANK TOPS, BUNKER END, CAB DOORS AND BEADING

Measure the height from the base of the smokebox to the bottom of the boiler with the handy little widget on the end of the Vernier calipers.

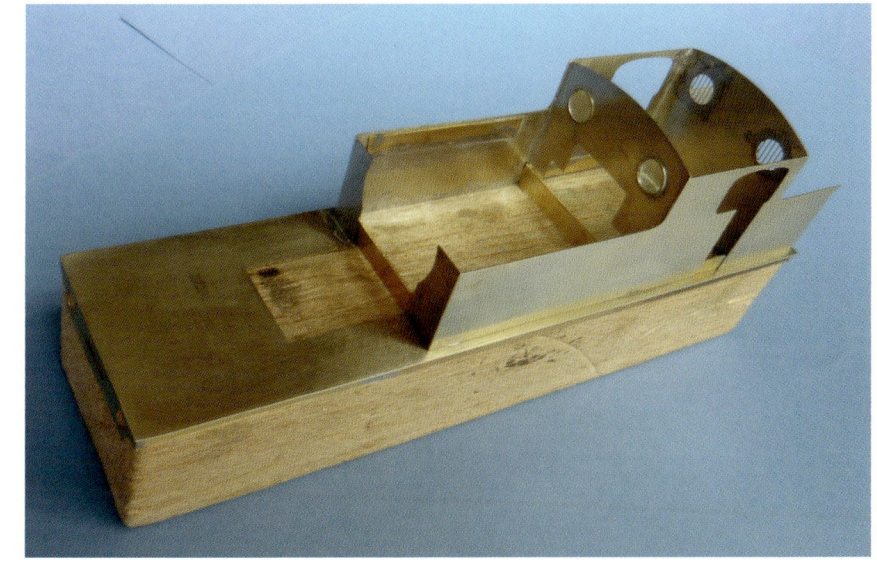

Cut two temporary spacer strips to the height you have measured and tack solder them across the front and back of the tanks.

be identical; don't worry if they're a tiny bit different.
- Make up two tank top strips from 0.015in nickel-silver strip and rest them on the strengthening strips inside the tank's sides and against the boiler sides.
- Mark where the top of the boiler meets the cab front.

- Remove the boiler and drill a hole 2mm down from the mark to allow the boiler to be bolted onto the cab (if you haven't done so already).
- If you are happy with the horizontal fit of the tank tops, solder them on from inside the tank sides. If they don't fit well, fettle them or make new ones until you are satisfied.

TANK TOPS, BUNKER END, CAB DOORS AND BEADING

Make up two tank top strips from 0.015in nickel-silver strip and rest them on the strengthening strips inside the tank's sides and against the boiler sides.

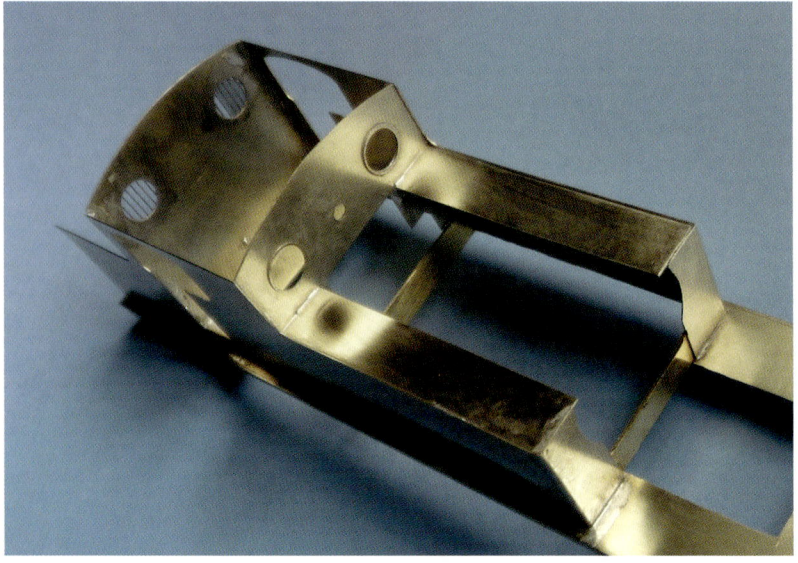

If you are happy with the horizontal fit of the tank tops, solder them on from inside the tank sides.

- Once that is done, remove the temporary supporting strips. Either push them carefully and quickly away with the soldering iron or, if you are worried about unsoldering everything around them, cut them off with the piercing saw or cutting disc in the mini-drill. (Watch your eyes.)

The photos show cruelly my original mistake in measuring the tank ends. They are nowhere near a good

TANK TOPS, BUNKER END, CAB DOORS AND BEADING

fit on the boiler. I fixed that little problem with a couple of thin overlays soldered to the originals.

SECURING THE BOILER

It's a good idea not to permanently fix the boiler to the cab front. This can be achieved by soldering a long 10BA bolt exactly central and parallel to the inside of the boiler. This allows the boiler to be bolted through a hole in the cab front.

Laying everything out on graph paper helps while doing this.

- Paint the part of the thread that you don't want to be soldered with marker pen – that's the bit that you want to bolt to the inside of the cab front.
- Leave a nut threaded on so that when you saw off the bolt head, the nut will cut the end of the thread cleanly making it easier to rethread later.
- Leave the bolt head on until the end as it's easier to hold while you're soldering.
- Once securely soldered, saw off the bolt head, file cleanly and run the nut up and down to clear the thread.

REMOVING THE BOILER CUT-OUT

In order to accommodate the motor and gearbox some of the metal needs to be removed from the boiler.

- Fit the boiler in place and mark where the boiler abuts the tanks. Remove the boiler and draw a cut-out in marker pen, starting about 10mm in from the tank fronts so that you can't see that the boiler suddenly stops being a cylinder. Leave some of the boiler sides for strength.

ABOVE: *A soldered bolt for bolting the boiler to the cab front, seen here prior to the removal of the bolt's head and nut.*

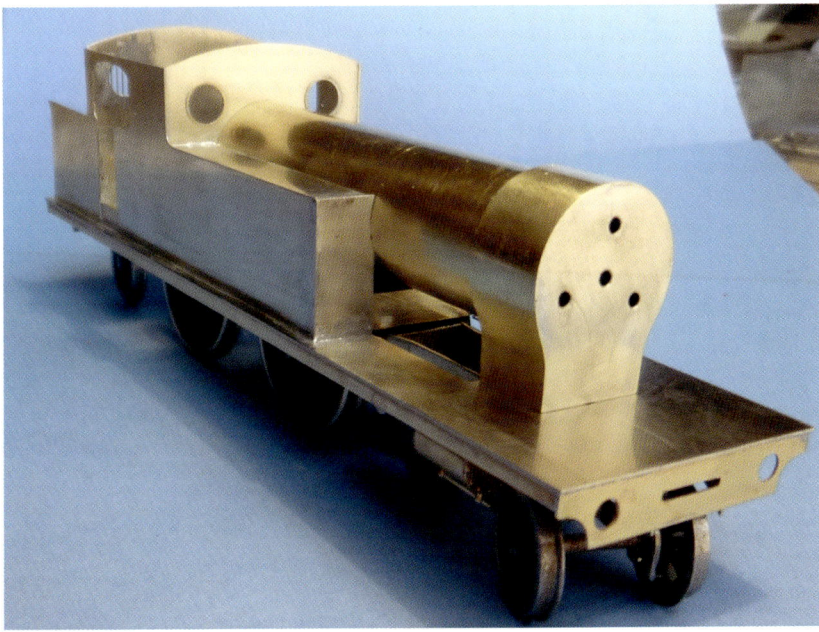

Cleaned up and reassembled, the loco has a charming toylike appearance.

104 TANK TOPS, BUNKER END, CAB DOORS AND BEADING

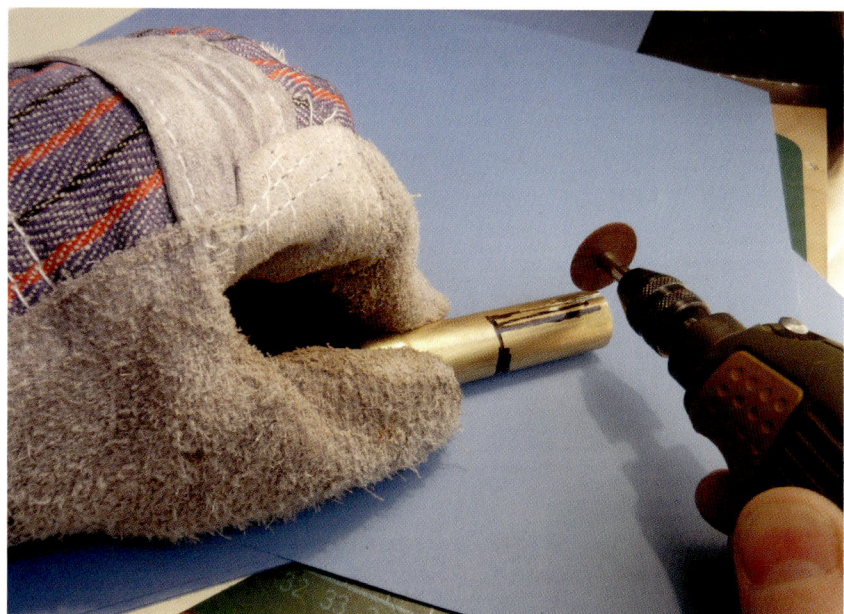

Better safe than sorry while removing the cut-out.

BELOW: *The crisp lines of Thundersley's rear end.*

- Remove the cut-out with a slitting disc in the mini-drill. Wear eye protection in case the disc shatters, which they do occasionally. For extra peace of mind wear gardening gloves, which adds a somewhat surreal air to proceedings.

The slitting disc and various burrs running in the mini-drill are very useful if you want to add a bit more clearance in other areas like the footplate or cab cut-out.

Now for the bunker rear.

FINISHING THE BUNKER

Unlike other railway companies, such as the Great Western, the Tilbury Tanks' bunker rear was flared in only one plane – that is, it only bends outwards at the top of the back edge. The flare doesn't go around the sides, either, which makes life easier as that means you don't have to fabricate fiddly little corners. However, you are going to have to form a curved top that fits nicely to the curves of the sides.

Forming curves is another one of those scary bits, but it's just a curve in a piece of metal and if you make

TANK TOPS, BUNKER END, CAB DOORS AND BEADING

a complete mess of it you can have a second more practised attempt – and succeed.

CURVING THE BACK OF THE BUNKER

Normally I produce flares such as the long ones on the sides of tenders by taping the edge of the metal to a suitably sized rod, clamping it in the bending bars and bending it, supporting it with a file. There are other ways: you can force the piece down into a yielding surface such as balsa wood with a rod; tweak it with long-nosed pliers (be careful as they can mark the metal); or fold the metal around the rod with your fingers if it's thin and narrow enough. (Evolution didn't predict the soldering iron but it certainly gave us the right stuff for metal-folding in miniature.) Let's take the plunge.

- Measure the width of the bunker at the bottom edge and transfer the measurement to the metal (0.010in nickel) with the caliper jaws.

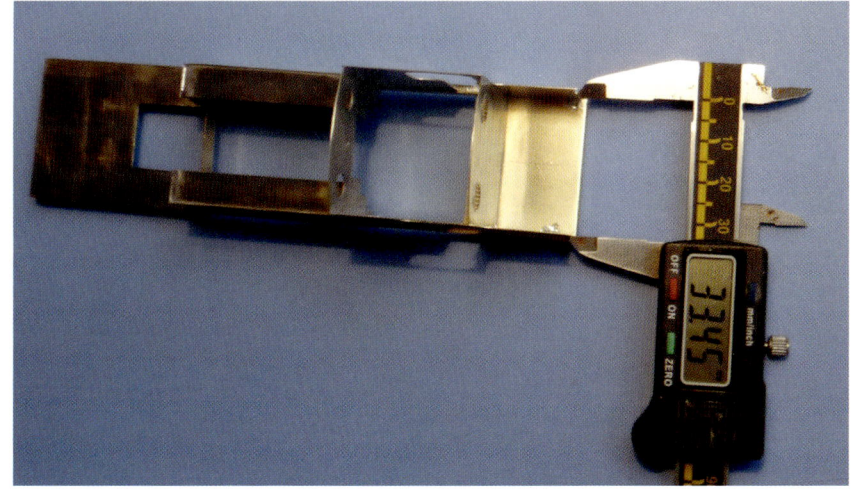

Measure the width of the bunker at the bottom edge and transfer the measurement to the metal (0.010in nickel) with the caliper jaws.

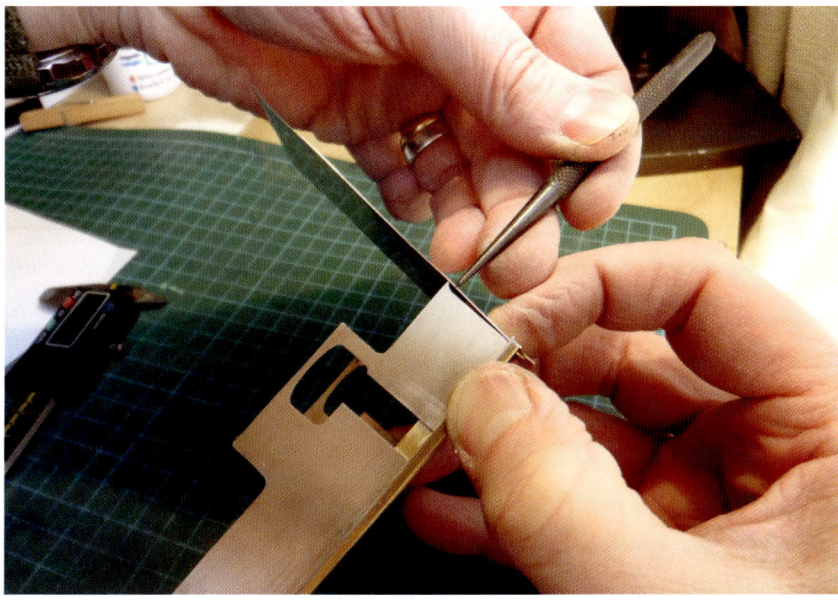

After breaking a longish strip, hold in place at the bunker bottom and mark a line at the position of the beginning of the bend.

TANK TOPS, BUNKER END, CAB DOORS AND BEADING

- After breaking a longish strip, hold in place at the bunker bottom and mark a line at the position of the beginning of the bend.
- Use double-sided tape to secure the strip to a squared cutting mat or graph paper, taking care to align the strip with the grid. Hold a 2mm-diameter rod parallel to the grid lines. Position it by eye so that the curve will start at the marked line.
- Hold down the rod firmly with your fingers and use your thumbs to produce the bend.
- Check for a good fit, tweak if necessary, then mark a line approximately 1mm above the bunker top.
- Using a square, score deeply and then carefully break the excess metal, using your fingers to flex it gently without disturbing the bend. Be patient,

Hold down the rod firmly with your fingers and use your thumbs to produce the bend.

Check for a good fit, tweak if necessary, then mark a line approximately 1mm above the bunker top.

TANK TOPS, BUNKER END, CAB DOORS AND BEADING

Using a square, score deeply and then carefully break the excess metal, using your fingers to flex it gently without disturbing the bend.

do lots of small flexes, and try to avoid the pliers unless absolutely necessary. You are aiming for a smooth curve that will fit nicely to the back of the bunker.

If things get a little out of hand, resist the urge for a hissy fit. Put everything down gently, switch off the soldering iron and take a break. When you return, tweak and tweak again. Or have another go at making the piece. If necessary, make the back slightly too wide – it will then be easier to fit and can be filed smooth later. Eventually everything will fit perfectly.

- Once you are happy with the fit, tack solder the back in position, supporting it with a piece of wood. Seam when you are satisfied.
- Clean up and file and sand the joints on the sides until you can't see the join.

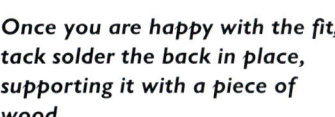

Once you are happy with the fit, tack solder the back in place, supporting it with a piece of wood.

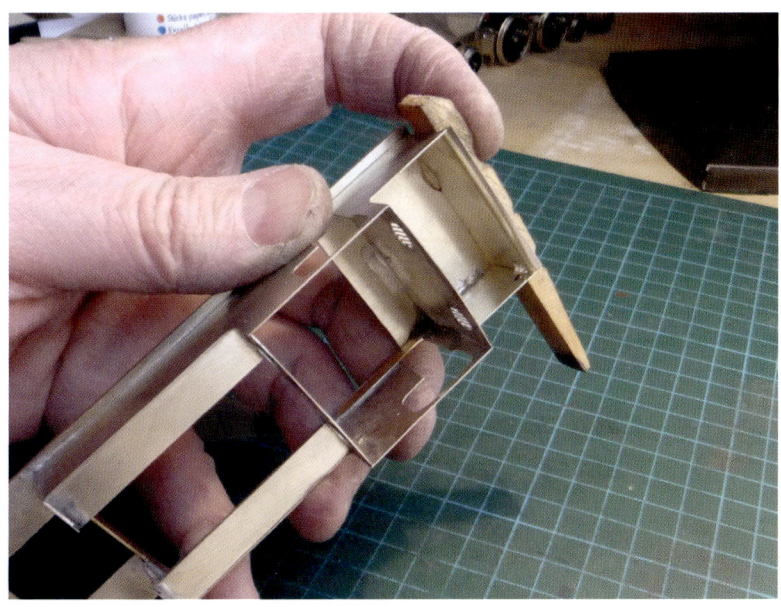

108 TANK TOPS, BUNKER END, CAB DOORS AND BEADING

File carefully to finish.

Frustrating though the process can sometimes be, it's worth persevering as the end result can be incredibly satisfying. Show people. Have a drink.

CAB FLOOR

Having gone to all of the trouble of making the doors look good, a representation, at least, of the cab floor can be easily produced. If nothing else, it gives you a ledge to stand the crew on.

- Simply cut a U-shaped piece of 0.020in nickel silver to fit inside the cab. It locates nicely on the door strengthening pieces and provides a ledge to stand the bottom of the doors on. Do make sure that the U-pieces are not too wide otherwise they will interfere with the wheels.

Tin snips cause much more distortion than breaking or sawing but with a bit of practice they can be very versatile.

CAB DOORS

I've plumped for not worrying about being unable to see into the cab of the model; it is, after all, full

The floor can be trimmed with tin snips. Note that you need to snip away in small strips so that the waste deforms and not the main piece.

of mechanism. Photos obligingly show the cab doors firmly shut and all you need is a complement of jolly cast-metal crew and nothing inside is going to be visible. Particularly once the roof is on.

So, to paraphrase *The Italian Job*, let's get the bloody doors on.

- Form the doors from two rectangles of 0.010in nickel strip broken to size. In order to inset them slightly from the sides, solder thin strips of metal just inside the door edges and then solder the doors onto them.
- The beading that you rest your arm on while leaning out of the cab is rounded for comfort. Make this by soldering on overlong lengths of copper wire – overlong because this allows you to hold the wire while you solder. Then trim to length with side-cutters, which leave a nice straight edge and won't force the wire to distort enough to break the soldered joint.

Thundersley's door from inside the cab.

CAB ROOF

We're going to tackle this now while you are in a mood to make some shapes. You can use your new-found confidence in curving to good use.

I was thinking of using thin brass to make the roof as nickel is rather springy. I didn't have a suitable thickness of brass so I used some nickel instead. This, I think, turned out to be a good idea. Thin brass is very soft and loses its shape at the least provocation. With springy nickel, if you make the bends very slightly tighter than they should be, the roof will cling neatly onto the sides. Also, it's dead easy and very effective.

- Make a roof template from card.
- Cut a rectangle from 0.010in nickel silver to match the card template. There should be an overhang of about 1mm on every side.
- Roll the rectangle on your thigh with a larger diameter tube than you did for the smokebox.
- Check for a good fit on the cab ends.
- Bend a pair of lengths of 0.7mm wire to the same curvature and bend down some 'legs' at each end to locate the roof into the sides. Make each leg a slightly different length to help when locating the roof.
- Mark the underside of the roof with the dividers to help you position the wire shapers then solder them on.
- Push-fit the roof onto the cab. Tweak the curvature a bit for a really good fit. Take care not to get any kinks. With this method of fitting there's no need to solder the roof on, which is always good if you need to get inside the cab later.

Make a roof template from card.

BELOW LEFT: *The wire shapers soldered to the underside of the roof. Their position is not critical as long as they fit within the cab sides.*

BELOW RIGHT: *The cab roof in place with lengths of thin wire soldered on as rain strips. Note the frame extensions on either side of the smokebox – we'll come to them later.*

TANK TOPS, BUNKER END, CAB DOORS AND BEADING

TRIMMINGS

Now all of the major body components are in place, the various accessories can be added.

BEADING

Beading, I am reliably informed, gets rid of sharp edges and protects them against corrosion. It is also decorative and may be painted or polished to taste.

On the model, particularly around the cab windows, it is preferable that the beading material is quite soft. Half-round brass wire, if you can get hold of it, is ideal.

As I had run out of my favourite soft brass half-round wire and couldn't wait until my order arrived, I spent hours trying out different things to replace it: nickel-silver strip (too hard and springy), thick copper wire (too thick, too round), flattened copper wire (too kinky). Thin copper wire is good and can be given a flat surface with a lick of careful filing once it's in position. I didn't have any thin copper wire.

Finally, I took my own advice and called it a day. The next morning the postman delivered my wire of choice.

The beading around **Thundersley's** *cab door.*

> **TIP OF THE DAY**
>
> Try not to get hung up on pining for your lost reel of half-round brass wire or whatever it is you pine for. Think about what qualities it had that suited the job you wanted it to do (thinness and softness), find something else that has those same qualities and use that. Or wait.
>
> Oh, and if you stop doing something and distract your subconscious it'll come up with a different answer – possibly waking you up in the middle of the night in the process.

AND SO TO BEAD

- Straighten lengths of wire first by stretching between two pairs of pliers; you can feel it 'give' as it straightens.
- Start with the long sides to get some practice in first.
- Use overlong pieces of wire and cut to length later.
- Form easy to reach curves around rods.
- Hold everything in place with masking tape.
- Support tack soldering with pegs.
- Tack solder bit by bit, working around the curves and then trimming at the end.
- Avoid unsightly kinks; use wood skewers or cocktail sticks to form the bends so as not to bruise the metal and carefully tack solder from the rear if you can or the front if you can't.
- Support the beading with flat surfaces such as pegs or cards to keep the amount that it projects consistent.
- Trim with side-cutters to prevent distortion.
- Don't forget to leave a 2mm or so overhang to accommodate the handrails.

TAPERED HANDRAILS

At the free ends of the beading on *Thundersley* there are some delightfully tapered handrails. The shape is quite subtle so if you don't want to taper, just use some straight lengths of 0.7mm brass wire.

If you do want to get down and taper, it's good fun:

- Clamp a short length (about 40mm) of 0.7mm wire into the collet of your mini-drill. Set it going and hold the wire gently down against a hard wood block.
- Run a file against the revolving wire so that you produce a gradual taper. Don't touch the revolving collet with the file, that's why there's a bit of extra length.
- Use the calipers occasionally to check how things are progressing. When the tip of the wire reaches 0.5mm you are done and dusted.

Soldering the beading along the tank tops.

TANK TOPS, BUNKER END, CAB DOORS AND BEADING

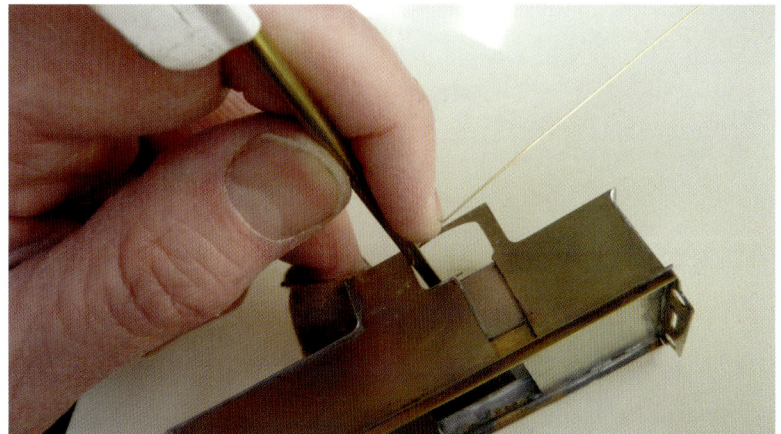

Curving the beading around the inside of the cab cut-out.

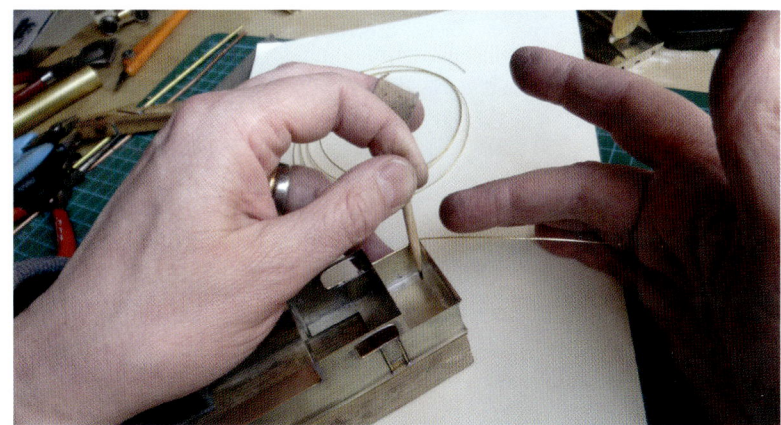

Adding the beading to the bunker tops.

- Repeat six times to create six delightfully tapered handrails.
- Polish them with a bit of wet and dry to a shiny finish.

I soldered them to the overhanging ends of the beading on the tank ends by passing them through 0.7mm holes drilled in the footplate. The ones for the cab doors were trimmed to length to fit between the beading and the footplate. They can be soldered up against the doorstep for extra strength. Finish by rounding the ends of the beading using an oilstone or fine file.

FRAME EXTENSIONS

To position the boiler neatly on the cab and footplate we need a pair of frame extensions. These are the fine knife-shaped blades between which the smokebox sits. As their name suggests, they are extensions of the frames of the chassis.

In OO gauge the frames are closer together than they should be so we have to cheat and place the frame extensions on top of the footplate with no real connection to the chassis. Which makes life a lot easier. They are quite tricky to make though as they are rather skinny.

- Tack solder two strips of 0.020in nickel together and draw or stick on a template of the frame extensions cut out from the main drawing of the Class 51 in Chapter 5.
- Cautiously saw the curve out; it gets very thin to the rear.
- File and clean up.

TANK TOPS, BUNKER END, CAB DOORS AND BEADING

Tapered handrails and frame extensions in evidence.

The frame extensions of Thundersley, *nicely lined out in red and black.*

- Position the smokebox securely and mark locating lines parallel to the footplate edge so that you can solder the extensions in straight lines too.
- Put a strip of cigarette paper between the smokebox and the extension, press it up to the smokebox and tack solder along the length.
- Do this for both sides, then remove the smokebox, check the extensions are parallel and seam them up.

- Clean off any excess solder (and there probably will be) – you can try the dodge of drawing the solder to the inside of the joint where you can't see it.

This really sets off the front end of the loco. Admire, and reward yourself. You're nearly there. If you can't wait to add your finishing touches then skip to Chapter 17 on detailing.

TANK TOPS, BUNKER END, CAB DOORS AND BEADING

A frame extension held in a jewellers' clamp for final shaping.

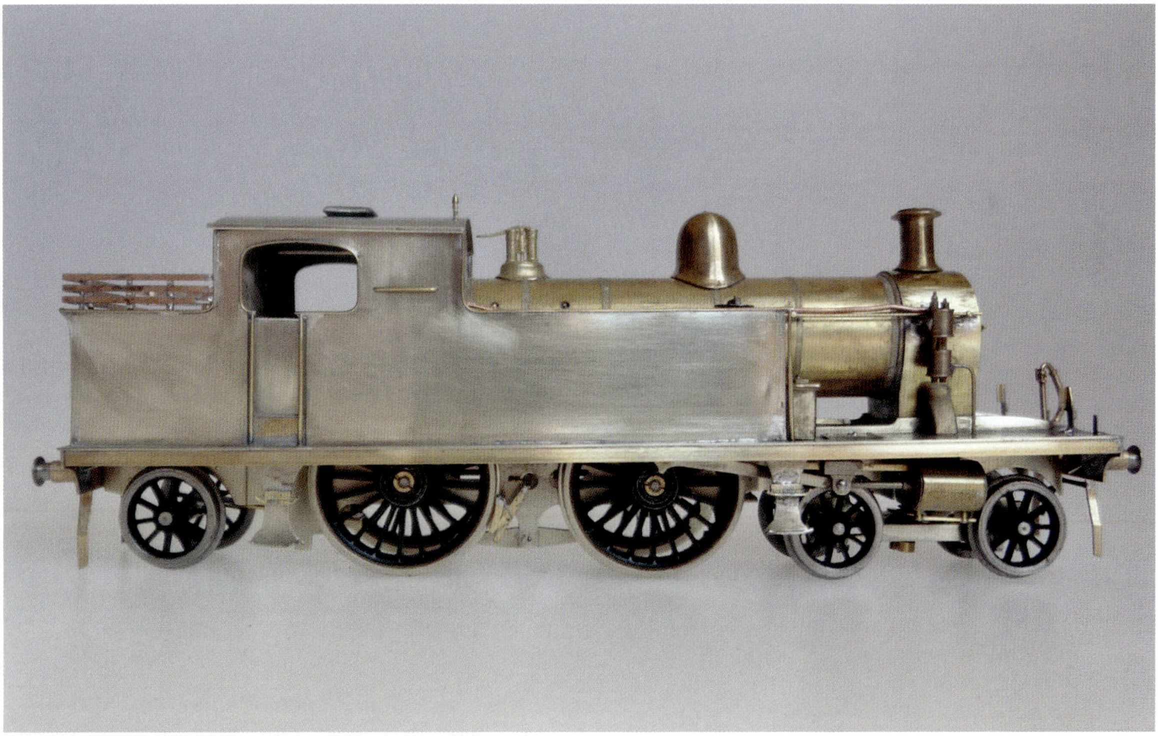

The Class 51 loco complete.

CHAPTER FOURTEEN

BUILDING THE CLASS 79 CHASSIS

VIVE LA DIFFERENCE

The Class 79 and rebuilt Class 37 tanks were slightly larger than Class 51 locos. Their boilers are a bit heftier and higher and equipped with extended smokeboxes. The cylinders are fractionally more robust and both classes had those newfangled wrap-around cabs. There are some other detail differences mainly due to the relative modernity of these later locos. The frames and chassis, however, are almost identical with the Class 51 tanks, which is handy in that we can build another of the same, gaining from the experience of building the first and using it as a test bed for some new ideas.

I actually did it the other way around, building the Class 79 first. I realized that I had employed arguably

Class 79 Tilbury Tank No. 41975. COLOUR-RAIL

BUILDING THE CLASS 79 CHASSIS

> **MAIN COMPONENTS**
>
> - Two pairs of Alan Gibson 6ft 6in driving wheels
> - Three pairs of Alan Gibson 3ft 6in bogie wheels
> - High Level SlimLiner+ 54:1 gearbox with D3 drive stretcher
> - Mashima M1220 can motor
> - London Road Models radial truck etch
> - Alan Gibson or High Level horn blocks
> - Selection of small diameter thin-walled brass tubes
>
> **Additional (and optional) tools**
> - GW Models (or other) rivet press
> - GW Models 4mm finescale wheel press
> - Hobby Holidays Master Chassis Jig

more complicated techniques and decided to swap the order in which they appear in the book. Feel free to pick and choose.

THIS CHASSIS INCLUDES

- Etched construction sprung radial axle box
- Scratch-built bogie
- Compensation beam between the front driving wheels and bogie
- Horn blocks and bearings for the front driving wheels
- Alan Gibson driving wheels
- Solid 'nested tube' construction cylinders
- Plunger-style pickups

The frames are much the same as those for the Class 51. Standardization of design made things easier and cheaper for the railway companies; the Great Western in particular embraced the idea, as did Mr Ford of Model T fame.

Note that the rectangular cut-outs for the radial truck are a more prototypical shape and that there may well be less clearance on tight curves as a result. The cut-outs for the front four-wheeled bogie stay the same. There is also a rectangular cut-out for the horn blocks, which include the bearings for the front pair of driving wheels.

First things first: a new technique.

RIVETS: THE EMBOSSED VARIETY

If you are as keen on obsessive detail as I am, you might like to consider embossing your rivets directly into the metal. There are a few dotted around the frames so you could get your eye in here first. I would suggest you practise on some scrap metal before you pepper a beloved model with unsightly encrustations – just in case.

The GW rivet press is, in my opinion, the Rolls-Royce of riveters. It is hand-machined by a gentleman from whom you have to order it by post or phone. It has a platform to clamp your work to and dinky little handled wheels that you can turn to move everything about with great precision. There are various additional pieces to provide a choice of rivet sizes and if you are really practised you can make rivets in exactly spaced circles. All you need do is press the handle down and a rivet magically appears. It's marvellous. It can be tricky to see what you are doing and it's a little cumbersome, particularly when trying to accommodate larger chunks of metal. It is also the most expensive option – perhaps you could split the cost with a friend, or ask your local club to buy one for everyone to share.

EMBOSSING THE RIVETS

All rivet presses operate in basically the same manner. A pointy 'hammer' presses a round rivet shape into the metal. If there isn't a corresponding 'anvil' to support the work you will need to do it onto a hard, yet yielding surface, like a piece of sheet lead or cutting mat, to prevent distortion. (Don't forget to wash your hands.)

If you don't have access to a press, rivets can be made simply by using a scriber, or even a sharpened nail, and a light tap with a small hammer. Even old-fashioned record player styluses were once pressed into use for the purpose.

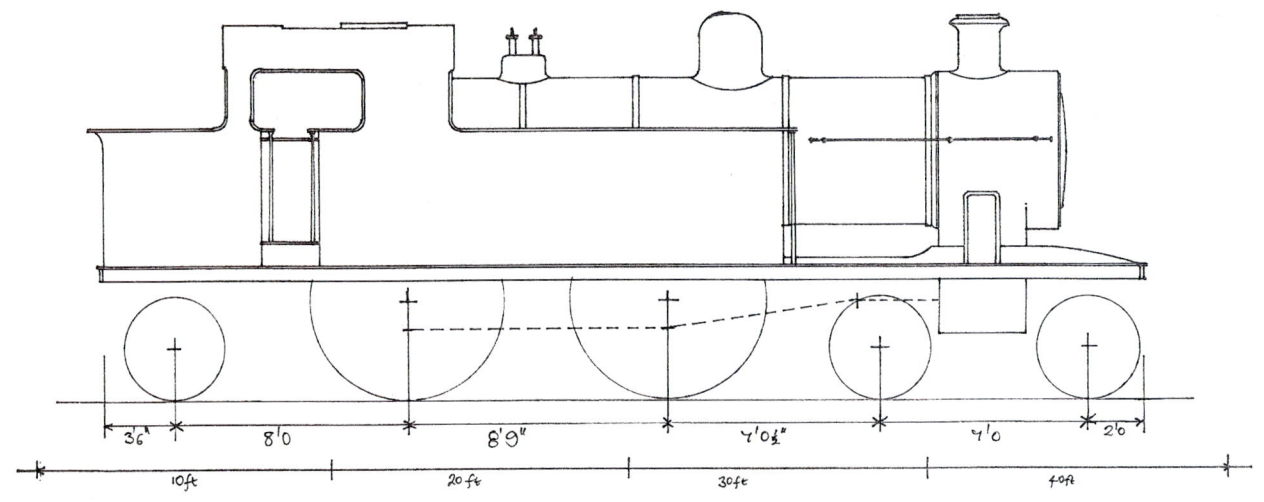

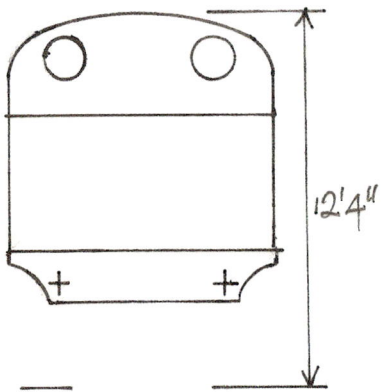

ABOVE: *Class 79 scale drawing. See Class 51 drawing for chassis frames.*

The GW Models rivet press.

A frame marked up for two rows of rivets, ready to be pressed.

BOTTOM LEFT: *A pleasingly riveted frame.*

POSITIONING RIVETS

Rivet positions are rarely marked on drawings so you'll need to study photographs to see where they should appear. If you can't see them, do you really need to put them on?

I generally mark out the rivet positions, even with the GW machine. When you get really good you can take a bit of a risk and do it all by eye.

Do remember that you are embossing from the back of the work through to the front. I've spent many hours pressing beautiful rivets into rear surfaces where they can never be seen. Or worse, they appear as rows of holes or anti-rivets, never a good look.

If you get them in the wrong place they are fiendishly difficult to get rid of. I try to poke them back in with a scriber and then file them flat, which can work. Sometimes. Also, you almost always need to make them before you assemble things so they can add lots more time to the building process.

Some people enjoy counting the rivets and putting them all on. I aim for an impression. Each to his own.

FORMING THE CHASSIS

When you have finished having fun with the riveter, you'll need to solder the frames together to form the chassis. This will be slightly different if you are using horn blocks and compensation beams. First you'll need to solder in the axle bushes for the fixed axle just as we did for the Class 51.

USING A CHASSIS JIG

There are a number of jigs available on the market, ranging from simple turned rods with pointy ends that accommodate the coupling rods to more complex systems. Find out if anyone at your local club uses any jigs and ask them to show you theirs, then you can plump for one that suits your requirements and wallet.

I'm describing the Hobby Holidays Master Chassis Jig because it's the one I use. I love it. It is reasonably priced, if you are going to use it a lot, and they come in 7mm and 4mm scales and more. Mine is a 7mm one that I have modified for 4mm with the aid of nested tubes (another fantastic use for the nested tube). This fine piece of equipment has moving wooden blocks that can travel along threaded rods, allowing you to set your axle distances to infinite finesse and keep them firmly in place.

Horn blocks with 'shoulders' are easier to locate as you have some leeway in soldering them to the inside face of the frames. Those from Alan Gibson fit inside the rectangular cut-outs you have carefully sawn. You just have to be a little more accurate in sawing out the frames. Follow the instructions.

The chassis is held in place on the jig, with one pointed rod passing through the bearings of the fixed axle and the other through the bearings in the horn blocks. The exact spacing is fixed using the coupling rods placed on the ends of the pointed rods, which can be cranked backwards and forwards until everything is just right. The horn blocks can then be

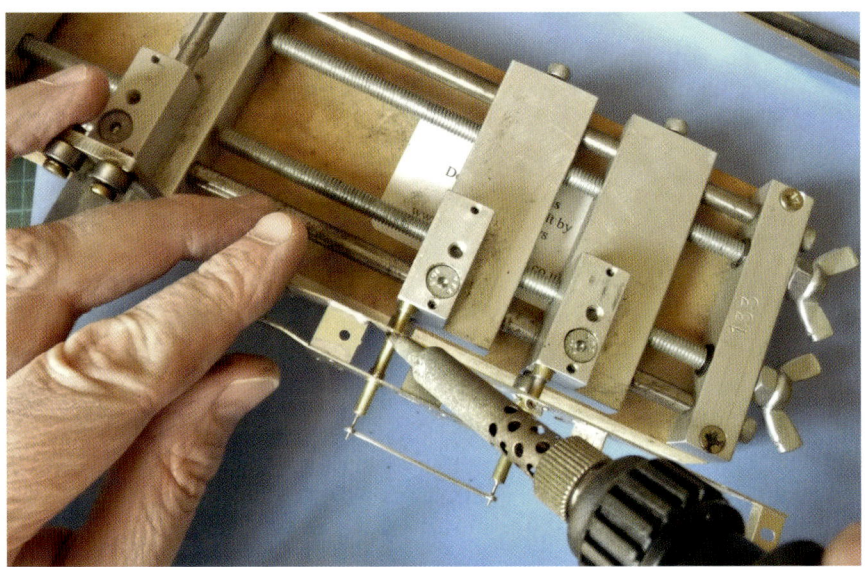

The master jig at work, soldering axle bushes in place.

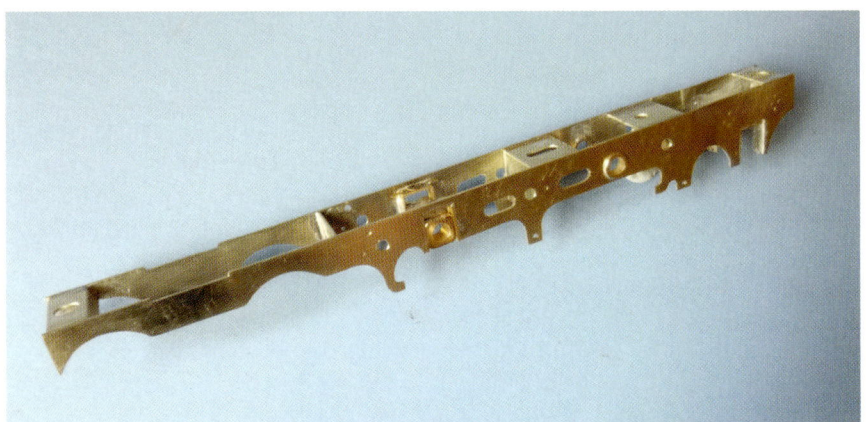

Horn blocks and spacers in place.

BUILDING THE CLASS 79 CHASSIS

soldered into the frames and then the spacers can be fitted. Remember that you'll need slightly narrower spacers for the joggled ends of the frames.

Great stuff. Take care as you try to get the assembled chassis off as it can be a little stiff. Slide it gently.

The Hobby Holidays jig is possibly a little more difficult to get to grips with than the Comet jig. Seek out their stall at exhibitions for a good look at the thing. They do other fantastic stuff too.

The horn block bearings are generally prevented from falling out using small staples of 0.5mm wire.

PLUNGER PICKUPS

Plunger pickups offer a different way of transferring track current to where it drives the motor. Some people love them, some people don't. They can be difficult to maintain and if too stiff in the spring department exert rather a lot of braking force on the loco. Though exquisitely fiddly, they are reasonably easy to instal.

These dinky little Alan Gibson pickups simply locate through holes drilled in the chassis frames that coincide with the back of the driving wheel tyres. If you haven't already drilled the holes, draw round the edge of the wheel, onto the frames, to help locate the correct drilling site.

The plungers are small brass turnings housed in plastic sleeves that insulate them electrically from the frames. They bear onto the rear of the wheel tyres with the aid of tiny pingy springs, which is why they are so fiddly. (Alan Gibson may be happy to sell you some spares.) The instructions suggest bending the rear of the plungers to keep them from exiting the plastic sleeves. I broke them when I tried to do this, so soldered some fine flexible wire to them, in the position that I would have bent them, instead. Then I Araldited them in place in the frames. If you make the holes a tight fit you won't even have to do that. The pressure of the wheels should keep them where they should be. Araldite if you want to be sure. Do check first that they are in the right place by sliding a wheel and axle into each position.

I connected the wires from each plunger to a short strip of printed circuit board (PCB) soldered to either side of the inside of the frames. A single connecting wire can then be run from each bus bar to the motor terminals.

Other forms of pickups are available. Lots, in fact.

FITTING ALAN GIBSON DRIVING WHEELS

Alan Gibson wheels can be as simple to fit as Romford wheels. They have a more scale appearance and

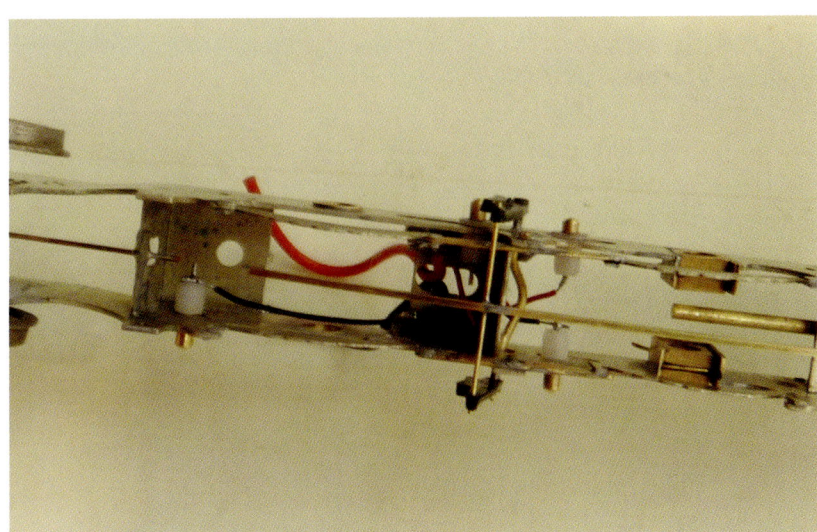

The horn blocks in place, bearings supported by wire staples. The plunger pickups can also be seen.

BUILDING THE CLASS 79 CHASSIS

The GW wheel press in action. I've got a back-to-back gauge in there too, just to check.

are possibly a little less robust. It is not recommended that you keep taking them on and off their axles as rough handling may pull the rims off. If you do so, click them back on and fix them with a tiny drop of Loctite. You also have to quarter them by hand as they don't have square-ended axles as Romfords do.

We can get away with fitting the wheels a couple of times. So we'll do a first fit to check for free running. They can be pressed on and quartered at the same time by using a dinky little jig from Mr GW (he of the rivet press) that is great for fitting Gibson wheels. He also does something that will pull the wheels off – he's a remarkably versatile man and very friendly on the phone.

Anyway, fit the crankpins to the wheels first, as per Alan Gibson's instructions, and then follow the instructions for the wheel press. Basically, the wheels are half pushed into the axle ends (with the frames between) and then everything is located in the jig. Gentle pressure is applied and 'Boom'. Pressed and quartered. Magic.

All this can of course be done by eye, peering through the spokes from one side to the other. Line the spokes up, with the right-hand wheel a quarter further round than the left-hand one. You can get remarkably good at it.

Now, fix the coupling rods on and away we go. The first test run of the chassis. Gentle finger pressure should do it, or tilt the track slightly and she should roll along under her own weight. Check and fettle until things are good.

Switch off the soldering iron, step away from the workbench and rejoin the real world. There are further things to fit but all in good time.

RADIAL TRUCK

This is an exciting little piece of engineering. The wheel bearings are held in a curved slide moving through correspondingly curved guides. They are elegant and agreeably easy to make, especially if you buy an etch from London Road Models. Follow their instructions to make life even easier.

The wheels are a doddle to fit. Check them with a gauge and adjust the spring for good running. Ta Da. Radial truck.

BUILDING THE CLASS 79 CHASSIS

Radial truck etch.

BELOW LEFT: **The guides and slide are folded up and soldered.**

ABOVE RIGHT: **The guides are soldered to the inside of the frame cut-outs.**

The slide is held into the guides with short lengths of 0.5mm wire and a length of phosphor-bronze wire locates in the top of the guide and acts as a spring.

124 BUILDING THE CLASS 79 CHASSIS

SCRATCH-BUILT BOGIE

This is another pleasantly simple challenge in scratch-building; it's very rewarding to make, too. Take a look at the simple shape that you can see between *Thundersley*'s wheels. At this stage we will concentrate on the bar; the rest, such as the spring, can be attached cosmetically later on.

To make the equalizing bar and to give a bit of strength to the bogie's sides, I built them up from various pieces.

ABOVE LEFT:
**Thundersley's *front bogie.*

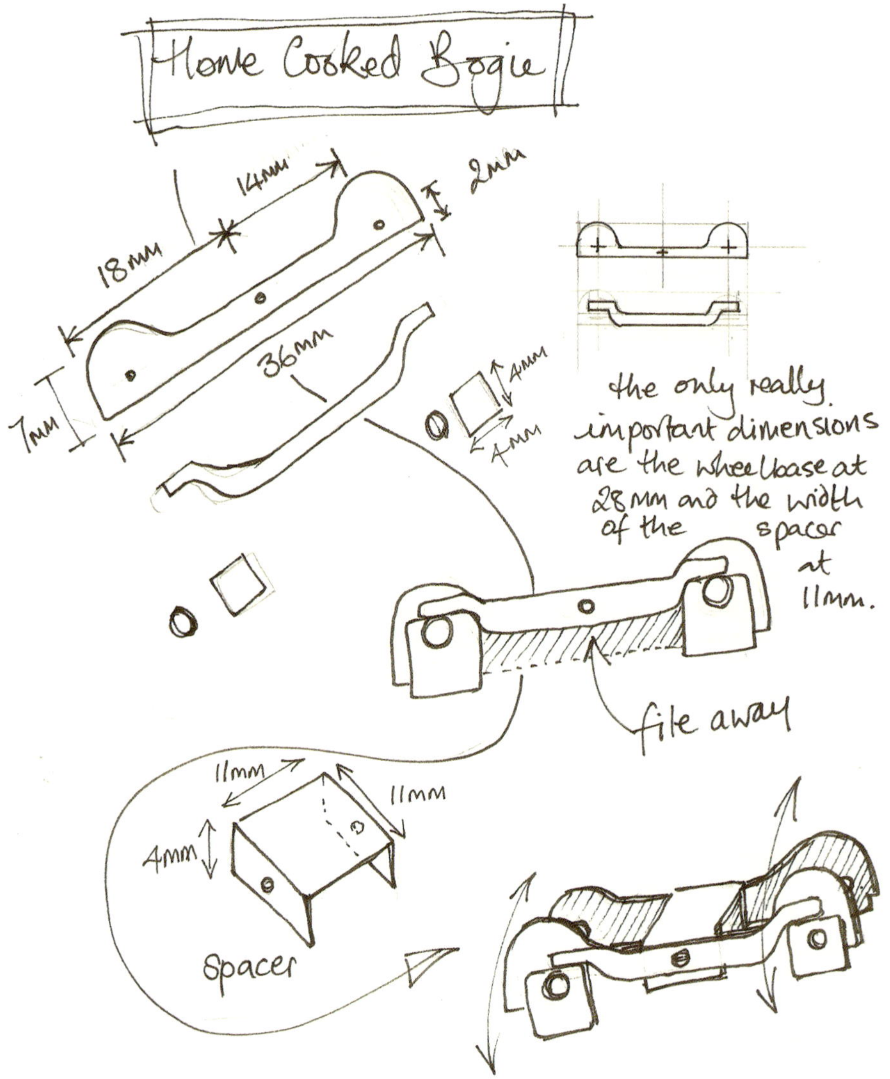

The components of the scratch-built bogie and how to build it.

BUILDING THE CLASS 79 CHASSIS

This is a pleasing construction exercise:

- Draw the bogie sides onto two pieces of 0.010in nickel silver tacked together.
- Drill and open out the holes. Separate the pieces.
- Solder all of the components together as in the sketch.
- File the main body of the bogie back to the outline of the equalizing beams and bearings (not essential, though it looks nice).
- Cut thin collars of 2mm inside diameter tubing as bearings and solder them in place.
- Cut out, drill and fold up the bogie stretcher. Use a triangular file to make the folds crisp and run a

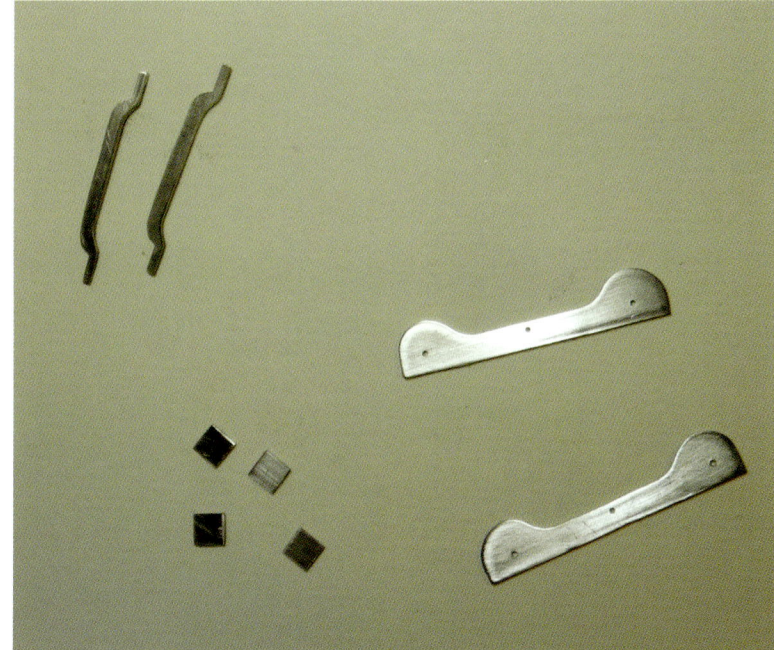

Drill and open out the holes. Separate the pieces.

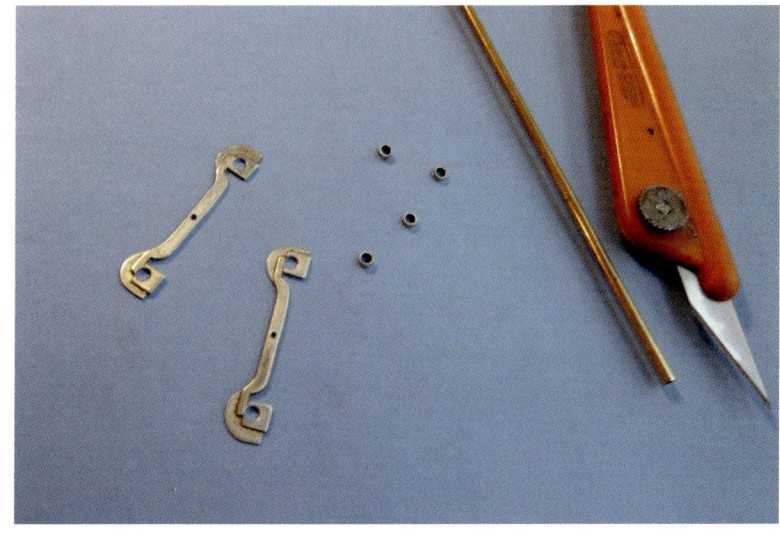

File the main body of the bogie back to the outline of the equalizing beams and bearings (not essential, though it looks nice).

126 BUILDING THE CLASS 79 CHASSIS

ABOVE LEFT: *Cut out, drill and fold up the bogie stretcher.*

ABOVE RIGHT: *Solder a 14BA bolt to the inside of the stretcher (using cigarette paper to stop the solder going anywhere else).*

The finished item.

filet of solder into the folds to strengthen them. You'll end up with a nice little open box.
- Solder one side of the box solidly to the stretcher. Pin the other side of the box to the stretcher using a 14BA bolt that has had its thread filed off in the mini-drill.
- Solder a 14BA bolt to the inside of the stretcher (using cigarette paper to stop the solder going anywhere else). The bolt acts as a pivot and gives the bogie some equalization, to simulate the real thing.

COMPENSATING THE CHASSIS

It could be argued that, as the radial truck is sprung and the pony truck has some simple rocking movement, it is unnecessary to add any more flexibility to the chassis. And indeed you may decide that you don't want to. However, I have assumed here that you do have an interest in adding compensation, and if you want to know the full Monty I can recommend Mike Sharmann's little classic on the subject, *Flexichas: A Way to Build Fully Compensated Model Locomotive Chassis*.

The form of compensation common to modelling in the smaller scales gives the chassis a 'three-legged stool' character. This means that however many lumps and bumps are present in your trackwork, three wheels of your chassis will always be in contact with the rails. The most compelling argument against the need for compensation is that your trackwork shouldn't have lumps and bumps!

A simple beam pivot can be made for a length of 1mm inside diameter tubing, cut to fit snugly between the frames.

- Solder a length of 1.2mm rod centrally and perpendicular to the tubing. Use a grid to help. The rod, or 'beam', must be long enough to bear down on the front driving axle at one end and the central pivot of the bogie at the other.
- Solder a 'pad' of nickel silver to the underneath of the bogie end of the beam, parallel to the pivot tube. This will bear on the bogie pivot bolt.
- Pass a piece of 1mm rod through the holes in the frames, trapping the pivot tube between the frames with scraps of cigarette paper between the ends of the tube and the inside of the frames.
- Use a quick blob of solder to secure the rod to the outside surface of the frames and remove the paper. The tube must remain unsoldered and free to pivot.

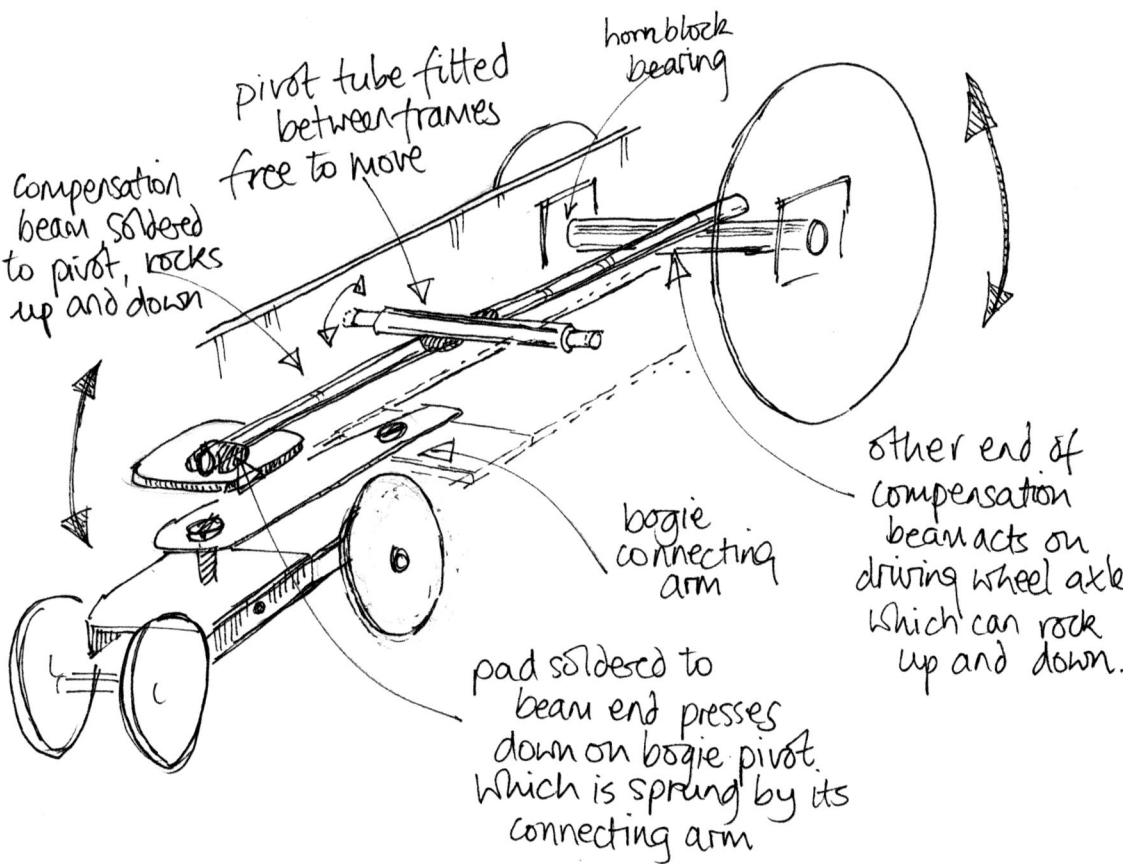

The basics of the beam compensation system for the Tilbury Tank.

You now have a nice little see-saw with a pad at one end. The other end is pushed up by the front driving wheel axle, which is also able to pivot at right angles to the beam. When this happens, the pad pushes down on the bogie, and vice versa. Any track undulations are dealt with effortlessly. Some people put matchsticks on their trackwork to test this. (People who are happy not to use compensation tend not to bother with the matchsticks.)

All that remains is to fix the bogie to the chassis. I used a bogie pivot plate etch produced by Comet Models. It has an ingenious U-shaped slot at the front that pushes the bogie slightly forward as it passes into a bend. I added a (not strictly necessary) phosphor-bronze spring to further control this movement. The long slot on the tail of the plate allows you to set the wheelbase of the bogie precisely.

The bogie bolts on to the plate and the plate bolts on to a frame spacer. The compensation beam presses down on the bogie bolt. And that's it.

It's all rather fiddly but a great deal of fun.

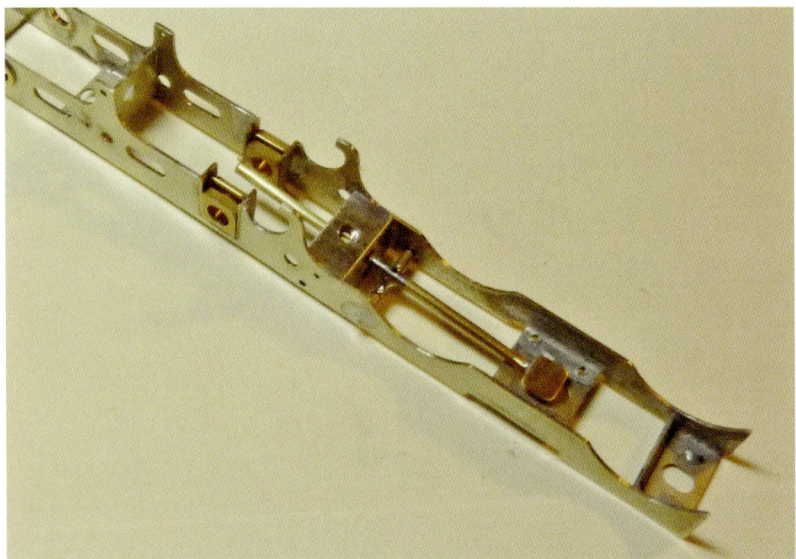

The compensation mechanism in place.

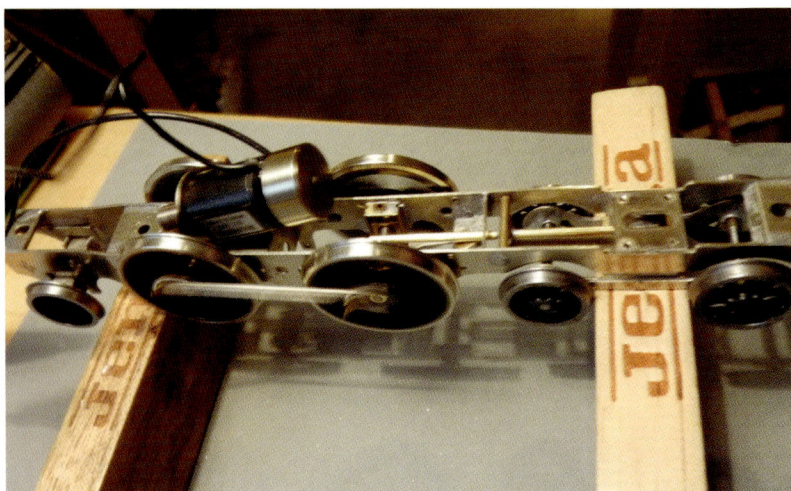

The compensated chassis in motion.

BUILDING THE CLASS 79 CHASSIS

SOLID CYLINDERS

For the rest of the locomotory motion we are going to knock up some perfectly cylindrical cylinders. It's a job that could be done in short shrift if you have a lathe, not if you haven't. So nesting tubes it is.

The aim here is to solder together a set of nesting tubes to form a pair of cylinders of the correct outside diameter with an exactly central guide tube for the piston rod. You'll need a lot of tubes – ranging from 1mm to 8mm diameter – but in my opinion you can never have enough of them. Just make sure you don't get your metric and imperial tubing mixed up. Make both cylinders at the same time by using just over twice the length necessary, 24mm.

- Start by cutting the 8mm outside diameter tube to size and solder the next tube inside it. Then saw that one to size and so on down to the smallest diameter tube. Things to be careful of:

- When cutting the tubing, keep the ends straight and at 90 degrees; check frequently with the square and use masking tape to make the cuts parallel.
- Use the previous cut tube to guide the saw for the next. You might want to try a razor saw to save time; take care to keep the cuts straight.

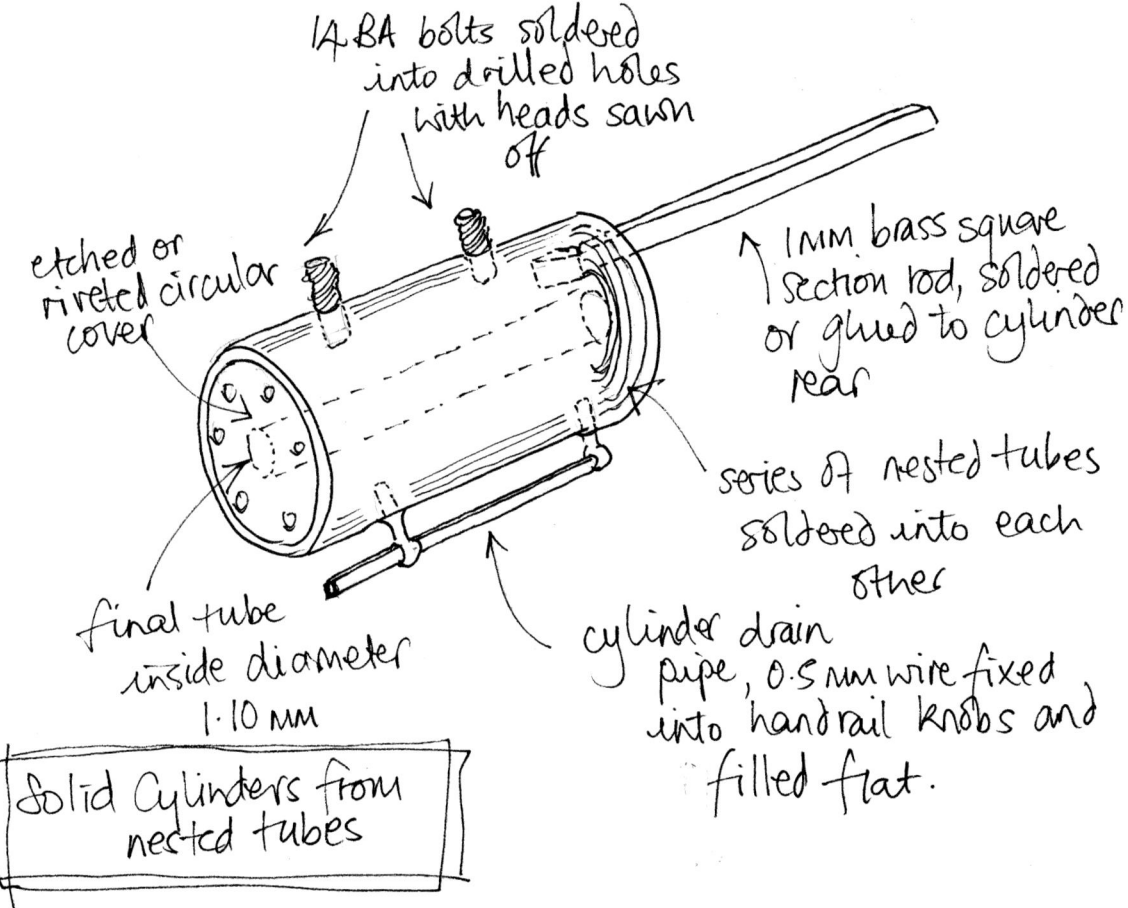

Solid cylinder construction.

- Keep things clean; abrade the outer surface of the tubing with wet and dry and inside with a rolled piece or sanding stick, or indeed a wire brush in the drill if the diameter doesn't stop you getting it in. Smooth the ends carefully after each tube is soldered.
- Take care to keep excess solder to the minimum on the inside of the tubes as you'll have to keep cleaning it out.
- Hold the tubing with a peg – it gets *very* hot and you'll need more heat as the amount of brass increases. Take great care every time you go to pick it up with your fingers. Think piranhas, hot piranhas.
- Watch out for the flux spitting out of the ends. Think vipers.
- Keep the last tube as a handle for when you divide your finished cylinder – it gives you something to hold on to.

What you end up with is a brass tube a bit like a Swiss roll with the outside and inside diameters you are after. All this rigmarole is good practice for soldering, sawing and keeping things straight and true. Then cut the tube in half across the middle with a razor saw to produce the cylinders.

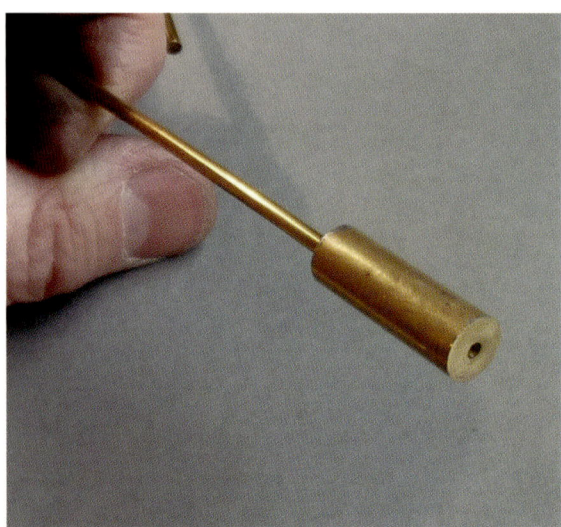

Soldered nesting tubes.

- Use the piercing saw to start the final cut around the outer tube and then continue with the razor saw to increase speed and accuracy. Keep turning the metal and checking your cut is true. I held it up against the stop on my saw block and clamped it when my fingers got tired. Take it gently and you'll be rewarded with two very cute little pieces of solid engineering.
- Clean up, file if necessary so that both cylinders are the correct length and solder at the cut ends to ensure they don't just fall apart. Again, be careful that you allow the metal to cool before you pick them up; they can take a long time to cool down. I know this because I have a cylinder-shaped burn embroidered on the pads of my fingers. A useful check is to spit on the cylinder and see whether it swiftly evaporates.
- Decorate the ends with etched pieces or washers. Again, watch out for the brass blocks acting as heat reservoirs.
- Finally, check that each piston rod slides freely in the cylinders. Give the internal tube a light whizz with a broach and polish the rod with wet and dry until you have a perfect fit.

FITTING THE CYLINDERS TO THE FRAMES

Now it's time to fit the cylinders to the frames. I decided to bolt the cylinders to a stretcher and then bolt that across the frames.

- Check the photos to help you.
- Cut a 30 × 12mm rectangle of 0.020in nickel silver as a stretcher. It should fit nicely into the slot in the top front of the frames. A small amount of filling might help.
- The cylinders are located by soldering two 8mm long pieces of 2 × 2mm L-angle onto the stretcher. The outer sides of the cylinders should be parallel to the ends of the stretcher. Use a square to help line everything up.
- There are now two options:
  - Option 1: use a flat needle file to file a 1mm wide groove, 1mm deep, along the top surface of each cylinder, parallel to the long axis. Then

BUILDING THE CLASS 79 CHASSIS

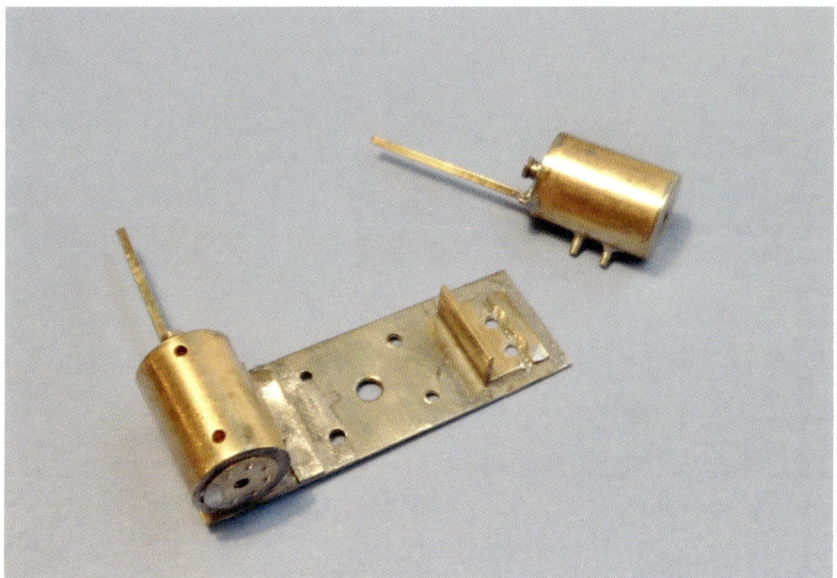

Locating the cylinders.

solder or glue in a 30mm length of 1mm square rod to act as the slide bar. Finally solder or araldite the cylinders to the stretchers, locating them against the L-angle pieces.
- Option 2: put a 90-degree bend in a 21mm piece of 1mm square rod 3mm along, to give an 18mm slide bar, and solder the short length to the front of the cylinder so that the slide bar projects from the top, continuing parallel to the long axis of the cylinder. I did this so that I could drill and solder in some beheaded 14BA bolts, which then bolt the cylinders to the stretcher.
- Once the cylinders are secure you can test locate the stretcher again on the frames.
- Fit the driving wheels, coupling rods, connecting rods and crossheads. The piston rod should locate into the pistons so that it is at the same height as the wheel centres and everything is parallel and horizontal. Adjustment by filing the chassis slot

The cylinders in situ.

to lower the stretcher or raise it by packing with thin pieces of scrap brass.
- Roll the chassis back and forth to check everything runs smoothly.

When you're happy with the fit, solder, glue or bolt the cylinder ensemble in place.

MOTORIZING THE CHASSIS

With the cylinders in motion, the chassis can now be motorized.

HIGH LEVEL GEARBOXES

Having used a pre-built gearbox for the Class 51, I thought I would describe one of the deluxe offerings that you have to construct yourself for the Class 79. High Level (who have a website full of advice and are always helpful at shows) do some great etched gearboxes and motor mounts. They even do one that will fold itself away into the frames so that it doesn't protrude into the cab, which means you can then detail the inside if you so wish.

The gearboxes are by no means simple and you need to follow their assembly instructions carefully. One of the more alarming procedures is having to force fit the worm gear to the motor shaft:

- Open out the hole in the worm gear microscopically with a tiny twirl of a broach to fit the driveshaft.
- Clamp the worm gear/motor assembly in a vice, taking care to protect the end of the worm gear with a block of wood and making sure that the shaft of the motor is perpendicular in the vice jaws so that no bending force is put on it. (If you hold the motor in the vice at either end of the shaft then the only pressure exerted will be along the shaft itself and not on the sensitive – and expensive – innards of the motor.)
- Gently force the worm onto the shaft. Be wary of bending the shaft; if you tighten a little each time and give the motor a quick spin with your fingers you will feel if the shaft is beginning to deform, so back off if it does.

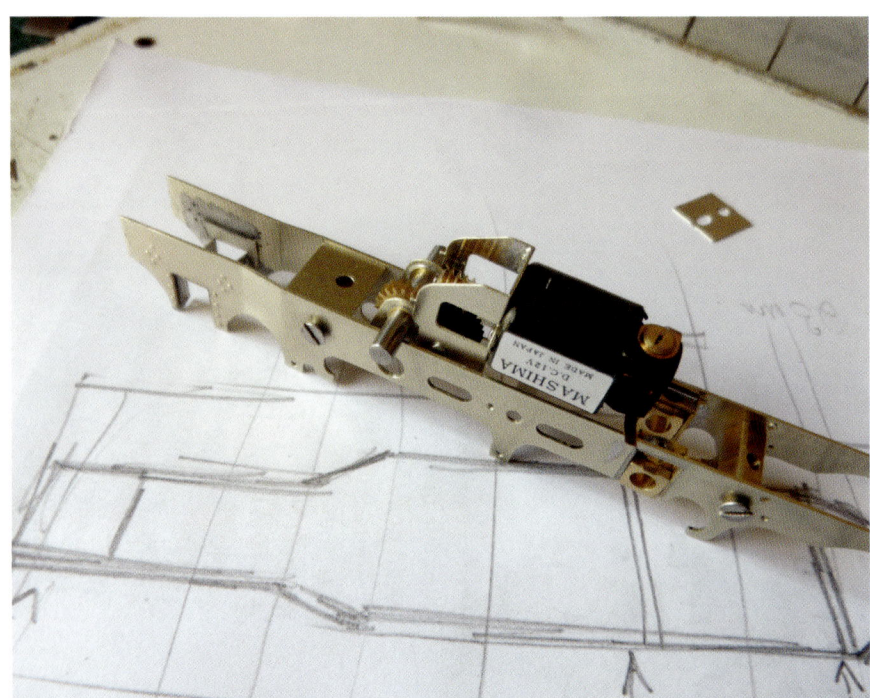

High Level gearbox and motor.

BUILDING THE CLASS 79 CHASSIS

Fitting the worm gear onto the motor shaft in the vice.

- Check for when the motor shaft is getting close to peeking through the other end of the worm so that you can accommodate it on its continuing journey with a hole drilled in the wood block.
- Use Vernier calipers to monitor the gentle movement of the worm along the shaft.

Once that is done and you have soldered up the gearbox, carefully following High Level's instructions and using all of your scratch-building skills, it's time to fit everything to the chassis.

ASSEMBLY

- Remove the fixed driving wheels, slip on the gearwheel, press the wheels back on and, hey presto, the loco is with motor.
- If you want to prevent any sideways movement of the wheels or the motor on the axle add some washers. These slip between the frames and the bearings and you have to put them onto the axle at the same time as all the other bits and pieces. Use tweezers. Thin axle bearings are a good alternative to washers as they have a shoulder that can be gripped more firmly with the tweezers.
- Wire up either temporarily or solder contact wires to the motor terminals.
- Have a go at fiddling and fettling until you are happy with the running – test run as suggested for the Class 51 chassis. Refinements to the compensation and springing can be left until the bodywork is in place as its added weight will affect the adjustments you make.

CHAPTER FIFTEEN

CLASS 79 BODYWORK

Having built the chassis, we can now build the body to fit. Here we depart from *Thundersley*'s classic lines as I wanted a more modern version, somewhat tarted up by the LMS. While the details are different, the fundamental shapes remain the same, so a mixture of sources is appropriate. Just keep an eye on which photos show the bits and pieces you want. If there's anything you don't like you might want to change it. For instance, I'm not keen on the rather angular domes that the LMS plonked on some locos, so when we get to the details I'm going for a more rounded shape. Apparently the domes were sometimes beaten into shape by hand so they were probably all slightly different. That's my excuse, anyway.

The different construction methods described are:

- Boiler rolled from sheet metal
- Extended smokebox
- Wrap-around all-over cab

The footplate and bodywork are pretty much the same as for the Class 51, although the sides and bunker are built up separately to accommodate the one-piece cab. They are simply rectangles of nickel silver soldered in place with a little bit of shaping at the

Three-quarter view of Class 79 locomotive 41940. THE TRANSPORT TREASURY

bunker rear. I'll describe this briefly in the section on building the cab roof.

First, though, let's roll a boiler.

ROLLING THE BOILER

When building 7mm O-gauge locos, I generally roll the boiler from flat brass sheet as it's difficult, if not impossible, to find tubing of the larger diameters needed. Thick-walled tubing also acts as a fabulously efficient heat sink for which more ferocious heat sources than a soldering iron may be required. Smaller scales such as the 4mm we are working in are better catered for by thin-walled tubing that is much easier to get hold of but can be quite expensive.

In the spirit of adventurous scratch-building, early masters of loco building like Guy Williams used to roll his boilers on his thigh. I've tried it and it hurts. As with many modern things, the thighs of old were obviously built of sterner stuff. You can try, but I reckon a set of rolling bars are the bee's knees.

The main disadvantage of rolling bars is the price. I have my own now, though I once took a set of flat etches from a kit to an exhibition and persuaded one of the demonstrators to roll them there and then. Or try your club.

Rolling bars are basically a set of solid bars geared together, with the ability to move them closer or further apart; rather like an old laundry mangle, though smaller. You insert a carefully cut and measured rectangle of brass sheet, turn a handle and out comes a tube. Magic.

As with every new tool, the process takes a little getting used to. You do have to load the metal carefully, keeping the leading edge parallel with the bars, otherwise you tend to get a rather art-deco spiral (which can be straightened out with a bit of brute force). The pressure of the bars running against each other also has to be set to determine the diameter of the tube produced. This really comes from trial and error and a bit of practice. So, if you get the chance, practise winding bits of scrap metal before you commit to the real thing. Just watch your fingers.

THE MATHS

How, you cry, do I calculate the dimensions of the rectangle of metal to be used? Well, you could try using card templates. Or you could employ some simple maths.

The dimensions of a boiler can be worked out using the formula for finding the circumference of a circle:

C (circumference) = π (3.14) × D (diameter)

The width of the rectangle of brass you want can therefore be worked out by multiplying the diameter

My GW Models rolling bars precariously perched in the vice in best Heath Robinson fashion.

of the boiler by 3.14. In this case the boiler diameter is 4ft 9in, which equates to 19mm in 4mm scale. Multiply by 3.14 and you get 59.66mm.

There is a catch: you have to remember that the metal has a thickness. So measure it (I'm using 0.25mm brass sheet) and double it because it's at the top and bottom of the tube – that makes 0.5mm. Take it off your circumference, which makes it 59.16mm. That can be rounded up safely to 60mm to give you your width.

The length of the rectangle is 82mm and so the piece of metal that you'll need to run through the rollers will be 82 x 60mm.

USING THE ROLLERS

Now to roll. Having played with your rollers a bit, you should have a feel for how they work. My set of bars has three rollers, is easy to use and comes apart to allow you to free the resultant tube from its metallic clutches.

- Adjust the bars using your fingers (instead of Allen keys) so that you can feel the bars resting gently together.
- Offer the long edge of the rectangle up to the bars and make sure it is parallel.
- Gently start to roll; you will feel the bars catch the edge of the metal.
- Run the brass gently back and forth through the bars a couple of times. This can be remarkably soothing.
- Increase the pressure gently and equally at both ends so that the bars are pressing more tightly together. While running the metal through, note the amount of curve produced. Don't be tempted to rush things by overtightening as you will only get a curve that is too tight and then you will have to straighten it out. If you are getting a slightly wider gap at one end, tighten that end of the roller slightly more than the other until the gap is equal.
- With three rollers you can get a slight flat along the straight edges so roll very carefully until you can feel the 'click' of the edge of the tube hitting the roller. (It can be eased back into the roller if it becomes disengaged.) This should give you a nice smooth curve throughout the tube.
- Repeat until you get a nice smooth tube. You'll know the tube is ready when the long edges touch. You don't need to do any more as things will distort if the edges overlap.
- Loosen the rolling bar's bolts at both ends and unscrew the bolt at one end. Watch you don't lose any springs or fixings.
- Release the tube.

Run the brass gently back and forth through the bars a couple of times. This can be surprisingly soothing.

Repeat until you get a nice smooth tube.

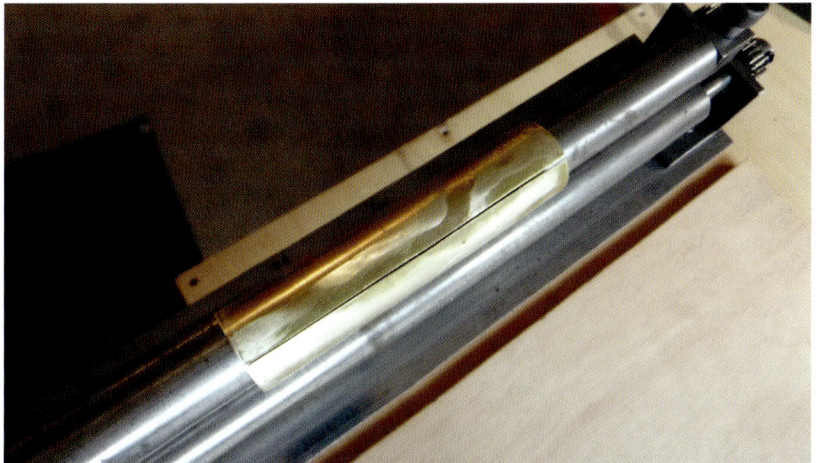

Loosen the rolling bar's bolts at both ends and unscrew the bolt at one end. Watch you don't lose any springs or fixings.

Release the tube.

The tube may spring apart slightly when you remove it from the rollers but that is easily remedied when you solder everything together.

- The tube may spring apart slightly when you remove it from the rollers but that is easily remedied when you solder everything together.

You are now the proud owner of a beautifully hand-rolled tube, but don't solder it until you have formed the rest of the boiler.

FORMING THE BOILER

A good way to start is to rustle up some discs from 0.015/0.020in waste nickel silver as formers that can be soldered inside your boiler. I loathe cutting circles and unless you can find some preformed ones – etched or, if you are very lucky, some coin of the realm that is an exact fit – you'll just have to fret some out yourself with the piercing saw. The discs have to fit *inside* the boiler so their diameter should be 0.5mm smaller than the outside boiler diameter.

I use an Olfa ratchet circular cutter bought from my local stationers to mark circles. Make a couple at a time or three if you want to really reinforce your tube.

- Solder some 0.015/0.020in nickel together, drill a 0.5mm hole in an appropriate place and mark out a circle using the hole as a stable pivot for the cutter. The blade scores a sharply defined circle in the nickel providing an excellent guide for the piercing saw. If you enlarge the hole to take a 10BA nut and bolt, the discs can be held tightly together if the solder doesn't.
- Saw out the discs, then clean them up with files or by holding them in a hand drill and rotating them against various abrasives. This will polish them although it doesn't seem to make them much more circular. Use calipers to check the diameter. Don't worry if they're very slightly off as the tube will average out small inaccuracies.
- Check that the discs fit within the tube; don't worry if you have a millimetre or so gap along the seam. A dodge to deal with a large gap is to solder a length of small diameter tubing into the gap. As long as the boiler is the correct diameter, all is good.
- If you haven't done so already, enlarge the holes in the discs to take a 10BA nut and bolt.
- Solder a 10BA bolt into the hole in the disc that will act as the rear former – this will enable the disc to be held easily while assembling the boiler and will also enable the boiler, once assembled, to be positioned accurately onto the cab front.
- Tighten the boiler tube around the rear former with a twist of copper wire. Using the pin vice to position the disc just inside the tube, tighten the copper wire with a pair of pliers. You might need three hands for this – evolution has yet to cotton on to the needs of railway modellers so persevere or bribe someone to help you. The slight rebate should be the same distance all the

Marking circles with an Olfa circular cutter.

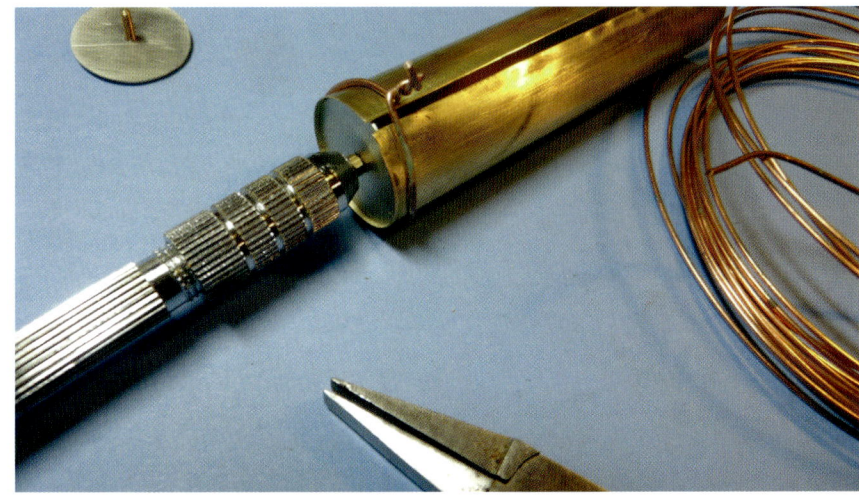

Preparing to solder up the rear former while holding it in place in the pin vice.

way around and allows you to solder securely. Take your time to get it right.
- Tack solder, check that everything is aligned correctly, then seam up.
- Solder a 10BA nut over the centre hole on the inside of the disc that will act as the front former. Screw in a 10BA bolt.
- Now loosen the copper wire slightly and slip it down to the other end. Slip in the front former, holding the disc in place with the bolt in the pin vice. Position the disc carefully, tighten the wire (not too tight) and solder in the same way.
- Slip off the copper wire and solder along the seam of the tube. If you've been particularly successful with your maths and measuring, this will be gap-free. If you are a bit more like me and have an accusatory gap grinning at you, don't worry, you really won't be able to see it later on. The tube may bulge slightly in the middle where it's unsupported and can be squeezed gently into submission with your fingers.

So now you have a boiler that is cheaper than a piece of tubing, more time-consuming to make but very rewarding.

SMOKEBOX

The smokebox is a slightly larger cylinder than the boiler and nestles familiarly around the front end of the boiler. If you are opting for ready-made nesting tubes, all you need do is cut a suitable piece of the next tube up in size. If you are rolling, it's another chance to practise this time-honoured scratch-building technique.

- Wrap a card template around the boiler to give you the correct length then cut a 17mm wide rectangle of 0.020in brass to the same length. Make sure the sides of your rectangle are parallel otherwise your smokebox will be out of kilter.

Looking at *Thundersley*, you'll see a very decorative brass ring encircling the joint between the boiler and smokebox – boy those Victorian engineers loved a bit of decorative brass. This can be simulated nicely:

- File a quarter circle along one edge of the smokebox wrapper piece before you roll it.

Thundersley's decorative brass smokebox trim.

BELOW LEFT: **Look along the rounded edge of the smokebox for a good shape before rolling.**

BELOW RIGHT: **Gently roll the rectangle of brass, following the same procedure as you did for the boiler – you should be beginning to get good at it by now.**

It's probably easier to rub the metal along a smooth file resting on the workbench. Take your time.
- Look along the rounded edge of the smokebox for a good shape before rolling.
- Gently roll the rectangle of brass, following the same procedure as you did for the boiler – you should be beginning to get good at it by now. The resulting cute little cylinder should fit snugly around the boiler – don't forget to have the decorative brass ring facing the rear. Give the cylinder a few tweaks if need be. If, like me, you've made it slightly too small, the edges might not meet, which is fine. Once you are happy with the fit and are pleased with the look of the thing, it's time to solder.
- Tin the inside of the front and rear of the smokebox with a very thin layer of solder. Leave a 0.5mm rebate to overlap at the front for a good cosy fit of the smokebox front. Get a really close fit with a good strong twist or two of copper wire. Solder around the inside of the rebate at the front and sweat solder at the back, using lots of flux and the minimum of solder.
- Now cut a brass disc to fit inside the front of the smokebox. The waste from cutting the disc should fit the outside of the smokebox to provide the support, which is known as the saddle. Some careful marking out of the disc will enable you to cut out two saddles – a dodge that demonstrates that the saw blade does have a small and significant width.
- Solder in the smokebox front and clean it up. A nice casting of the smokebox door will later adorn the face of the loco.

The smokebox cylinder soldered to the boiler showing the 0.5mm rebate for the smokebox front. I don't think it's particularly good engineering practice to have the gaps in the seams lined up, they really ought to overlap for strength. However, the saddle will hide all sorts of ills.

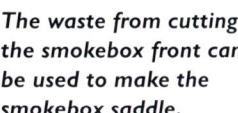

The waste from cutting the smokebox front can be used to make the smokebox saddle.

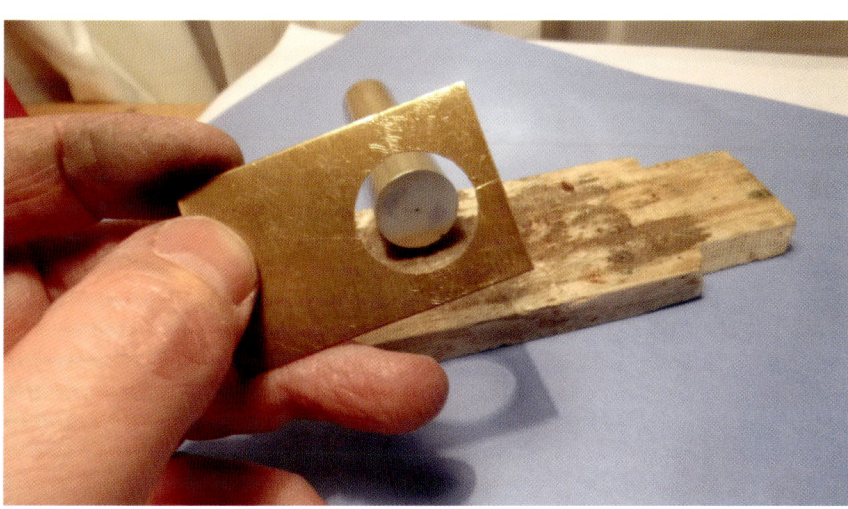

142 CLASS 79 BODYWORK

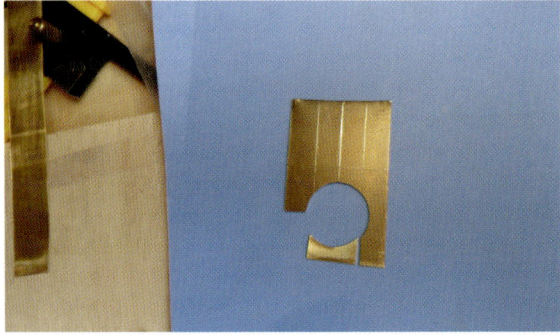

SMOKEBOX SADDLE

This is the rather splendid name for the structure that supports the smokebox at the front of the boiler. Most locos have very similarly shaped saddles; those of the Tilbury Tanks had parallel sides, which makes life easy when constructing them. As there was so much clutter obscuring *Thundersley*'s smokebox saddle, I've included a fine example sported by GWR No. 1450.

ABOVE LEFT: **You'll need to cut two pieces, one from the top and one from the bottom is easiest.**

A Great Western smokebox saddle in all its glory.

CLASS 79 BODYWORK   143

Let's get on:

- File the smokebox saddle ends that you have just made carefully to shape. (If you want them to be truly identical, solder them together before final shaping.) Check them against the smokebox occasionally and use fine wet and dry paper wrapped around the box itself to finish off.
- Solder the saddle ends to a carefully cut rectangle to form the base of the saddle. If you drill a hole in the centre of the base, a 10BA nut can be soldered in to allow you to bolt the saddle to the footplate. Make sure everything is square.
- Solder the saddle onto the smokebox. Try to do it on the inside surfaces in order to avoid having to do too much cleaning up.

It does start to look like a very racy loco at this point and I can never resist the temptation to balance boiler fittings precariously on top. This has a purpose as you get to see how they fit and whether or not they are the right ones. The downside is that every time you pick up the model the fittings fall off and head for the darkest corners of your modelling space.

To finish off, the smokebox needs a wrapper to give it that riveted look and to close up the sides of the saddle.

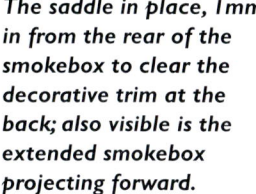

Finishing the saddle off for a close fit.

The saddle in place, 1mm in from the rear of the smokebox to clear the decorative trim at the back; also visible is the extended smokebox projecting forward.

SMOKEBOX WRAPPER

Creating a wrapper and getting it onto the smokebox can provide endless hours of fun. It's quite tricky. Take it gently, keep a close eye on what you are doing and do it a little at a time.

RIVETING AND ROLLING THE WRAPPER

Looking at photos of Class 79 locos in later life, many have smokeboxes that are peppered with rivets. Even *Thundersley*, normally a model of decorum in being without unnecessary adornments, has them. So here we have to make a decision. Do you want all those rivets and, if you do, how are you going to create them?

Araldite Steel is good stuff for adding forgotten ones, but not so good for all of those closely spaced ones in regimented lines. Archer Transfers are much better for that and can be put on last, although you'll have to navigate all the nooks and crannies. Or you could manufacture a pre-riveted smokebox wrapper.

I should warn you that this could be the most challenging bit of the build so far. It is possible to sidestep it completely by soldering a couple of plain rectangles to the saddle sides and cleaning up. Where's the fun in that though? Solder on.

I chose a piece of 0.010in nickel silver as I find thin brass sheet a bit too fond of crumpling and showing unwanted dings and dents. Nickel is a little more springy – sometimes almost unmanageably so.

As the smokebox is extended, it projects forward of the saddle. It's a look I rather like, giving the loco an air of forward purpose – grit, perhaps. What this does mean is that your smokebox wrapper has to be quite an unusual shape in the 2D plan. Most of it wraps around the smokebox and then hugs closely to the sides of the saddle. The front third takes a different route, continuing around the underside of the protruding smokebox.

- Use a piece of card to produce a template for the smokebox wrapper.
- Transfer the dimensions to a strip of 0.010in nickel silver, leaving a little bit of extra length that can be tidied back easily when everything is soldered up.
- Cut the metal to shape, either with a sharp knife or very carefully with a piercing saw. You can saw very thin metal if you support it on a piece of hard wood and keep the saw blade at an acute angle, or use a piece of card to bulk the metal out.
- Mark the positions of the lines of proposed rivets on the back of the metal. Space the lines 1mm apart for those around the edges of the boiler and use wider spacing elsewhere. The closely spaced squares of rivets at the front of the wrapper are 1mm apart.
- Now start riveting. Don't get too frazzled by all those rivets. What we're aiming for is an impression here – and rather impressive it is, too.

Use a piece of card to produce a template for the smokebox wrapper.

CLASS 79 BODYWORK 145

Roll the riveted wrapper, using either rolling bars or your thigh and a rod.

Drill a 2mm hole in the top of the wrapper.

- Create slits at each end of the wrapper to allow the front to continue around the underneath of the smokebox – slice them with a sharp knife or cut them with the piercing saw.
- Roll the riveted wrapper, using either rolling bars – with a piece of card to protect the rivets from being squished – or your thigh and a rod if you want a bit of a change from heavy machinery. Try not to catch and bend the narrow 'legs' you have just created. The wrapper will try to spring back out of shape – it's not essential to achieve a neat cylinder, just roll it enough so that it will wrap around the smokebox held in place by light finger pressure.
- Drill a 2mm hole in the top of the wrapper where it will be hidden by the chimney. Support the wrapper on a broom handle while you are drilling, starting with a small drill and gradually getting larger. The hole will allow you to anchor the top of the wrapper with solder, keeping it strongly centred and in place while you attend to the rest of the job.

FIXING THE WRAPPER

The problem with soldering is that the brass smokebox and boiler will act as a heat sink, making soldering the wrapper difficult. You might therefore want to consider gluing the wrapper to the smokebox.

If you use a five-minute epoxy resin such as Araldite you will have time to position the wrapper carefully before the glue sets. Once set it is strong and it isn't too badly affected by heat so you can solder nearby reasonably safely afterwards. The glue can be incredibly messy in the wrong hands (like mine) but it has the benefit of giving you a short window of time after it has just set to clean it off while it is still semi-hard. Gluing is probably easier than soldering and undeniably less prone to disaster. It's definitely not as quick.

The steps that follow assume that you are set on soldering but the information relating to the positioning of the wrapper is applicable to both soldering and gluing:

- Tin the rear surface of the wrapper very thinly with 145°C solder.
- Hold the wrapper centrally so that the edges are parallel with the front of the smokebox and there is 1mm or so of the brass trim showing at the back.
- Position the wrapper by teasing the 'legs' into position underneath the smokebox; if they are reluctant you might need to file the slots a little.
- Twist some copper wire around the front of the wrapper to hold things in place.
- Add a dab of flux at the front of the top of the smokebox and tack solder (very quickly if you are

Position the wrapper.

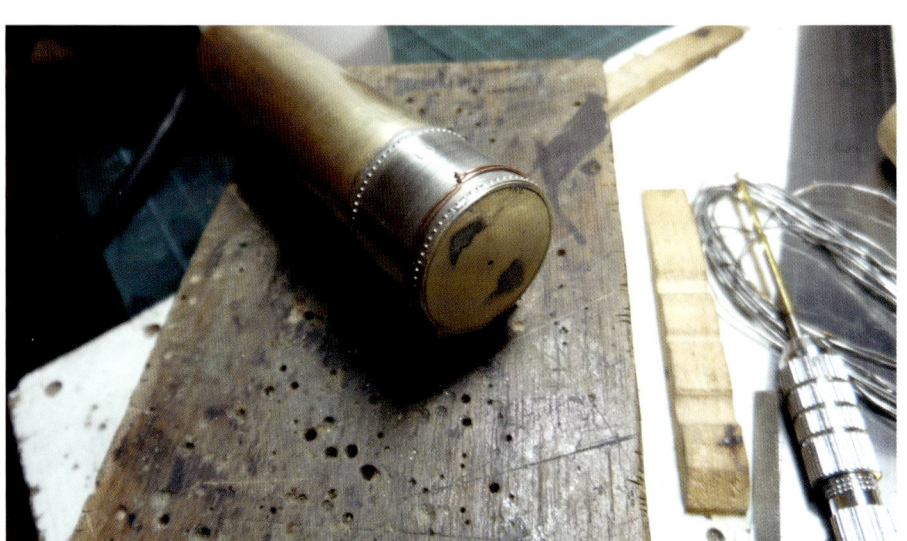

Twist some copper wire around the front of the wrapper to hold things in place.

still holding it with your fingers). Once the front is tightly attached, apply the solder through the hole at the top to secure the wrapper centrally.
- Tease everything else decisively into shape with your fingers and then more firmly with wooden implements such as cocktail sticks or pegs. (Metal implements will mark the wrapper and blunt your rivets.)
- Hold firmly and solder around all of the edges down to the bottom of the saddle.

Fixing the wrapper takes rather a lot of resolute brute force and can sometimes feel like wrestling with a boa constrictor. Once you've managed it, though (and it may take a few goes), it is extremely fulfilling.

It can be very messy in the solder department.

REMOVING SOLDER

Soldering the wrapper can be a messy business. It's almost impossible to avoid coating quite a few rivets in the silver stuff and it's very difficult to dislodge without losing rivets. This is where the dreaded fibreglass burnishing brush becomes my go-to tool, so here are a few provisos:

- Try to get as much solder off as you can first with scrapers and then perhaps with a wire brush in a mini-drill.
- Finish off with wet and dry paper and old files without losing rivet detail.

Hold firmly and solder around all of the edges down to the bottom of the saddle.

The finished article – there's quite a lot of solder to clean off, most of it in difficult-to-see places once the boiler is in its proper position.

- When using the fibreglass brush, wear medical rubber gloves to prevent fibres getting in your fingers, and use eye protection.
- Work over a sheet of kitchen towel to catch the bristly gunk; carefully fold it and dispose of it immediately after you have finished.
- Rub the brush gently and patiently across the soldered surface.
- Never blow on the work; use an old brush if you want to clear any muck off.
- Wash the work thoroughly when you have finished.

The end result of all this labour is a really pleasing riveted, extended smokebox and boiler. Celebrations are in order.

The dreaded burnisher being used to clean a pair of chassis frames.

The finished smokebox and boiler.

CHAPTER SIXTEEN

BUNKER, TANKS AND A WRAP-OVER CAB FOR THE CLASS 79

Here we come to tackle a distinctive feature of the Class 79 Tilbury Tank, the wrap-over cab roof, which appears to be a continuation of the cab sides, tanks and bunker. This presents a number of modelling challenges.

THE WRAP-OVER CHALLENGE

The roof and sides could in theory be made as one piece, which as a bit of a completist I'd rather like to do. (It might be simpler if produced as an etch but would still be difficult to fit accurately.) As an exercise in fret sawing, though, creating a one-piece would be rather absurd: you would have to cut out a very complex shape and then bend it to fit, and if you tried to make the sides wrap around to form the back and front of the cab as well, then you'd have an impossible shape. Even the real thing doesn't go to this extreme, so we won't go there.

Careful study of photos shows that after a brief curve upwards the cab is joined to the sides horizontally with rivets. And by sheer chance I found this cab roof lying around at Bewdley on my last trip to the Severn Valley Railway. Perfect.

The rear end of 41937. THE TRANSPORT TREASURY

150 BUNKER, TANKS AND A WRAP-OVER CAB FOR THE CLASS 79

A wrap-over cab; goodness knows what it's from. It was in the car park at Bewdley.

What we'll go for here is the easiest and most sensible option, similar to that of the Class 51, except cutting each tank and bunker side as separate pieces, joining them with a bunker back and adding the roof as a single folded-up structure. The slightly out of place join on the model between the cab and the sides can be hidden by solder and sanding, while the join between the wrap-over cab roof and the sides on the real thing can be represented cosmetically by a few hefty rivets to add interest. There is also a perfectly placed cab handrail.

We will later need to tackle the problem of the door cut-outs, as they curve inwards towards the roof. This is solved quite simply when adding the beading.

The constructional methods for the main body and footplate are essentially identical to those for the Class 51. The footplate and buffer beams are exactly the same. You can try out your new-found riveting skills on them if you wish before you solder them together.

CAB BACK AND FRONT

In contrast to the Class 51, the cab front and back are soldered in place first, before the sides are soldered to them. This is merely a different order of doing things; I find it facilitates the construction of the wrap-over cab. Other solutions are available.

The cab back and front soldered in place.

BUNKER, TANKS AND A WRAP-OVER CAB FOR THE CLASS 79

The smokebox boiler assembly can then be bolted to the cab front and footplate in exactly the same way as the Class 51.

TANK SIDES AND FRONT

The tank sides and fronts are made in one piece.

- Use a card template to determine the rounded edge of the tank front, then transfer the shape to an overlength strip of 0.020in nickel, the width of which should correspond to the height of the tank sides.
- Take two pieces of 0.020in nickel silver, solder together, mark, saw, drill, file, separate and clean up carefully. Take your dimensions from the drawing and see the following photos to help you.
- After filing, offer the tank front cut-out to the model to check the fit.
- Fold the tank fronts at 90 degrees to the sides using the previously described procedures.
- Check the folded front and sides for a good fit.

After filing, offer the tank front cut-out to the model to check the fit.

Check the folded front and sides for a good fit.

CAB FLOOR

I thought it would be a good time to add the cab floor, such as it is, before any further soldering took place. The method is the same as for the Class 51 except that pieces of 2mm L-shaped brass were used for extra strength. They are soldered between the cab sides for the floor to rest upon. I removed the boiler while all this was going on.

Check that the motor and wheels have sufficient clearance by locating the body temporarily onto the chassis.

BACK TO THE CAB SIDES, FRONTS AND TOPS

- Mark a line along the footplate with the dividers to help locate the tank sides.
- Tack solder the side in place, parallel to the footplate edge and against the cab front.
- Bolt the boiler back in place, check all fits well and add the tank top as for the Class 51. Then repeat with the other tank side and top.

The cab floor soldered to two lengths of L-shaped brass section.

Mark a line along the footplate with the dividers to help locate the tank sides.

BUNKER, TANKS AND A WRAP-OVER CAB FOR THE CLASS 79

Tack solder the side in place, parallel to the footplate edge and against the cab front.

Bolt the boiler back in place, check all fits well and add the tank top as for the Class 51. Then repeat with the other tank side and top.

BOILER CUT-OUT AND REINFORCEMENT

Once the boiler is back in place mark and remove the cut-out needed to clear the motor and anything else that might get in the way. The method is the same as for the Class 51 except the tube may spring open a little – especially if, like me, you didn't manage to get the edges of the rolled tube to meet. Help is at hand:

- Once you've made the cut-out, apply a copper wire tourniquet to restore the tube to its correct diameter.
- Hold or clamp a small diameter brass tube to fit snugly into the gap.
- Tack solder, check and seam.
- Trim the tube back to the cut-out.
- Clean up.

BUNKER SIDES

This is basically the same as for the tank sides.

- Take two pieces of 0.020in nickel silver, solder together, mark, saw, drill, file, separate and clean up carefully, checking that your verticals are indeed vertical.

154 BUNKER, TANKS AND A WRAP-OVER CAB FOR THE CLASS 79

Reinforcing the boiler seam.

Keeping the bunker sides square with a packing piece.

BUNKER, TANKS AND A WRAP-OVER CAB FOR THE CLASS 79

The completed bunker and tanks.

- Tack solder the bunker sides to the footplate, following either a scribed line or packing pieces previously soldered to the footplate. (Ensure that the rear of the cab is upright at 90 degrees as you add the sides.) It's a good idea to use a rectangular packing piece to keep the sides parallel (but don't accidently solder it unless you want to cover it with coal later on). Remember to tack solder with quick dabs of the iron.
- Check that the sides are vertical and that both ends are exactly the same distance from the end of the footplate otherwise you'll get a wonky back.
- Correct and seam.
- Add the bunker back as on the Class 51. Job done. Excellent.

CAB ROOF

Before the cab roof goes on, solder in a nice set of cab doors as per the Class 51. It will be difficult, though not impossible, to get inside afterwards so have a think about what else you want lurking in there. If you are keen for some interior detail then now might be the time to make it.

Tape a rectangle of card squarely to the top of the tank sides and fold it firmly around the cab.

FORMING THE BENDS

Ready for some exciting metal shaping?

- Tape a rectangle of card squarely to the top of the tank sides and fold it firmly around the cab.
- Mark the position of the other side.
- Cut a template from the card, then use the template to cut a piece of 0.010in nickel silver to shape to form the wrap-over for the roof. Mark in the shape of the windows but *don't* cut them out yet. Add any rivet detail now if you want to.

Mark the position of the other side.

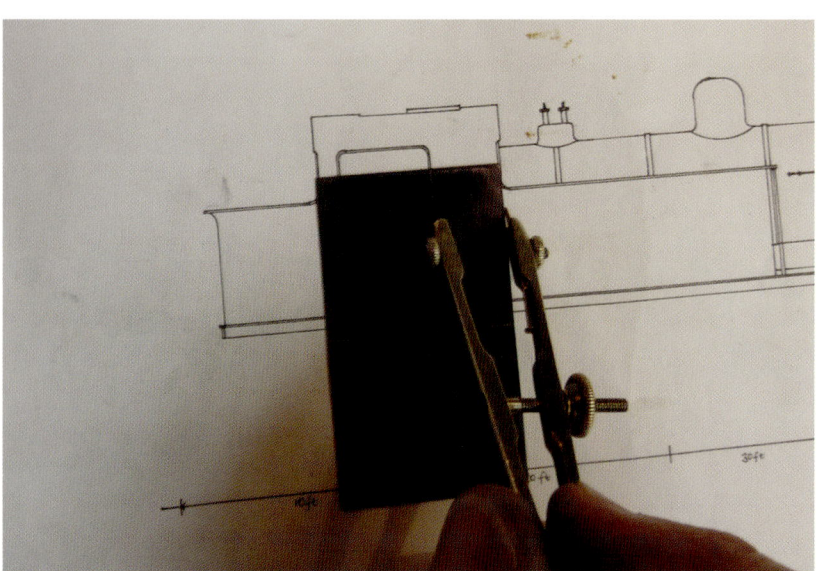

Cut a template from the card, then use the template to cut a piece of 0.010in nickel silver to shape to form the wrap-over for the roof. Mark in the shape of the windows but don't cut them out yet. Add any rivet detail now if you want to.

BUNKER, TANKS AND A WRAP-OVER CAB FOR THE CLASS 79

Roll a gentle curve in the roof, check for a good fit, ensure everything is central and mark the midpoint of each tight curve.

Keeping everything parallel, roll each tight curve using a bar of the same diameter. Line up the pencil mark with the centre of the rod.

- Roll a gentle curve in the roof, check for a good fit, ensure everything is central and mark the midpoint of each tight curve.
- Keeping everything parallel, roll each tight curve using a bar of the same diameter. Line up the pencil mark with the centre of the rod.
- Keep checking for a good fit and finish fitting by pressing with a wood block.

This exercise requires patience. If you are lucky you might get it right first time, which is fantastically satisfying but doesn't always happen. The metal will

Keep checking for a good fit and finish fitting by pressing with a wood block.

survive quite a lot of tweaking before it becomes unworkable, but you might have to make another one. No matter, it takes practice.

CUTTING THE CAB WINDOWS

When all is good (I think I managed on attempt two) it's time to cut out the cab window. If you had done it before it would have been even more difficult to form the curves satisfactorily.

What you don't want is to ruin your lovely curves, so this next part takes a bit of delicacy and finesse. Keep the work supported carefully as you drill, cut and file and you'll be fine.

- Drill relieving holes in the corners of the window aperture using a wood block for support.
- Support the cab and cut out the window with a fret saw.

Drill relieving holes in the corners of the window aperture using a wood block for support.

BUNKER, TANKS AND A WRAP-OVER CAB FOR THE CLASS 79

Support the cab and cut out the window with a fret saw.

File the window into its final shape – to support the delicate cut-out, I wedged the edges gently in a slot cut in a block of balsa.

- File the window into its final shape – to support the delicate cut-out, I wedged the edges gently in a slot cut in a block of balsa.

FITTING THE ROOF

When the windows are finished it's time for some stout soldering work.

- Secure the cab roof firmly in position prior to soldering. Using lolly sticks and copper wire, I trussed up the roof and body sides until the whole thing looked like emergency repairs following a skiing accident. What you want is a tight fit with no gaps or bulges anywhere. If the roof is slightly too big, file tiny amounts from either of the lower

Secure the cab roof firmly in position prior to soldering.

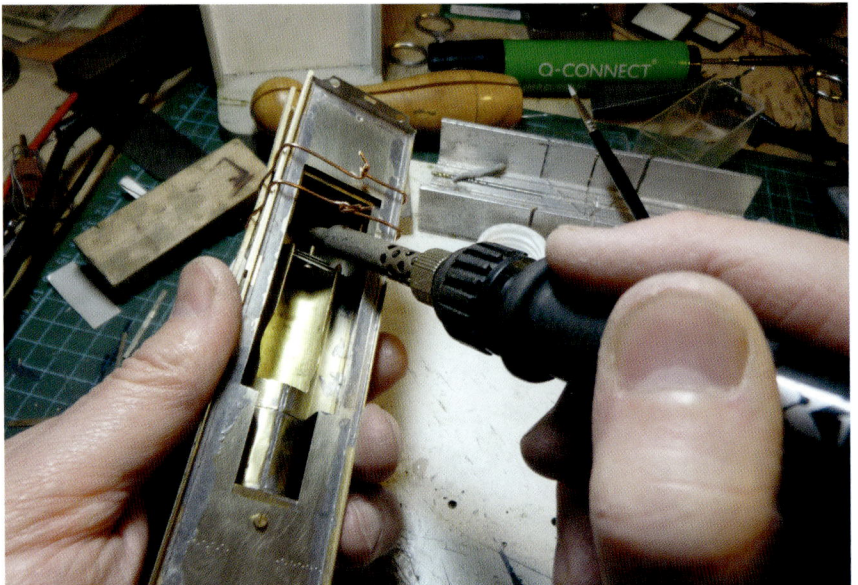

First solder on the inside.

edges to keep everything equal until the bulges disappear. If it's slightly too small, some packing strips can be soldered on the inside of the joint. Take your time with is as it will pay dividends.
- First solder on the inside.
- Then solder on the outside. Dab on or 'puddle' Carr's 224°C gap-filling solder, trying to avoid swamping the rivets. Clean up the solder to hide most of the joint – if this involves using a burnishing tool, take all the usual precautions.

And very good it is too. If you remember the Hamlet cigar advert, it's that sort of feeling you're aiming for here. Relax and enjoy. It's just the details left to do.

Then solder on the outside. Dab on or 'puddle' Carr's 224°C gap-filling solder, trying to avoid swamping the rivets. Clean up the solder to hide most of the joint – if this involves using a burnishing tool, take all the usual precautions.

And that's that: a 'comb-over' cab.

CHAPTER SEVENTEEN

DETAILS, DETAILS

The details are the bits that really bring your model to life. Look carefully at photos and decide what you would like to include and what you can live without. It's completely up to you. And you can always add more later on.

A COUPLE OF QUANDARIES

Which bits first? How shall I make them? These are quandaries faced by all modellers when coming to the details. The second is easier to tackle than the first.

HOW TO MAKE THE DETAILS

If you want, you can build up all of the detail parts from scratch. It takes longer and can be ineffably fiddly, yet the end result can be very satisfying. On the other hand, there are many manufacturers out there eager to part you from your children's inheritance with some lovely time-saving etches and castings – and why not?

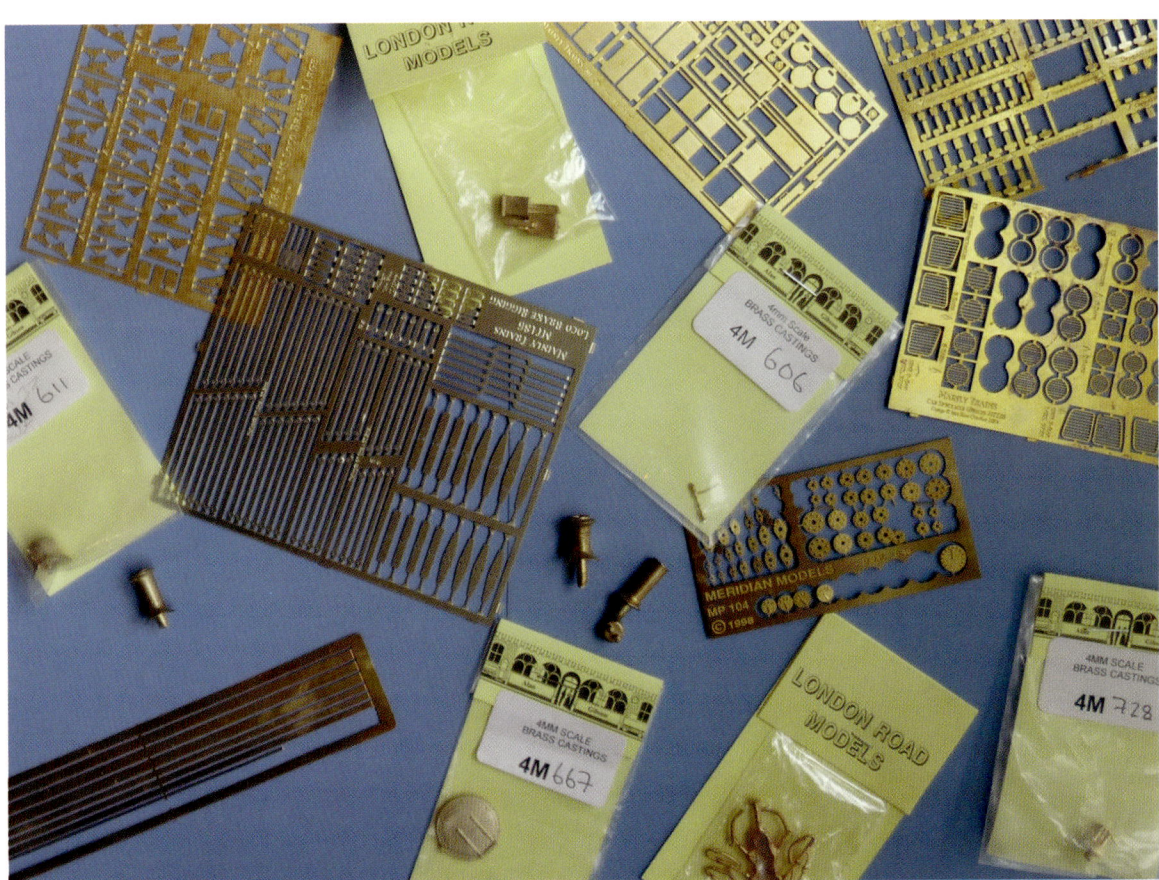

Lots of details, all ready to apply.

DETAILS, DETAILS

In the following pages I have sketched how I would make some items, even if I haven't in this instance actually soldered them myself. It's up to you to do as I say or do as you wish.

WHICH BITS FIRST?

Now, though, back to the first dilemma. Hindsight is a wonderful thing, and that certainly applies in scratch-building. You usually know if you should have done something first *after* you have done something else.

Consider the following:

- Will something you've just done or added on get in the way or actually block you from adding something else?
- How delicate and easily broken, or broken off, is a component?
- Do you want to glue, screw or solder something on? (How long can you wait for it to fix?)
- Is there a hole for it drilled already or will you have to drill precariously around existing fixtures?
- Can you mark the position of components reasonably easily?

- If you want to rest the loco on its sides or ends, will bits get bent or broken off? (Some people like to hold their models between their knees; I'm not sure about that.)
- Plus many other unexpected events, the solutions for which only experience or luck will supply.

Soldering small details can be done with a quick splash of 145°C solder, which won't disturb other solder joints. When building up details use 180°C before you solder them onto the main body of the loco.

Basically, as you have no instructions to ignore you have to work out in which order to construct your little masterpiece.

It's a good idea to start in one place and move gradually sideways and upwards. If you begin with the footplate, leave the buffer beams till later as many of the details here are delicate and easily broken off. However, the buffer shanks are chunky and you could get them on straightaway. They are also useful to balance the loco on when adding bits and pieces to the back or front.

Class 79 with all of its bits and pieces in place. Pretty eh?

The loco balanced on its sturdy buffer shanks with various blocks of wood to prevent damage to the more fragile parts.

ADDING THE DETAILS

Detail parts can be classified by their construction or how you choose to apply them. The sketches that follow demonstrate a mixture of both approaches.

SOLID BITS
Including:

- Chimney
- Dome
- Safety valves
- Smokebox door
- Steam pipes
- Sand box

Solid castings can be successfully glued to the model – soldering is tricky and can be messy as there is a lot of metal around to soak the heat away. Five-minute epoxy gives you time to adjust the fittings.

The **dome**, **chimney** and **safety valves** in particular need to be in line and perpendicular. A mirror is great to give you a different view. Keep looking from all angles and nudge things along until the glue sets.

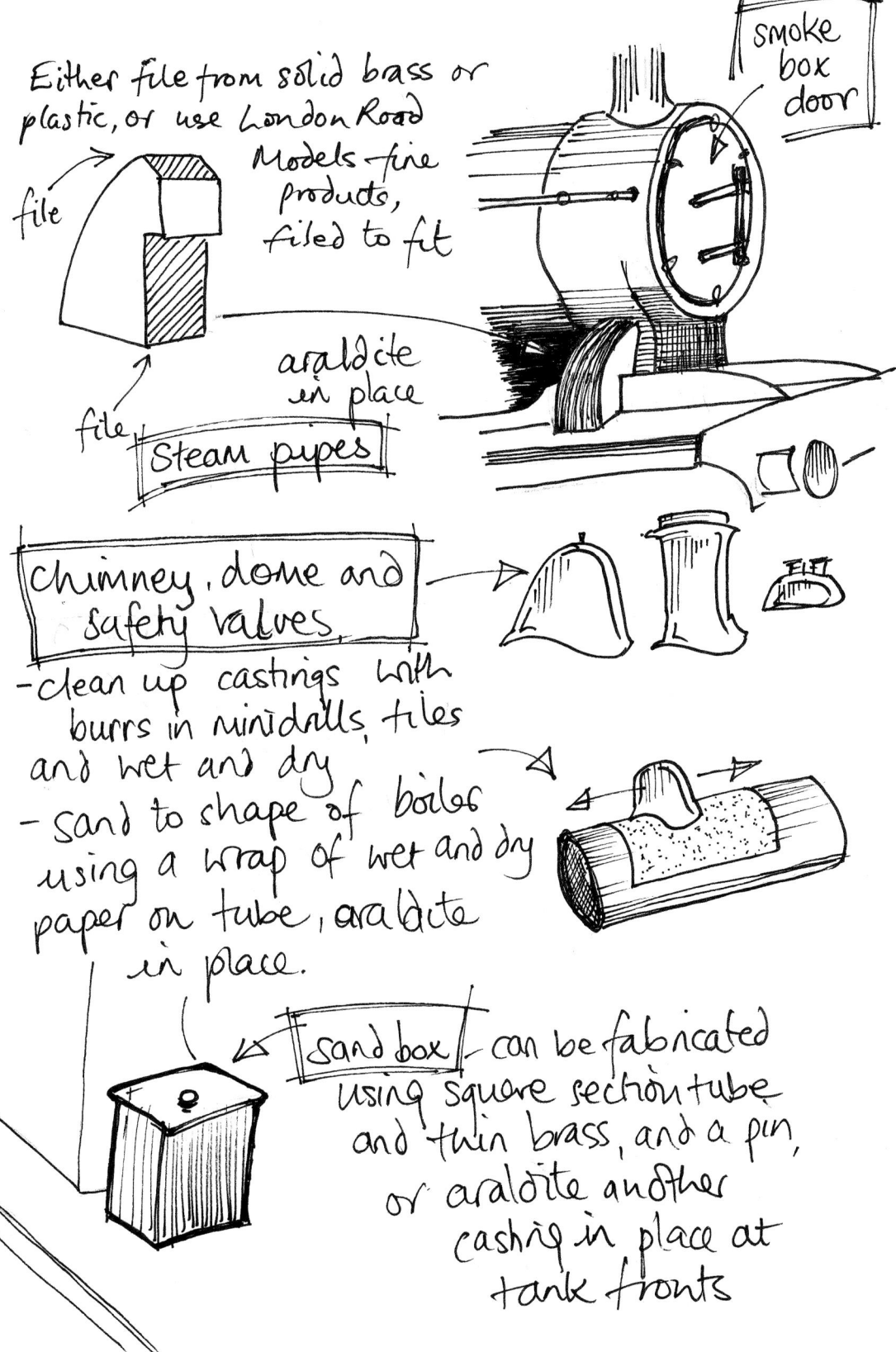

Big solid bits.

DETAILS, DETAILS

Looking away and coming back to look again helps too. After about fifteen minutes, any excess glue can be poked away using a cocktail stick. This also fills any small gaps.

Do give the castings a good file and polish as they are very obvious. Small casting seams and bumps and dents can be removed with a bit of elbow grease. More extreme tactics can be employed to remove larger lumps of unwanted metal, such as when trying to get castings to sit properly. A dental burr in the mini-drill can be a particularly effective tool for this.

Before you add the boiler fittings it is a good idea to fit the four **boiler bands**. These can be soldered on from thin brass strip (Alan Gibson and Markits both supply suitable etches). Or you can stick on strips of Scotch Magic tape, which is extraordinary stuff, seemingly unaffected by most cleaning products,

Using a dental burr to remove excess metal from a dome casting. Clothes pegs make good clamps for this sort of operation. Watch your eyes.

Marking the position of a boiler band using dividers. Two of the bands, made from tape, are already in place.

unwary brushes with bristles, nearby soldering or paint – do test it out first just in case.

Whichever method you decide on, you will have to remove a chunk of material from beneath the dome and safety valve to get them to sit properly. The tape is easier. The brass is possibly more stable but it's more difficult to apply. I tin the brass strip first, tack solder one end underneath the boiler, loop it around the boiler and solder it in exactly the same place. When satisfied you can deftly sweat the remainder in place and clean up. Both methods benefit from marking the positions on the boiler with the dividers.

If you haven't yet finally fixed the boiler in place you may find it easier to separate it for this job. Some people ignore the bands altogether and just add some transfer paper of suitable thickness during the paint job.

TUBES AND PIPES

Including:

- Handrails and pipes
- Clack valves and pipes
- Cylinder draincocks
- Vacuum brake ejector
- Whistle

Details such as these can be pleasingly built up from nesting tubes and from various castings adapted with copper and brass wire. Small bits and pieces can be soldered or glued in place. This is about the only time I might use superglue. I hate the smell, it irritates my eyes and I invariably glue myself to immovable objects, but it is very good for tight fits for small objects like **handrail knobs** and wires. Use it only when all soldering has been finished.

As an alternative to superglue, a Resistance Soldering Unit (RSU) can come into its own here. It's great for pushing and prodding and holding things in place. It's also good for burning metal surfaces and melting delicate pieces. Use solder paste applied with a pin to leave a nice clean joint.

I should make a special mention of Alan Gibson's beautifully crafted brass handrail knobs. They are perfectly in scale and come in different lengths for different applications: short for the cab sides and smokebox fronts, medium for the boiler and shoulderless for when the others don't fit. The cab-side handrails are merely bent-up lengths of 0.5mm wire.

BUILT-UP ITEMS

Including:

- Bunker coal rails
- Simple lamp irons
- Guard irons
- Lamp and buffer guards
- Destination board brackets
- Chassis equalizing beam and springs
- Reversing rod

In the absence of available etches or tiny castings these items can all be built up from scraps of sheet metal. However, there are some lovely detail etches from Markits that cover many of these fittings.

As an unexpected bonus, I discovered that Markits' brass etched strips were set apart on the fret correctly for the **bunker coal rails**. Upright spacers were simply soldered across the strips using a card guide for the correct positions. The strips were then cut to length, bent and soldered into the bunker. Alternatively you could hold down separate lengths of strip with masking tape for the same effect.

SMALL CASTINGS AND ETCHES

Including:

- Lamp irons
- Roof hatches
- Brake hoses
- Brake shoes (plastic pieces or metal etches)
- Mud holes
- Washout plugs

Things like these can be the essence of fiddly to fix on. The **lamp irons** are preferably soldered as they are very prone to breakage. Deft use of the soldering iron or – perhaps better – the RSU is required here.

The RSU can also be used to solder white-metal items, like the **cab hatch**, if you don't touch the

Tubes and Pipes

Alan Gibson casting with soldered wire additions

loop of 0.5mm wire

1.2mm tube

1mm dia wire

Class 79 Vacuum brake ejector and Clack Valve

TANK SIDE

16 BA nut

0.5mm copper wire

1.2mm dia. tube

Clack valve: LRM casting or built up from tubes, wire and washers

0.5mm handrail curves around clack valve

file top

0.5mm wire

brass tube

shape top of whistle body

form gap and lower part of whistle body

Whistle

0.5mm wire soldered into 0.5mm inside diam. tube. Rotated in mini-drill and shaped with triangular needle file.

1mm square brass wire

tank filler cap

Large washer or brass disc

slice of 5mm diameter brass tube

Tubes and pipes.

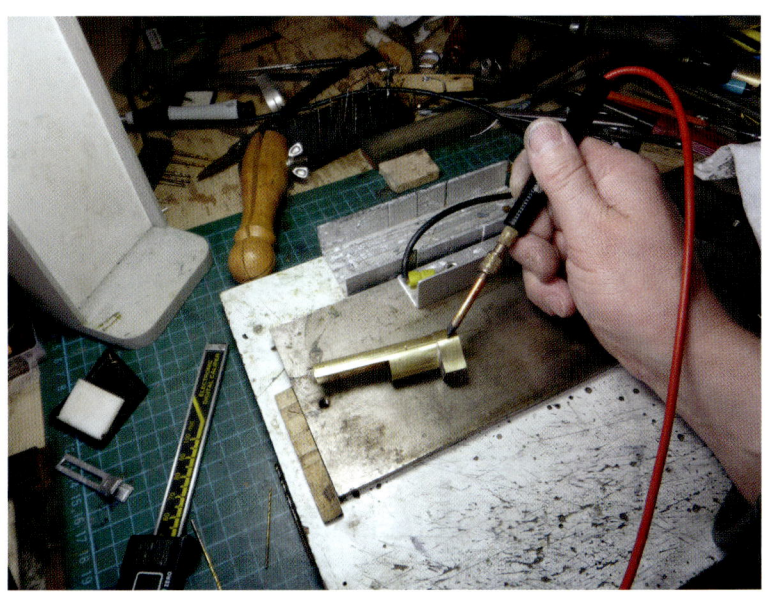

Resistance soldering the handrail knobs. Use dividers or Vernier calipers to help you mark out their positions.

casting with it. Tin the metal surface using Carr's 179 No Clean Solder Cream with the conventional iron and apply some flux. Position the casting and apply the resistance probe close by until the flux fizzes. Soldered. Not a lot of people know this.

If you take a close look through *Thundersley*'s cab window on page 79, some **washout plugs** can be seen in the foreground. These are actually clamps. When you wanted to give the inside of the firebox a good wash out you undid the clamps and lifted off the cover to get your hosepipe in for a swoosh around.

These LMS ones are very distinctive and quite the devil to model. People happily represent them with their most distinctive feature, the little rounded end, at the top. But Alan Gibson, as ever, has come to the rescue with some beautiful little castings. They are comparatively expensive but do the job superbly.

There is a hefty brass stalk on each one that has a nice little raised rim to finish off. All you need is a fairly large hole: 2mm, opened out very carefully with a reamer until they fit perfectly. Make sure you mark the positions of the holes carefully and do check from photos that you have positioned them correctly. Fiendishly, the LMS didn't always have them symmetrically placed on either side.

Separate the castings from the sprue with the piercing saw about halfway up the stalk. If you leave it too long it will be tricky to solder as it will act as a heat sink and it might get in the way of the motor/gearbox. Too short and they get very fiddly to handle.

The Class 51 has much smaller washout holes that are simply made by drilling 1mm-diameter holes in position on the boiler and gluing a backing sheet of lead inside the boiler (which is good for weight too). Holes of 0.5mm diameter are then drilled centrally in the lead sheet, siting through the boiler holes, and 0.5mm brass wire soldered in. The ends of the wire just poke through level with the boiler surface. Take a good look at some LMS locos when you next come across them for more washout plug details. (Don't forget to wash your hands after handling lead, or indeed washout plugs in general.)

Brake shoes can be added by soldering 0.5mm wire into the correct holes in the chassis frames and then soldering (or gluing) plastic or etched brake shoes. Plastic ones are good if you want to avoid short circuits. In any case, bend them sufficiently clear of the wheels.

Finally, solder, glue or screw on your favourite choice of **couplings**.

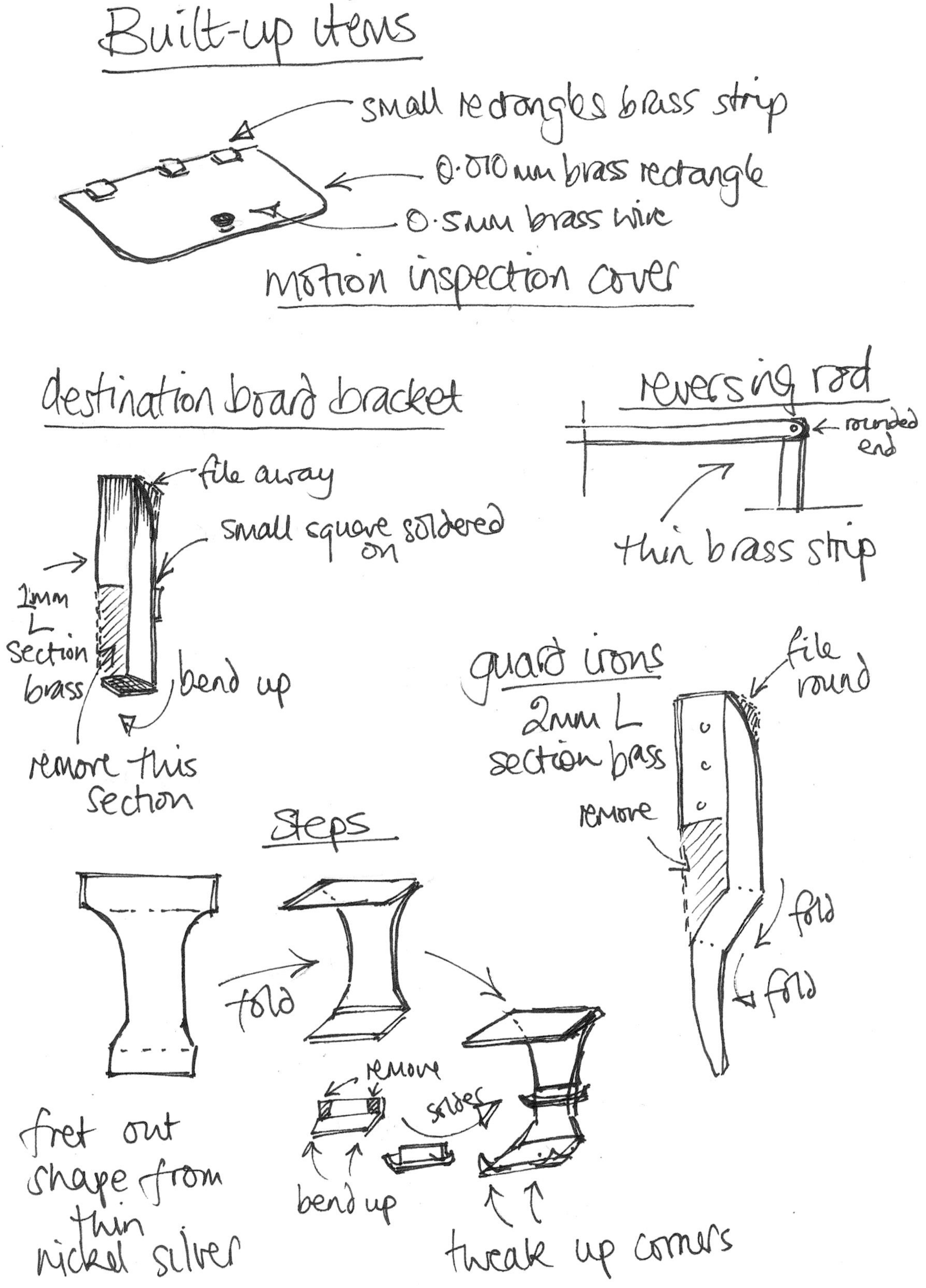

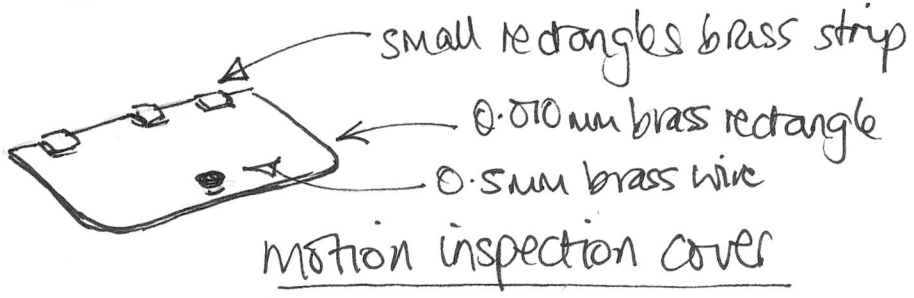

Built-up items.

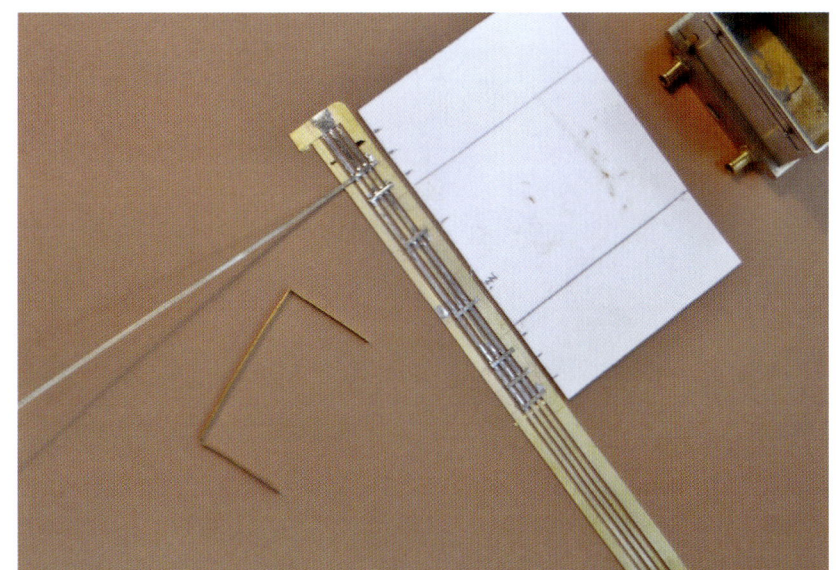

Soldering up the bunker coal rails.

The detailed bunker.

Resistance soldering the white-metal cab hatch on the Class 51.

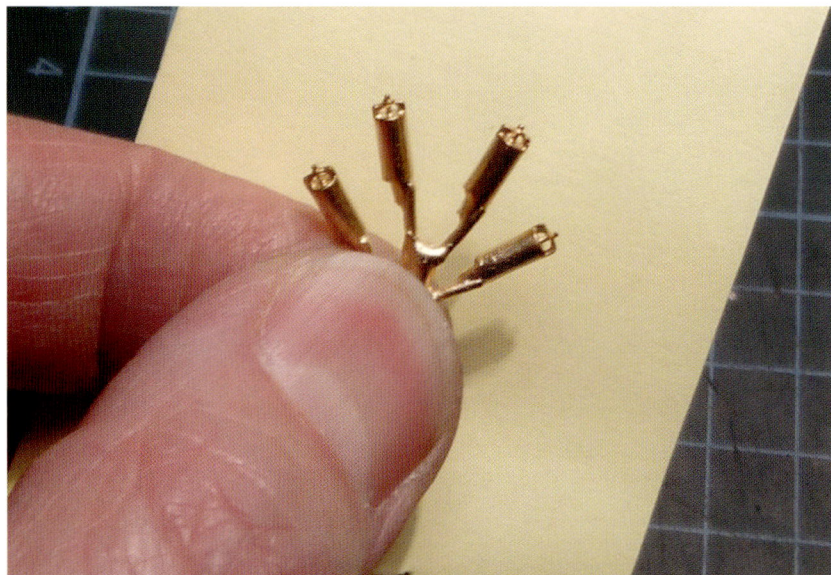

Alan Gibson's washout clamps.

Boiler details.

And that's it really. It's been a long journey and very well worth it. Sit back and admire. Show your models to people. Bask in their astonishment. You deserve it. You have a beautiful Tilbury Tank – or two.

Finally, we finish off with a brief revisit to the J15 to show how I painted her. You can see evidence of cosmetically added rivets in the photos. Added just prior to painting, they can be from beautiful sheets of resin transfers by Archer Transfers or carefully sited, tiny blobs of Araldite. You can do something similar for your Tilburies if you so wish. Enjoy.

Class 51 washout plugs under construction.

Class 79 and 51 Tilbury Tanks front.

Class 79 and 51 Tilbury Tanks rear.

CHAPTER EIGHTEEN

PAINTING AND DECORATING

In my previous book I rather smartly sidestepped the process of finishing and painting by directing the reader to various works of genius, such as those by Martyn Welch and Ian Rathbone. For this volume I thought I'd let them have a little rest (although you will still find them in the bibliography at the back) and describe a simple and rather effective alternative.

I'm not at all keen on brush painting models. I have some fine examples of badly painted models I made as a kid to remind me just how easy it is to ruin a reasonable model with a few sticky brush strokes. I like to spray. However, I no longer have an outside space available to fill with noxious fumes and, as I live in a rental property, the overspray that probably still adorns parts of my last home would be inappropriate here.

So in search of a solution I discovered that various paint manufacturers now make spray primer paints in a variety of colours and not just the classic light grey. There are all sorts, including black, white and red, and they come in acrylic, which is much less injurious to both residents and soft furnishings. They are strong, smooth and hard-wearing, designed as an undercoat for plastic and metal surfaces, and they dry very quickly. Choose the colour you want and it can be a one-stop shop.

PREPARING TO PAINT

The victim in this instance is the J15 I built for my previous book. It was last seen in reasonably shiny metal finish; nice to look at though a bit odd running around a layout. While the Victorians – particularly those in Swindon – liked a bit of bare brass here and there, most other locomotive surfaces were given a thorough and decorative painting for protection against the elements and to let the travelling public know who they were travelling with.

Find a colour photo of your chosen loco, or something that's near enough to it, work out what colours you need and start looking for your rattle can of choice. You could start by nipping down to Halfords. Games Workshop do a very well-regarded Chaos Black primer or try Vallejo black primer, which I used. This was appropriate for a J15 in BR ownership which is black – with some dust and grime to taste.

CLEANING UP

If you've been good with your hygiene routine and cleaned up after each modelling session you will have less to do here. The ferocious power of atmospheric oxygen will still tarnish surfaces and your grubby fingers will leave paw prints of grease, so you'll need to do some extra cleaning before you paint. Also, your model will have accumulated dust however clean your home is.

Having previously warned against the venomous bristles of the fibreglass brush, they can be good for stubborn stains and places that are difficult to get at. Take adequate precautionary measures, then have a good scrub at your beautiful model, trying not to remove your fondly applied details, until you can see your face in it. *Never* blow the dust about – eyes, people, eyes.

Finally, give the model a good scrub with a toothbrush, warm water and something like Bar Keepers Friend that smells suspiciously brutal and will remove any leftover stains and hopefully not your carefully applied rivet detail. You might want to test it out first. Some brave souls put the non-mechanical parts in the dishwasher. Try it once for fun, if you dare.

Rinse the model thoroughly and dry it with a hairdryer, which will also help to blast dust, dog hair and other small particles from the shiny surfaces. Keep the model covered in a plastic tub until you are ready to paint.

Now is the time to say goodbye to the gleam.

PAINTING AND DECORATING

A beautifully atmospheric photo of a nicely weathered J15. COLOUR-RAIL

METAL BLACKING

There are places where you might not want to paint at all, maybe because you don't want a synthetic layer of pigment over a metal surface. Metal-blacking liquid will remove the shine to leave a pleasant metallic sheen. This is a potentially lethal chemical so don't drink it (obviously); wash your hands thoroughly if you come into contact with it; and before you start using it make sure you have a receptacle full of water to hand in which you can rinse off the compound.

I like to dip things into the bottle, gripped firmly in tweezers. Watch the surface blacken, then rinse to stop the process. Repeat as necessary. A better effect is produced by cleaning and burnishing the metal before and after applying the liquid. I blackened the brake gear and the coupling rods in this way. And very pretty they are too.

The shiny wheel rims, axle ends and crankpin collars can be similarly blackened although I'm unsure of the chemical effects on the plastic wheel rims and their smooth running. I would suggest that it's probably safer to just touch these in with a permanent black marker, which is also very useful to dot in any paint knocks that expose bright metal.

SPRAYING TIPS

- When you are ready to paint, first make sure your chosen environment is not too windy,

Blackening the coupling rods.

certainly not dusty, cold or damp. It should be well lit, too, preferably by natural light, although you can simulate this with blue 'daylight' light bulbs from art shops.
- Ventilation is paramount. You and yours do *not* want to inhale the fumes of doom. Throw open all your doors and windows, or step outside if the weather is good and space is available.
- If you are inside and the weather is a bit cool you can warm things up a little with a hair drier set on cool and directed towards the window. This helps the paint dry and wafts the fug outside.
- You might want to wear a mask, although if you can smell the chemicals you are inhaling them. Fresh air is what you are after.
- Rattle the can for the appropriate time (follow the instructions on the side of the can).
- Practise spraying onto a test piece of card or metal so that you can see what the coverage will be like. Too close and it might land too wet and you will get unsightly runs. Too far away (or too hot a day) and the paint will dry as it hits the metal, resulting in that unmistakable and unsightly orange-peel effect reminiscent of woodchip wallpaper.
- If splattering occurs there may be a build-up of paint clogging the nozzle of the can. Wipe with a cloth and a dab of cellulose thinners (more nasty chemicals).
- When satisfied with your test piece, pass the spray over the model starting the paint stream before you reach the model and finishing after passing the other side. A few passes should do. Aim for a liquid, not runny, coat. You will know when you get it right: it will look shiny and firm. You will also know when you get it wrong; don't panic, finish painting first, let things dry thoroughly and deal with mistakes afterwards.
- Most acrylics dry very quickly but don't be tempted to return to your model too soon. If you try to wipe or pick while the paint is still wet you will only make matters much, much worse. If all else fails dunk the whole thing in cellulose thinners and start again.
- Look carefully to see if all surfaces have been covered, particularly in the shadow of detail components such as handrails and chimneys. Spray from different angles until satisfied. If you find you haven't noticed a bare patch you can always have another go later.

PAINTING AND DECORATING

- Once fully hardened, runs and dust specks can be carefully sanded using fine wet and dry.

PAINTING THE CHASSIS

I dismantled the chassis completely, which you don't need to do, although it is at least advisable to remove the motor and wheels – some people don't and merely spray merrily away with the wheels turning, it's up to you.

The inner surfaces of steam locomotive frames were often painted red. This is thought to make things like oil leaks and cracks easier to spot, allowing maintenance to be a more relaxed affair. Whatever the reason, it does

The inside faces of Thundersley's frames showing red beneath the boiler.

Spray the insides red and wait to dry.

178 PAINTING AND DECORATING

Rebuild the chassis and you have a thing of beauty.

make a pleasant splash of colour visible deep in the loco's interior and it's very easy to effect using red primer.

- Dismantle the chassis and place the frames with the insides uppermost on a flat surface, having protected the surroundings with copious amounts of newspaper.
- Spray the insides red and wait to dry.
- Replace the newspaper, turn the frames over and spray the outside surfaces black.
- Rebuild the chassis and you have a thing of beauty. Run a reamer very gently through the bearings to get rid of any unwanted paint.

This is a good test of your prowess with the spray can as everything is helpfully flat and accommodating.

PAINTING THE BODYWORK

MASKING

Any sparkly bits that you would like to keep sparkly need only to be given a quick dab of masking fluid. A particularly useful bottled variety comes from Hobby Holidays as the bottle can be fitted with a fine tip, which is excellent for application, though something similar from the local art shop and a cocktail stick will do the job just as well.

Masking in progress. I have covered the clack valves and piping, whistle and safety valves.

The liquid dries clear so you will need to remember where you have applied it. If any unwanted spots and splodges occur, let it dry and then whip it off with a cocktail stick.

COMPLETING THE PAINTWORK

Having masked the shiny bits, we are now ready to complete the paintwork. Before doing so, you will need to decide how to support the bodywork while you are painting it. It's best to handle the cleaned model as little as possible – it's amazing what complex chemicals our bodies manufacture that seem specifically designed by evolution to spoil painted surfaces.

Some people grip the model by a part that doesn't require a coat of paint, using a medical rubber glove to protect the hand (and model). Others buy special clamps. My way of doing things is to prop the model on a rotating cake stand.

Whatever your method, spray away. Take care and enjoy yourself.

Wait until everything is completely dry then remove the masking fluid to show off the shiny bits of naked metal below. After a few days the stuff can become very gooey and difficult to get off satisfactorily. However, if you try to remove it too early you may risk peeling off the adjoining paint. A cocktail stick or something similar is a good tool for this as it won't scratch the paint surface.

If your loco is black, like mine, you are just about done. If it's a different colour I would use grey primer and then the closest match for the top coat that you can get in Halfords or from other car paint suppliers. There are useful paint-matching lists on various websites including www.rafkinlossmrc.co.uk, who have a really wide-ranging selection from many different railway companies' liveries. Anything more fancy and you might want to head back to the welcoming works of Messrs Rathbone and Welch.

Are you still with me? Well, if your top coat is black, and your primer is black, who needs a top coat? Wait until your primer has had a good chance to dry and harden off and then buff it up with a stiff paintbrush or toothbrush if you want a bit more shine.

EXTRA COLOUR

There are various places that you can leave black, if you wish, like the cab interior. If you want to paint them more authentically, cabs are generally creamy yellow or dirty white and a good acrylic, like Vallejo, can be neatly brush-painted inside. Be careful not to allow paint onto the outsides or through the windows. Wet paint can be wiped off effectively with a damp cotton-wool bud.

Removing the masking fluid.

Just one coat of black primer – job done.

The buffer beams should be painted red; they get black and dirty very quickly. If you want pristine you will need a few smooth brush coats. Another way of doing this is by careful masking of the buffer beams with masking tape and using the red primer for them first. The cab interior could be similarly primed in white or grey, then masked off and the rest of the loco primed in black.

APPLYING TRANSFERS

Keep the model safe and still by resting it on a small pad of foam rubber while you apply the transfers, or 'decals', as they are sometimes called. I usually use HMRS Methfix transfers, which you cut out, soak for a bit and then allow to swim gently on a small slick of methylated spirits to get them in the correct position. This time I thought I would have a go at Pressfix transfers.

I've never been keen on these transfers as I didn't like the idea of pressing the transfer onto the surface as it sounded like you would have to get it in exactly the right place first time (which is definitely not one of my superpowers). They actually turned out to be easy and simple to use; I had just been put off by the name. I am told that the fresher they are the easier they are to use.

Make sure you read the instructions, whatever your choice of transfer. You need a nice smooth surface if you want the transfers to sit properly as they don't like it rough. Gloss paint is good; as we are not using it here, a small piece of fine abrasive on a stick can be used to burnish the paint surface on which you want to place the decal.

- Polish a small area of paintwork to create a smooth surface on which to apply the transfer.
- Cut each transfer out carefully with a sharp blade. Position it exactly, then press down with a cotton bud or a not too pointy cocktail stick.
- Blob a bit of water on and wait about thirty seconds.
- Peel the carrier film away with cautious use of the tweezers.

For long numbers, as found on the cab sides of the J15 (No. 65462), start in the middle and move outwards either way so the spacing is uniform. Use a piece of card to position the bottom of the numbers and space them out by eye; all very satisfying.

- Use dividers to position the central number.
- Once applied and dried, position the second number using the card template to ensure everything is level.
- Repeat for the next number and so on.

Polish a small area of paintwork to create a smooth surface on which to apply the transfer.

Cut each transfer out carefully with a sharp blade. Position it exactly, then press down with a cotton bud or a not too pointy cocktail stick.

Blob a bit of water on and wait about thirty seconds.

Peel the carrier film away with cautious use of the tweezers.

Use dividers to position the central number.

Once applied and dried, position the second number using the card template to ensure everything is level.

PAINTING AND DECORATING

Repeat for the next number and so on.

BELOW RIGHT: *A set of Guilplates for BR J15 No. 65462.*

BOTTOM RIGHT: *Using the oilstone to finish off – it doesn't catch as much as a file might.*

If you want to glaze the cab windows, a couple of small circles of transparent plastic glued on from the inside will do fine. Use PVA or Clear Glaze sparingly so as not to spoil the plastic.

PLATES

Various metal plates can be found attached to locomotives telling you who built them, where and when and what numbers they may have carried in their varied lifetimes. Again, a number of manufacturers supply these and my favourite is Guilplates, who do a great variety in a large number of scales. In fact, they will etch almost anything for you, particularly if you give them a good photo to work from.

The plates come as small etches and you may have to cut them out – and small can be very small. I use the piercing saw, very carefully supported to go around the edges as close as I dare. Files and oilstones are used to finish off, holding the plate in the jewellers' vice. If you leave one edge as a larger chunk of metal, things are much easier to hold until the final fiddle at the end.

These delightful little works of art are stuck on with Micro Kristal Klear (a PVA glue).

WEATHERING

If you want to do a bit of weathering without using any more paint, I can thoroughly recommend commercial weathering powders, or simply buy a set of artists' pastel crayons. Give your chosen colours a good rub on a coarse file to make your own powder. I generally use black, grey, white, blue, yellow, orange and brown.

Apply sparingly with a small stiff brush (paint or make-up brushes are ideal) and remove as much powder as you want. Look at your photo carefully and don't overdo it. The surface will gradually become polished by the brushwork and the colours will blend imperceptibly into a pleasing whole. For authenticity, work the brushstrokes generally downwards from top to bottom, the direction in which most weather weathers. There may be some streaks in the direction of travel but not, it would appear, on the rather unhurried J15.

If you want a hard-water streak or two, very carefully draw them in with the sharpened edge of a grey crayon and then buff up with a brush. Any mistakes can just be polished off, then you can start again. The occasional fingertip can be used to good effect too. I would keep water well away from the process as you could end up with unwanted streaking.

FINISHING OFF

You don't need to varnish if you'd prefer not to. It really depends on how much you want to handle the model. Do try to keep your greasy digits off the flat surfaces, though, as you may create a giant fingerprint effect over time.

If you do decide to use varnish, take care that your spray-on varnish doesn't make your transfers crinkle. Spray test onto a transfer on a spare painted surface first. Testors Dullcote is often recommended, but so too are various makes of floor polish, so I'll repeat myself: test it out safely first.

And that's it – quick, simple and effective, and a good base to improve your skills. Or you could buy an air brush and compressor – they're fun too.

All of these painting and decorating processes apply equally well to finishing off your Tilbury Tank if it's in unlined LMS livery, particularly if it's black. Lining using transfers is a very similar procedure, just a little more tricky. So practise with the numbers and emblems and then move on. Do the corners first and fill in with the straight bits; after all, that's how most people do jigsaws and they're not too hard are they?

Use the small stiff brush first and polish off with a larger softer one. Keep looking at your prototype photo to get things just right.

PAINTING AND DECORATING

The fully painted and decorated J15.

POSTSCRIPT

I ended my first book thinking about further scratch-building projects and included a photograph of a locomotive that looked more like a large chicken shed on wheels than the rather charismatic Bo-Bo Ford Diesel shunter that it turned out to be. I thought you might like to see how I got on with it.

And finally, I started this book by dedicating it to a man who inspired and encouraged me to begin to scratch-build model railway locomotives – Don Wilson. I would like to finish it by mentioning another man who has inadvertently continued the process.

Having recently joined the Shropshire & Herefordshire Area Group of railway modellers, I must have met John Bailey two or three times. I can just remember him as a calm and quiet man who had a reputation as a gifted and meticulous modeller. When he died in February 2015 he left the results of a lifetime's achievement in railway modelling to the group.

I was delighted to be given a half-finished scratch-built locomotive from John's workshop in the hope that I might complete it. And I will. It is quite exquisitely built in a style that is recognizably similar to how I would like to do it, only with the benefit of

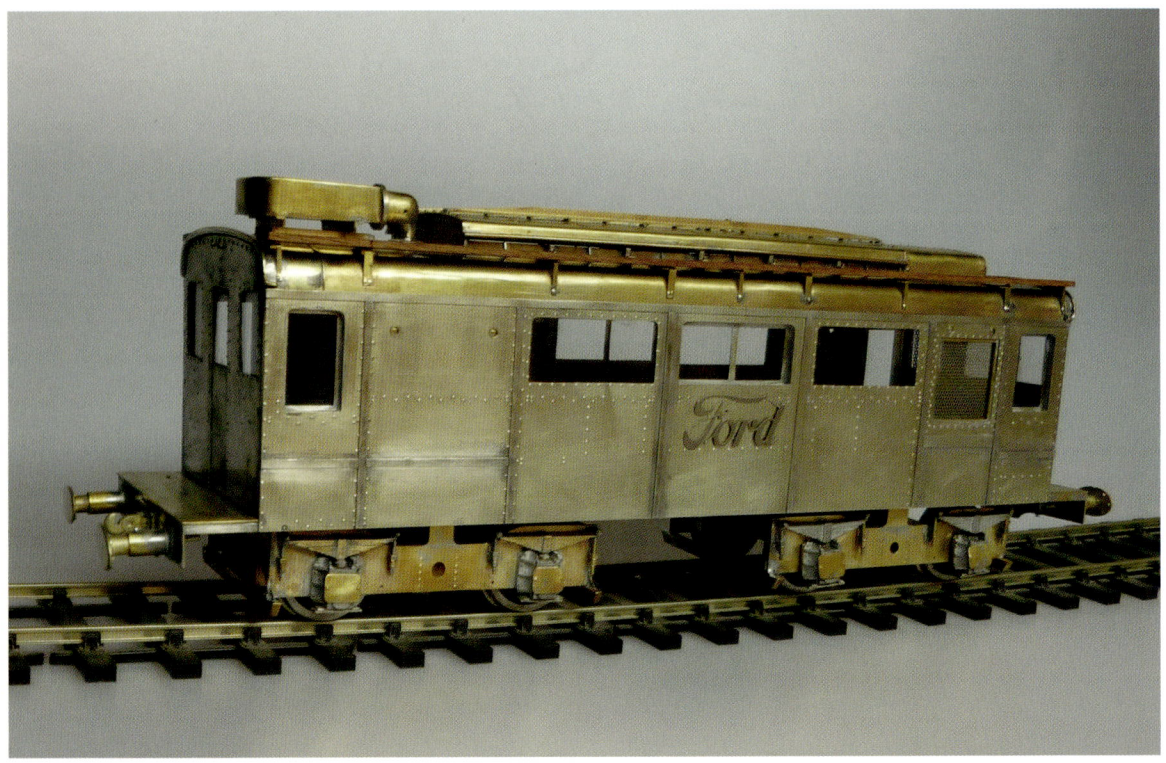

Ford Bo-Bo Diesel shunting locomotive in 7mm scale.

craftsmanship and experience that I hope one day to achieve.

Now I'm looking forward to researching LNWR locomotives. We think it's a coal tank, and building it to the Scalefour 4mm standards will allow it to run on 'Kerrinhead', a layout for which John was one of the key instigators. It will also need to be DCC fitted, which is another thing entirely and very new indeed for me.

So my scratch-building journey continues, helped along by the enthusiasm, expertise and support of others, just as it began.

John Bailey's scratch-built LNWR tank loco. Don Wilson would know which loco this was purely by touch.

FURTHER READING AND RESOURCES

BOOKS AND PUBLICATIONS

Modelling how-to books:
Ahern, John H. *Miniature Locomotive Construction*
Bolton, Simon *Scratch-building Model Railway Locomotives*
Holt, Geoff *Locomotive Modelling From Scratch and Etched Kits*
Holt, Geoff *Locomotive Modelling From Scratch and Etched Kits, Part Two*
Rice, Iain *Etched Loco Construction*
Rice, Iain *Locomotive Kit Chassis Construction in 4mm*
Roche, F. J. and Templer, G. G. revised by Stevens-Stratten, S W *Building Model Locomotives*
Sharman, Mike *A Guide to Locomotive Building: From Prototype to Small Scale Models*
Sharman, Mike *Flexichas: A Way to Build Fully Compensated Model Locomotive Chassis*
Williams, R. Guy *Model Locomotive Construction in 4mm Scale*
Williams, R. Guy *More 4mm Engines*
Williams, R. Guy *The 4mm Engine: A Scratchbuilder's Guide*
Wright, Pete *Loco Bits and Pieces* (The 2mm Scale Association)

Books on finishing models:
Rathbone, Ian *A Modeller's Handbook of Painting and Lining*
Welch, Martyn *The Art of Weathering*

Books on operating and running locomotives:
Fermour, Drew *GWR/BR (WR) Castle Class (Owners Workshop Manual)*
Semmens, P. W. B. and Goldfinch, A. J. *How Steam Locomotives Really Work*
Topping, Brian *The Engine Driver's Manual: How to Prepare, Fire and Drive a Steam Locomotive*
Way, R. Barnard *Meet The Locomotive*

Specific publications on Tilbury Tank locomotives:
Essery, R. J. *London, Tilbury & Southend Railway and its Locomotives*
Leech, Kenneth H. *Loco Profile 27: Tilbury Tanks*
Rowledge, J. W. P. *Locomotives Illustrated 101 London, Tilbury and Southend Railway Locomotives*
Welch, H. D. *Locomotives and Rolling Stock of the London, Tilbury and Southend Railway*

Further sources of drawings of Tilbury Tanks:
Beattie, Ian *Drawn and Described: A collection of locomotive drawings and monographs*, Railway Modeller Magazine August 1982
Blyth, John D. and Cook, Arthur F. *Second Book of Locomotive Drawings*, Stephenson Locomotive Society
Roche, F. J. *Historic Locomotive Drawings in 4mm Scale*

Modelling journals:
Model Railway Journal
Finescale Railway Modelling Review

Other reading:
Harari, Yuval Noah *Sapiens: A Brief History of Mankind*
Lieberman, Daniel E. *The Story of the Human Body: Evolution, Health and Disease*
Roach, Mary *Gulp: Adventures on the Alimentary Canal*

LIBRARY AND ARCHIVE CENTRE

National Railway Museum Search Engine
www.nrm.org.uk/ResearchAndArchive.aspx

Science and Society Picture Library
www.scienceandsociety.co.uk

FURTHER READING AND RESOURCES

MODELLING PARTS AND TOOLS SUPPLIERS

247 Developments
www.247developments.co.uk

Alan Gibson Model Railway Products
www.alangibsonworkshop.com

C & L Finescale Modelling Limited
www.finescale.org.uk

Comet Models
www.cometmodels.co.uk

Eileen's Emporium
www.eileensemporium.com

G.W. Models
11 Croshaw Close, Lancing, West Sussex, BN15 9LE.
Tel: (01903) 767231

High Level Kits
www.highlevelkits.co.uk

Hobby Holidays
www.hobbyholidays.co.uk

London Road Models
www.traders.scalefour.org/LondonRoadModels

Mainly Trains
www.mainlytrains.co.uk

Markits
www.markits.com

Meridian Models
www.meridianmodels.co.uk

Metalsmith Ltd.
www.metalsmith.co.uk

RMweb
www.rmweb.co.uk

Roxey Mouldings
www.roxeymouldings.co.uk

Sharpening stones
uk.rs-online.com

Worsley Works Models
www.worsleyworks.co.uk

MODELLING SOCIETIES

The Central London Area Group of the Scalefour Society
www.clag.org.uk

Gauge 0 Guild
www.gauge0guild.com

The Scalefour Society
www.scalefour.org

PRESERVED RAILWAY SOCIETIES

Bressingham Steam and Gardens
www.bressingham.co.uk

Severn Valley Railway
www.svr.co.uk

INDEX

chassis frames design 26–27
Class 1 Tilbury Tank locomotive
    outside working parts sketch 20
    picture 14, 83
    research 19
Class 37 Tilbury Tank locomotive 15, 19
Class 51 Tilbury Tank locomotive
    complete model picture 115, 173
    drawings 34
    General Arrangement drawing 13
    research 19, 21
    sketch 33
Class 51 boiler
    construction 83–84
    fitting to smokebox 87–89
    main components 84
    removing cut-out 103–104
    securing to cab front 103
Class 51 bunker
    back curve 105–108
    finishing 104–105
Class 51 cab
    beading 111–112
    dimensioned drawing 80
    doors 108–109
    floor 108
    frame extensions 113–115
    front and rear 79–82
    front cab cut-out 81–82
    handrails 112–113
    roof 110
    window frames – etched 80–81
    window frames – homemade 80
Class 51 cab sides and tanks
    building the body 95–97
    cutting 91–93
    folding tank fronts 93–95
    GWR 2-6-2 side tanks picture 100
    marking out 90
    soldering to footplate 97–99
Class 51 chassis frames
    Adams Radial frames 28–29
    breaking metal by bending diagram 36
    choosing the gearbox/motor 34–35
    coupling rods 44–45
    cutting and sticking 32
    designing 27–29
    drawing 29–30
    drilling the frames 44–47
    driving wheel axle holes 45–47
    filing curves diagram 43
    filing the frames 41–44
    filing tips 41
    frame spacers 50–51
    joggling the frames 47–49
    opening axle holes out – tips 46
    piercing saw tips 40
    preliminary design sketches 31
    preparing the frames 38
    preparing the metal 35–38
    requirements affecting shape 27
    sawing the frames 38–40
    scribing axle hole positions 47
    separating the frames 47
    setting up for sawing diagram 39
    shaping 30–32
    soldering tips 37
Class 51 connecting rods
    construction 69–70
    fault finding 73
    fitting the crossheads 70–72
Class 51 cylinders
    building 64–69
    fault finding 73
    forming the formers 64–65
    main components 64

INDEX

slide bars 65–66
templates diagram 64
wrappers 66–68
Class 51 driving wheels 59–60
Class 51 footplate
  buffer beams 76–79
  construction 75–79
  dimensioned drawing 75
  shape 74–75
  valances 76–79
Class 51 front bogie
  Comet 7ft bogie etch 56
  construction 55–58
Class 51 motorization
  attaching the motor 60
  current pickup 60–61
  top-acting wipers 61–63
Class 51 pony truck
  fitting 54
  main components 52
  making a shouldered bolt 54–55
  tube and strip construction 52–54
Class 51 smokebox
  construction 84–87
  wrapper 85–87
Class 51 tank tops
  cutting 100–103
  removing boiler cut-out 103–104
  securing the boiler 103
Class 69 Tilbury Tank locomotive 19
Class 79 Tilbury Tank locomotive
  completed model picture 163, 173
  details sketch 17
  picture 9, 16, 116, 134
  research 15, 19, 21
  scale drawing 118
Class 79 bogie
  components diagram 124
  scratch-built 124–126
Class 79 boiler
  cut-out 153
  forming 138–139
  rolling 135–138
Class 79 bunker 153–155
Class 79 cab

  back and front 150–152
  floor 152
  windows 158–159
  wrap-over roof 149–150, 155–161
Class 79 chassis
  beam compensation system diagram 127
  comparison to Class 51 116–117
  compensating 126–128
  embossing rivets 117–119
  main components 117
  using a chassis jig 119–121
Class 79 cylinders
  attaching to chassis frames 130–132
  construction 129–130
  solid cylinder construction diagram 129
Class 79 motorization
  Alan Gibson driving wheels 121–122
  assembly 133
  high level gearboxes 132–133
  plunger pickups 121
Class 79 radial truck
  etch 123
  fitting 122–124
Class 79 scale drawing 118
Class 79 smokebox
  construction 140–142
  saddle 142–143
  wrapper 144–148
Class 79 tank 151

General Arrangement drawings 12–13, 15

J15 locomotive 174–175, 180–185

LMS Ivatt Class 4 locomotive 28
locomotive details
  boiler bands 166–167
  boiler details 172
  brake hoses 167
  brake shoes 167, 169
  built-up items sketch 170
  bunker coal rails 167, 171
  cab roof hatch 167, 169, 171
  chassis equalizing beam and springs 167
  chimney 164

clack valves and pipes 167
cylinder draincocks 167
destination board brackets 167
dome 164
guard irons 167
handrails, knobs and pipes 167
lamp and buffer guards 167
lamp irons 167
mud holes 167
order of attachment 163
reversing rod 167
safety valves 164
sand box 164
scale 14
smokebox door 164
solid details sketch 165
steam pipes 164
tubes and pipes sketch 168
vacuum brake ejector 167
washout plugs 167, 169, 171
whistle 167

National Railway Museum, York 11–12, 15

painting and decorating
  finishing off 184
  metal blacking 175–176
  painting the bodywork 178–180
  painting the chassis 177–178
  plates 183
  preparing and cleaning 174
  spraying tips 175–177
  transfers 180–183
  weathering 184

Riddles BR 3MT tank loco 26
rivets
  embossed 117–118
  GW rivet press 117–118
  positioning 119

scratch-building
  general advice 9–14
  research process 15–18
  kit bashing 14

tools and materials
  basic materials chart 25
  basic toolkit chart 24
  taps and dies 25

workplace
  dangers 23–24
  workbench organization 22–23